# THE NAPOLEONIC 'DAD'S ARMY'

## THE BRITISH VOLUNTEER MOVEMENT, 1794–1814

PAUL L. DAWSON

FRONTLINE
BOOKS

THE NAPOLEONIC 'DAD'S ARMY'
The British Volunteer Movement, 1794-1814

First published in Great Britain in 2024 by Frontline Books
An imprint of Pen & Sword Books Ltd Yorkshire – Philadelphia

Copyright © Paul L Dawson
ISBN 978-1-39903-772-3

Typeset by Lapiz Digital Printed and bound by CPI UK

Pen & Sword Books Ltd incorporates the imprints of Pen & Sword
Archaeology, After the Battle, Air World Books, Atlas, Aviation,
Battleground, Discovery, Family History, History, Maritime, Military,
Naval, Politics, Social History, Transport, True Crime, Claymore Press,
Frontline Books, Praetorian Press, Seaforth Publishing and White Owl

For a complete list of Pen & Sword titles please contact:

PEN & SWORD BOOKS LIMITED
47 Church Street, Barnsley, South Yorkshire, S70 2AS, England
E-mail: enquiries@pen-and-sword.co.uk
Website: www.pen-and-sword.co.uk

Or

PEN AND SWORD BOOKS
1950 Lawrence Rd, Havertown, PA 19083, USA
E-mail: uspen-and-sword@casematepublishers.com
Website: www.penandswordbooks.com

# THE NAPOLEONIC 'DAD'S ARMY'

# CONTENTS

*To my Twin, Anthony Leslie Dawson.*
*It is well over 20 years since we began this odyssey together, delving into the contents of the Minster Library in York. About time it was finished!*

# LIST OF PLATES

15. Naïve impression of a Volunteer c. 1805. With yellow facings, turned back in imitation of an officer's coat, black leather equipment and clubbed and queued hair, the Volunteer presents a marked divergence from the appearance of a 'traditional redcoat' soldier of the era.

16. Portrait of an officer of the Loyal Leeds Volunteers c. 1795. The coat, with its waist-length lapels and buttons in threes, is a marked divergence from how we expect an officer's coat to look. Two officers' coats for this unit exist, one in Leeds City Museum and another in the National Army Museum.

# ACKNOWLEDGEMENTS

I must start by thanking all those who have encouraged my return to studying this topic. After suffering a severe traumatic brain injury in 2016, as part of my rehabilitation I took up again a part-completed scheme of work, to 'ease' myself gently back into the process of research and writing. This coincided with the Covid 19 epidemic, which closed off the world of archive research in France and the UK. The digitisation of records by The National Archives at Kew, and making these free to download allowed me to re-immerse myself in the late eighteenth century and to study the numerous Volunteer forces of the era and to 'pick up' where my twin and I had left off, 20 years earlier.

In addition, I must pay posthumous thanks to my much-missed friend and co-religionist, John Goodchild for his patience with a pair of teenage twins stepping out into the world of archive research in the summer after completing their GCSEs. His death before I could recommence this book put much of the research in his collection on hold. Hopefully in due course, now the collection is part of the West Yorkshire Archive Service, a catalogue will be produced to endeavour me to 'pick up where I left off', as without John's detailed knowledge of his holdings, finding the material I previously consulted has proved so far almost impossible. I must also thank my much-missed friend Kate Taylor MBE: without John or Kate's sage advice and guidance, and love of all things Wakefield, historical and Unitarian, I would not be a historian or Unitarian lay preacher, and this book would not exist.

Dr K.B. Linch of the University of Leeds needs to be thanked for his support and interest in my research on Volunteers: our correspondence on the subject goes back to the late 1990s.

Richard Warren must be thanked for his support, advice and quality discussion and critique of my research, so too Ben Townsend. Robert Cooper must be thanked for his support and company on our many research trips to handle original Volunteer uniforms housed in museums across the country. Antonia Philips of the National Army Museum deserves praise for her help, and allowing access to original items of clothing and equipment held in that museum's collection. Staff at Wakefield Museum and Leeds Discovery centre also need to be thanked, so too the staff at Sheffield City Archives and York Library.

Finally, to my twin Anthony. Thank you for letting me complete what was in essence 'your idea' all those years ago, and to our lamented and much-missed grandmother, Jeane Cresswell, who ferried her grandsons to various archives and museums, whilst we hunted down archive references about the Wakefield Local Militia and other Volunteer units in Doncaster, Derby and the Minster Library York.

# PREFACE

2021 marked the 200th anniversary of the death of Napoleon Bonaparte: a man loved and hated by millions across the world. For much of the British press and government he was the 'devil incarnate' against whom the government sought to rally a nation. The cartoons of Cruickshank and Gillray glamourised John Bull, nationalism and xenophobia, summing up the vision of England against the evils of democracy and Napoleon.

Yet at the time these acts of propaganda were created, Great Britain was a nation at war with itself, being torn apart by the very forces that drove France to revolution in 1789. The political tensions set in motion by the American and French revolutions were the same in Barnsley as they were in Oxford, Norwich, Exeter and London. Radicalism amongst the middle class had been awakened in the 1770s and the response to the American War, characterised by the petitions of 1775, the Yorkshire Association of 1783–4 as well as radical groups like the Society for Constitutional Information and the London Corresponding Society: these groups were identified by the British government as an existential threat to the sovereignty and status of the British king, Parliament and constitution. Radicals represented the total usurpation of sovereignty. In government eyes this constituted a very genuine and real political threat. This was a long drawn-out battle over the very nature of society. Loyalism grew from ideas of 'Britishness' espoused by Edmund Burke, one-time Whig and champion of political reform. Loyalists saw citizenship in terms of 'traditional' British values – property, social order, church, and monarchy. They believed that the long-established British political system was the wisest and most reliable form of government. Politics and governance were best handled by the social elites and in consequence, those elites fought tooth and nail to restrict the electoral franchise: change was permissible but slowly and cautiously and instigated from the top down. The radicals, by contrast, thought that citizenship came from universal 'natural rights'. John Horne Tooke in 1792 declared 'that all civil and political authority is derived from the people. That equal active citizenship is the unalienable right of all men; minors, criminals, and insane persons excepted.' With a small army, committed to fighting the Flanders campaign and no police force at home, the Government had had to raise a mass army 'on the cheap' as quickly as possible, which resulted in the Volunteer Act of 1794. It witnessed the formation of hundreds of loyalist Volunteer regiments: by 1798 over 100,000 men had volunteered. The force was finally disbanded in summer 1814, 20 long years later. This book seeks to explore the history and development force of the Volunteer force in England 1794–1814.

As hundreds of different corps existed across the country, it is impossible to write a broad history that encompasses quite literally hundreds of thousands of men. The nature of the archive record means that The National Archives at Kew has been a primary point of consultation, as well as the Fitzwilliam Muniments in Sheffield. The papers of Earl Fitzwilliam, the Lord Lieutenant of the West Riding, are some of, if not the, most complete records for any Lord Lieutenancy in the country for the wealth of documents for Volunteers and Yeomanry. The book is therefore perhaps overly reliant on my home county of the West Riding of Yorkshire, to look at the development of the Volunteering movement, its strengths and its weaknesses across the period. This is the approach taken by Dr Glenn Steppler for Rutland and Leicestershire in his seminal work nearly 30 years ago.[1] The themes encountered in the West Riding are no doubt paralleled throughout the country which we explore at various points across the text to provide, hopefully, some sort of national coverage.

Paul L. Dawson,
Wakefield, 15 August 2023

# Chapter 1

# DEFENDING THE NATION

The 40-year period from 1780 to 1820 was overshadowed by the generation-long Revolutionary and Napoleonic Wars. Sometimes referred to as the Great War, it was a war on a worldwide scale with a level of mobilisation and a loss of life proportionally greater than the First World War of 1914 to 1918.

Final victory in 1815 was in no small part due to Britain's wealth, the result of industrialisation from the latter half of the eighteenth century. The war with France in many ways aided the growth of industrialisation, and the demand for military goods – muskets, shot, cannon, scarlet cloth – and the opening of new world markets – notably southern America and India – for British exports fuelled growth. Large areas of the North of England became heavily urbanised: Manchester became the first industrial city based on cotton, followed by Birmingham for engineering, Sheffield for steel, Leeds for textiles.

The process of industrialisation witnessed the emergence of the world's first labour movement: the climax of the wars of the coincided with the worst excesses of industrialisation and laissez-faire economics. The appearance of the United Englishmen, militant trade unions and Luddism were all symptomatic of the increasing wealth inequality in society, and desire by working men to have a say in how their community and country was governed. Robert Raikes' Sunday School movement had made the urban poor increasingly literate and aware of political rights, notably through the work of Thomas Paine and working-class organisations like the London Corresponding Society and regional groups like the Sheffield Constitutional Society. Through these societies and embryonic trade unions the working class demanded the right to vote, and challenged the old privileges of monarchy, aristocracy and gentry as well as creating conflict with the new industrialist class over working hours and fair pay. As factories that supported new and more mechanised industries grew, so too did the need for a labour force that had the requisite skills and abilities to perform such jobs. That labour force did not exist, but was created through an unprecedented shift of labour from the agrarian jobs of the country to the urban jobs of the city. Suddenly new urban areas were flooded with an eclectic mix of social and economic classes, including those from other countries looking for work in these new industries, and that tended to fuel the engines of associations, clubs and societies. The common thread for many of these men was that the social and economic constructs they were so accustomed to had been severely disrupted. The formation of these organisations, whether for political, cultural or other reasons, served to connect people of similar interests, but not necessarily the same backgrounds. The desire for equality and religious toleration, as well as political representation, drove reform. Concurrently, Whig opposition to the Tory party by a solidly middle-class body corporate also sought political reform and the right to vote, led by men like Rev. Christopher Wyvill and Major John Cartwright.

Religious opposition to the Test and Corporation Acts and the Blasphemy Act, which made perhaps 20 per cent of the English population and 90 per cent of the Irish population second-class citizens, had been growing in strength since the 1770s. Driven largely by middle-class and wealthy Unitarians – a religious group which denied the Trinity – who allied themselves with Catholics in Ireland, they also understood that political reform and universal human rights were essential next steps in creating a more equal and balanced society. In this the likes of Rev. Dr Richard Price and Rev. Dr Joseph Priestley, as well as Rev. Theophilus Lindsey and laymen such as Benjamin Vaughan, John Hurford Stone, Thomas Muir and Archibald Hamilton Rowan figured large.[1]

A radical political culture rapidly took hold in London and the North of England which was preached from Unitarian pulpits from Edinburgh to Taunton and disseminated via lectures and newspapers.[2] The democratic ideals of Thomas Paine, which had been forged in the crucible of the American Revolution, blended with religious dissent, trade unionist ideals and early socialist experimentation, stood in opposition to the oligarchic, 'Church and King' establishment, championed by successive Prime Ministers and men like Wellington. The cosmopolitan and universalist idealism that emerged after 1783 was in direct contrast to Tory sense of Britishness, which was forged with an ever-increasing Francophobia – Britain and France were almost continuously at war between 1689 and 1815. More than anything, this battle of ideology defined the conflict between Britian and France

1793–1815 both at home and abroad. Crucially it must be stressed that in the early nineteenth century, many radicals conceived themselves as being illegitimately excluded from the public space of political debate and appropriated patriotic language and actions to stress their loyalty to the nation and its history in order to legitimise their claims to participate.

For those opposed to reform of any sort, dissent from the Anglican Church – headed by the King – equated with dissent from the state and therefore branded such individuals as 'disloyal'. Failure to support the national church meant failure to support the King. In many respects, the Anglican Church was an intimate mouthpiece of the Tory party. Loyalist elites, in general terms, were pro-slavery and the slave trade, educated at grammar schools as well as schools like Eton and Harrow. They belonged either to the landowning classes, who believed in their natural superiority and right to rule, or were rich 'merchant princes' and industrialists. Burke in seeing the events unfold in France, realised that liberalism needed limits and institutions to support the state. In supporting the American Colonists, Burke had understood that *laissez faire* ideals whereby the state did not interfere in economics etc, when tested through the prism of the events in France from 1789, was in need of revision. Burke and his allies were loyal to the status quo and the Crown, and strongly opposed any social reform, believing that it would bring the ancient British 'constitution' into danger. Liberalism needed limits, and the state needed strengthening by institutions, yet consistently fought against any law that hindered economic progress and capitalism.

The governing elites believed themselves to be under direct threat from France and from radical activity at home. Indeed, alarmed by the emergence of the Revolution Society and the growth of radical groups like the London Corresponding Society as much by the events taking place in France, William Pitt and his ministers convinced Parliament and the British people of the need to use extreme and novel measures to eradicate the radical threat and protect the political status quo. In the climate and context of the time the Prime Minister and his colleagues believed that political reform was dangerous, French republican idealism intolerable, and posed an existential threat. The British Crown both encouraged and prompted loyal Britons to help to quell radical activity at home by means of propaganda, loyal associations, militarisation and intimidation. To this end, the Crown enlisted the support of a significant proportion of the population, through coercion, to voluntarily form loyalist associations, and left the status quo unaffected by harnessing 'people power'. For Burke

3

and his supporters, war was the only solution; war against all those who wanted political and social change and France as the originator of these problems. Between 1791 and 1792, there was a wave of thirty-eight strikes in which troops were deployed on twenty-five occasions against Luddites in Wiltshire, colliers of Coalbrookedale and Liverpool dock workers.[3] Anti-enclosure riots broke out across the country almost simultaneously to the strikes, most notably in Sheffield during 1791 which witnessed cavalry being deployed against the protestors. During the crisis year of 1792 when war against France was at its closest, loyalist groups such as the Bull's Head Association in Manchester and a variety of societies and associations of 'Loyal Britons' were set up throughout Britain. Their aim was to organise patriotic, anti-French forces in defence of king and country. Ordinary people, as well as the rich and powerful, supported these groups. This was a battle for the moral soul of a nation: it was to be a war of ideology.[4] Judging by the number of loyalist declarations by the alehouse keepers themselves, this warning was taken very seriously. Between May and September 1792, councils and boroughs across the country issued 386 loyal addresses saying they would do more to fight radicalism.[5]

On 1 December 1792 the government issued a Royal Proclamation embodying the Militia to meet the 'radical invasion'. A week earlier John Reeves, the former governor of Newfoundland, had announced the formation of a loyalist association to counteract the groundswell of sedition and encouraged like-minded souls to do the same. Within months his call, assisted by the government's press network, was answered by 1,500 local societies, creating a movement of prodigious proportions. Reeves campaigned against Jacobinism by founding at the Crown and Anchor tavern on 20 November 1792 the 'Association for Preserving Liberty and Property against Republicans and Levellers'. Reeves was backed by Pitt and his government, who had conceived a programme of deliberate persecution of the voice of opposition. The public, stirred by Reeves' populism for 'Church and King' and 'John Bull and England', rose in opposition to political reform. Several loyalists who would later participate as Volunteers who corresponded with John Reeves in 1792 advanced the concept of 'armed associations' for the purpose of 'dispersing rioters' and preventing the 'seditious assemblies of the people'.[6] Many of the northern corps shared this view: John Beckett, a wealthy Leeds banker, hoped that by mobilising the town's wealthy middle classes, 'our necks kept from the Guillotine'.[7]

One such Loyalist Association was founded in Wakefield by Henry Peterson. A slave owner born in Pennsylvania in 1729, he had emigrated to the Netherlands in 1776 due to his opposition to the independence of

4

the American Colonies. He had left the Netherlands with the creation of the Batavian Republic and settled in Wakefield. It was he who had organised the effigy burning of the Quaker Thomas Paine, the author of the *Rights of Man*, in the town and had declared at a 'meeting of the Clergy and loyalists' in the Moot Hall Wakefield, that:

> the deceptive, seditious doctrines are propagated among us with such malicious industry that it is high time for every sober man and loyal subject to use his best endeavours to counteract this EVIL tendency but uniting heart and hand in support of our most excellent constitution of government in aiding and assisting the Civil Magistrates in the execution of the laws against all traitors, rebels and seditious persons who endeavour to or attempt to subvert the government.[8]

The petition attached to the declaration attracted 1,660 signatures from the people of Wakefield.[9] Given that the 1801 census suggests the town's population was around 8,000, about a quarter of the adult populace signed! Indeed, in a letter to John Reeves, Peterson recounts that together with Jeremiah Todd Naylor, he had gone from house to house over six days and had collected over 1,000 signatures to the Loyalist Associations' resolutions to sniff out sedition, concluding that such was the level of support shown for 'Church and King' that 'the friends of Tom Paine were crestfallen'.[10] How representative these petitions really were of public opinion we cannot say, but it seems likely coercion was indeed used: refusing to sign marked one out immediately as a traitor, a target for the loyalist mob. Therefore, it took those of firm resolve not to sign and be stigmatised by the wider community.

Broadly speaking, loyalists hoped to close down radical space. Legal prosecutions or their threat were only part of this strategy. Equally important was the active propagation of loyalism, by address, sermon, tract, and festival. The Associations and allied publications, by claiming reform to be 'Jacobin' or 'French Treason', gave the Loyalists control of the debate. It placed the radicals in a defensive position. If private property, wealth and religious inequality as part of the social order were to be maintained in England, nothing short of exporting anti-revolutionary sentiment at the point of a bayonet would do.[11] To this end the Crown declared war on reform-minded groups who, using 21st-century terminology, had been 'radicalised' into becoming 'home-grown terrorists'. Despite opposition from Whig and Radical alike, war was declared on 1 February 1793: commencement of hostilities had as much to do with the alarm caused by the surge of radicalism in Britain itself as from the threat from

France. The British Crown and the Tories believed that the British system of a parliamentary monarchy and the rule of law, combined with a property-based social order and the Established Church, were the bastions which guaranteed British liberties and commercial prosperity. Charles Grey, Thomas Erskine and Whigs both in Parliament and the nation as a whole opposed the war. Another who expressed their anger at the recommencement of war was Anna Laetitia Barbauld. She was the daughter of a Unitarian minister, raised to believe she was equal in every way to her brethren. She was close to Rev. Dr Joseph Priestley during his time at Warrington Academy, and supported the revolution in France and reform at home. In 1793, when the British government called on the nation to fast in honour of the war, anti-war Dissenters such as Barbauld were left with a moral quandary: 'Obey the order and violate their consciences by praying for success in a war they disapproved? observe the Fast, but preach against the war? defy the Proclamation and refuse to take any part in the Fast?'. She continued 'We have,' she wrote, 'just calmly voted for slaughter and merchandized destruction . . . for maiming . . . for the making of widows and orphans . . . and for corrupting citizens and subjects into spies and traitors.' Barbauld took this opportunity to write a sermon, *Sins of Government, Sins of the Nation*, on the moral responsibility of the individual. For her, each individual is responsible for the actions of the nation because he or she constitutes part of the nation. The essay attempts to determine what the proper role of the individual is in the state, and while she argues that 'insubordination' can undermine a government, she admits there are lines of 'conscience' that cannot be crossed in obeying a government. It was a polemic against Burke and one-nation conservativism. Barbauld's essays demonstrated that it was possible for a woman to be publicly engaged in politics, and other female authors such as Elizabeth Benger emulated her. Barbauld's literary career spanned numerous periods in British literary history: her work promoted the values of the Enlightenment and of sensibility, while her poetry made a founding contribution to the development of British Romanticism. Her career as a poet ended abruptly in 1812, with the publication of *Eighteen Hundred and Eleven*, which criticised Britain's participation in the Napoleonic Wars. She was shocked by the vicious reviews it received and published nothing else in her lifetime.

The uncovering of a plot in spring 1794 which linked British émigré radicals in France to radical groups like the Constitutional Society in England and Ireland terrified Pitt and his ministers: the Government had proof that reformist groups were arming themselves and were openly sponsoring a French invasion.[12] Many on the Whig benches in Parliament actually doubted the evidence that Pitt presented. Samuel Shore opined to Rev. Wyvill 'you will undoubtedly see the reports of the secret committee . . . but fails in proving what is confidently professes to do, that there has been a long formed settled scheme to overthrow the government and constitution of this country – some imprudence's and [illegible] improper conduct in some individuals or societies appear to be all that be fairly made out.' Shore continued that he was worried that the Crown would use the report as an excuse to extinguish civil liberties.[13] Shore, Wyvill and the Whigs had legitimate concerns to be alarmed about the Government's next steps. All too predictably the Government embarked on a campaign of repression: over 200 men were arrested and tried for treason. As E.P. Thompson comments, the resulting trials, although they were not Government victories, served the purpose for which they were intended: many more moderate reformers and radicals were terrified and withdrew from active politics, fearful of governmental retribution. Few took their place.[14]

## The Militia

To defend the nation from both internal and external threats, the Militia was embodied between 1 December and 15 December 1792 for those counties nearest the coast, with further orders for embodiment of more county regiments, and many notices for their call-out, being published in January and February 1793. The militia was organised according to an Act of 1757 whereby every English and Welsh county had to supply (and pay) a given quota of men aged between 18 and 45 who had been selected by ballot to serve for a period of five years, although the buying of substitutes who could serve in your place was legal and widely practised; the Militia ballot and procuring a substitute becoming seen by some as an unjust tax on the well-to-do. The total sought by the government in 1793 was 32,000. Those balloted would be under military law during active service, and in peacetime they were obliged to do a month's military training. To avoid excessive taxation and corruption, men were to be raised relatively cheaply by local ballots which drew a proportion of adult males from each community into the county militias. As quotas of men were theoretically drawn at random from each locale, from a broad cross-section of society. As could be expected, the 'ballot' was despised by those called up, especially given the massive expansion of the system in the following years. Each of the Militia Acts, passed from 1757 onwards, included an important clause which allowed balloted men to pay a fine, or to provide a

7

substitute, in order to avoid personal service. The clause was intended to differentiate the Militia ballot from conscription by ensuring that gentlemen were not compelled to serve against their will.[15]

The Supplementary Militia Act of 1796 demanded an additional 60,000 men be drawn for the Militia. Unlike the initial formations, however, the Supplementary Militia was a 'top down' development. It was not funded by central government and quotas were by and largely filled by members of the middling and upper class – in essence those who could afford to pay for their own uniforms and weapons. In many parts of the country this act of compulsion resulted in anti-Militia riots. A year later, the third Supplementary Militia was levied, but not embodied till February 1798. Ultimately the West Riding had five regiments of Militia, to which would be added from 1794 dozens of Volunteer regiments. This was not a unique pattern in many counties and shires. Indeed, 'As in other major European states,' historian Linda Colley noted, 'in Great Britain, it was training in arms under the auspices of the state that was the most common working-class experience in the late-18th and early-19th centuries'.[16] It is undeniable however, that the hated ballot system had become so much abused via the purchase of substitutes that the quality of those balloted for the Militia was very poor, and may have joined the regular army anyway.[17]

In returning to the thesis of 'An Armed Nation', as Colley notes, militarism and the concurrent militarisation of society – just as in 1939–45 – shaped society as a whole. We often think of France as 'An Armed Nation' or moreover a state that was subservient to the needs of the military. Yet, it is undeniable that under William Pitt, the British Nation became obsessed with presenting a Francophobic sense of nationhood that had to be defended by use of arms. This hatred of all things French lingers to our current day. As the following chapters show, the militarisation of society did not always mean an end to opposition to government or harsh critiques of the government and Crown.

Chapter 2

# THE VOLUNTEER INFANTRY

Embodying the Militia had gone some way to providing a 'local defence force'. But if the French were coming as Pitt believed and the radical societies were 'in league with the French', in order to release regular troops to defend the nation, a new force for local defence was needed: the Volunteers were born. With the nation whipped into an anti-French and anti-Jacobin hysteria by the media, Pitt sought to harness the middle class to his cause whilst at the same time providing a defence force for towns and cities across the Kingdom, mobilising the middle-class 'Church and King' supporters as had been done during the invasion scare of 1780 with the formation of gentlemen Volunteer corps. These had been raised to guard against internal threats as a militarised arm of the magistrates as a quasi-paramilitary police force. For the state, the increasing spectre of discontent at home following the riots of 1792 and the Treason Trials of 1794, the need to provide an internal defence force was of paramount importance.[1] This strategy was buttressed by a strict surveillance of taverns and alehouses, whose landlords were threatened with the loss of their licences if they permitted radical groups to meet on their premises.[2]

In order to create his internal defence force William Pitt ironically emulated the French. The French nation had declared *'La Patrie en danger'* and had thus urged its citizens to volunteer to fight for France and the cause of the Revolution. Tens of thousands of men joined the army as volunteers as part of the newly-levied National Guard. It was a whole nation in arms: it was nothing short of 'a total war' where the nation and armed forces became fused. The sudden increase in the armed forces of France with over 100,000 volunteers flocking to the colours so alarmed the British Crown that Pitt had little option but to emulate the French National Guard: France was fighting in a new way, and the British armed nation had to follow suit.[3] Through the British media, Pitt issued a similar war cry to that in France: 'For Church and King'. This saw a mobilisation of largely Anglican loyalist Tories against Whig reformist Dissenters: divide and rule was order of the day. 'You are with us or you are against us' became the watchword.

The rallying effect of the Government's cry to defend 'Church and King' had sufficient impact that in March 1794 the well-to-do inhabitants of the West End of London formed an 'Association for the Parish of St. George's Hanover Square' to defend it against any possible invasion and, equally importantly, against any 'seditious' activities. On the back of this 'spontaneous' outpouring of public 'loyalty', a few weeks later an Act was passed empowered counties and cities to raise Volunteers for 'local defence' (i.e., to operate as local police force) and as soldiers 'in actual case of invasion'.[4]

## Forming the Volunteers

In order to create the Volunteers, two Acts of Parliament were passed in 1794. The first, in March, authorised that anyone who volunteered to be enrolled in the Militia was to receive the very handsome bounty of £10. A second Act authorised the formation of Volunteer companies and battalions. And, in order to encourage Volunteers to sign up, they were specifically exempted from the Militia ballot if they could prove 'adequate' attendance at drills and exercises of the corps to which they belonged. Not only did this provide an incentive to join the Volunteers, but furthermore encouraged individual members, and Volunteer units as a whole, to attend drills and remain 'efficient' so as to avoid the Militia ballot. Many county notables jumped at the opportunity to raise a battalion of Volunteers, as means to further their own status by being able to add the sought-after title of 'Colonel' or 'Lieutenant-Colonel' to their names. Further additional inducement to join the Volunteers was a scheme of pay and allowances for when a unit was on 'active service' for its mandatory period within the United Kingdom.[5]

The process of forming the Volunteer army began on 14 March 1794, with the following measures being authorised by Parliament:[6]

1.  An increase in the Militia through the formation of Volunteer companies, as had been practised in the American war, or by increasing the number of private soldiers in each company of Militia.
2.  The formation of Volunteer companies in particular towns, notably those on the coast, for the purpose of local defence.
3.  To form Volunteer troops of Fencible cavalry, each troop to muster thirty to eighty men per troop. Officers were to only

have temporary rank, and were not entitled to half pay. The arms, accoutrements and uniform were to be supplied by the government, the officers and men were to supply their own horses, which were purchased from them by the government. A Major was to command two troops, four troops by a Lieutenant-Colonel and six by a Colonel.

4. To form other bodies of Volunteer cavalry within counties, with approval from the Lords Lieutenant. The officers and men were to provided their own clothing and mounts, and recruited from the gentry and county yeoman. Their duties were to act in their own or adjacent counties for riot suppression, and receive pay whilst on such active service.

5. Volunteer pioneers and infantry to man the coast guard artillery were to be created, to consist of one captain, two lieutenants, three serjeants, three corporals, two drummers and sixty private men, one-third armed with firelocks and the remainder with pikes.

From this call came the formation of Volunteer corps across the country: ninety-six urban corps were formed by 1795 as well as thirty-two largely rural ones.[7] The 1794 Act was concerned with two main spheres:

1. Raising a body of troops as an aid to the magistrates.
2. Establishing discipline amongst society and those who joined the Volunteers.

These men would receive pay only when called out on actual duty and requirements for attendance at drills were set by the various Volunteer corps themselves. The 1794 Act required that these Volunteers were already to be householders, those 'citizens' already in good standing in their communities, and therefore ready to defend the existing social order and their stake – however small – in it. The preoccupation with local policing can be seen in the men's terms of enrolment, with most of them only agreeing to serve in a very limited area, usually just their town or parish.[8] In so doing, as historian Peter Hicks cogently argues, 'the government preferred arming a wealthy (and so establishment) amateur rather than a peasant whose loyalties might be unpredictable'.[9]

The Acts were not universally greeted with enthusiasm. In North Yorkshire, the veteran political reformer and lapsed Anglican vicar the Rev. Christopher Wyvill considered them unconstitutional and 'an unwarranted departure from the usual practice of Parliament'.[10] One of Wyvill's correspondents felt that in the wake of the Treason Trials 'the alarm seems to have been transferred from without to within', that the Volunteers were for internal defence and not against France.[11] Wyvill felt that 'I cannot at present discover anything that can be considered as constituting an emergency of national danger'.[12] The Rev. William Dealtry made his views crystal clear on both the war and the formation of the Volunteers in a letter dated 10 June 1794: 'my wishes to be for an honourable peace . . . I am often surprised at the madness of the minister and the blindness of the people'.[13] As well as written opposition, at a public meeting held to discuss the forming of Volunteers and the opening of a subscription list in Northallerton chaired by the Lord Lieutenant, 'Young Mr Hutton of Marsk surprized everyone in court by suddenly rising up and speaking with great warmth against the measure' and 'inveighed against Mr Pitt who he accused of treachery, and laid many things at his charge'.[14]

The formation of the Volunteers and Yeomanry was not greeted with universal support, and any suggestion that this was the 'will of the people' is clearly wrong. Wyvill started to gather around him a group of influential anti-war liberals, opposed to war with France and the militarisation of society: Samuel Shore of Sheffield, Thomas Brand Hollis, Richard Slater, MP for the City of York, and other MPs such as James Martin and Joshua Grigby. Dissenting clergy, notably William Wood of Leeds, Theophilus Lindsey of London, Dr Joseph Priestley, John Ralph of Halifax, George Walker of Nottingham and Newcome Cappe of York, as well as that most remarkable of women Anna Barbauld, all agreed with Wyvill, and were determined to end the war and remove Pitt from power. The creation of the Volunteers which some modern historians see as a nation-building exercise – e.g., Linda Colley – for men like Wyvill was nothing more than a power-grab by the executive.

The new Volunteer corps occupied an awkward position, not quite soldiers and not quite civilians: they constituted a part time military force under civilian control. Only when called out at times of invasion or for riot suppression did the Volunteers come under military law, and receive the same pay as the regulars, but were also subject to the Mutiny Act. The Volunteer system was overseen by the Lords Lieutenant, and ultimately by the Home Office. The War Office was only to assume control in the case of invasion and the Volunteers were placed under the military authority of the General Officer commanding the local military district. Officers' commissions were recommended to the Home Office, and thence to the Commander-in-Chief; arms came from the Board of Ordnance; pay came from the War Office. Being under civilian control, Volunteers were requested to attend training and permanent duty by the Lords Lieutenant or magistrates rather than being directly ordered.

## Organising Corps

Rather than being overseen by the regular armed forces, the new Volunteer units were organised by committees: control was ultimately in the hands of mayors and magistrates. Public meetings were held to raise these units, and subscription lists were opened to pay for uniforms and equipment. In the West Riding, in each of the major towns – Wakefield, Leeds, Bradford and Huddersfield – during April and May public meetings were called, chaired by the 'Chief Citizens' of each town, and attended by the 'Gentlemen, Clergy, Traders and Respectable Inhabitants' to form a local Volunteer corps.[15] One such meeting was in Bradford:

> At a meeting of the select committee of the Constitutional Society, held at the Sun Inn, in Bradford, the seventeenth Day of April 1794,
> H Wickham, Esq. Chairman
> The Necessity of forming a Volunteer Corps with this town and neighbourhood having been suggested, and this meeting thinking it an object deserving attention,
> Resolved, that a meeting of the inhabitants of the Town and Neighbourhood be held at the Sun Inn on Wednesday Next, the twenty-third day of this Instant April, at Eleven O'Clock in the forenoon, to take into consideration the propriety of establishing such a Volunteer corps.[16]

The meeting, held on the 23rd, agreed that:

> it appears highly necessary that a Volunteer Corps should be established for the defence of this town and neighbourhood, against insurrections and sudden commotions.
> Resolved, that such corps consist of a Major, Two Captains, Two Lieutenants, Two Ensigns, Four Serjeants, Six Corporals, Two Drummers, Two Fifers, and one hundred and fifty rank and file.
> Resolved, that a subscription be immediately entered into for defraying the expenses of establishing and supporting such a corps, to be paid by such instalments as the Committee to be appointed at this meeting feel fit.
> Resolved, that Henry Wickham, Johnathan Atkinson Bousfield, Benjamin Ferrand, Joshua Field, Joseph Stephen Pratt, Richard Hodgson, and Richard Houghton Esqrs. Mr John Sturgers, Mr John Hodgson, Mar Barber, Mr Thomas Lister and Mr Joh Jarratt be appointed a committee to carry out these resolutions into effect.[17]

A corps was founded in Halifax at a meeting held in the Talbot Inn, on 26 April 1794, 'for the security of the Town, Parish and its Neighbourhood'.[18] In the *Leeds Intelligencer* on 14 April the following appeared:

> A meeting is appointed by Alex. Turner Esq; the Mayor of this town, to be held at the Rotation Office on Thursday next, to consider of proper means to carry into effect the raising of a Volunteers corps with this borough.[19]

Elsewhere in the same edition we find that the purpose of the corps was 'for the express purpose of the internal defence of this Borough, against insurrection or any sudden Commotion'.[20]

In nearby Wakefield, townsfolk were stung into mobilisation by harsh criticism from the Lord Lieutenant about them lacking loyalist spirit. Initial membership stood at 570 in two classes, one of 'independent' who received no pay from the Government and took up arms, and the other 'gentlemen' who could not provide the time to actually Volunteer, but still subscribed fiscal backing.[21] Yet, organising a meeting to discuss the formation of a Volunteer corps did not always mean a corps would be formed. In Doncaster a meeting was held on 31 May to form Volunteers in the wapentakes of Strafforth and Tickhill, yet nothing came of this.[22] At a meeting in Pontefract it was resolved that:

> upon mature consideration of the local Circumstances of the Riding, it appears expedient, that the substantial inhabitants of the Market Towns and Neighbourhoods, be invited to enrol themselves into Corps of Infantry according to the laudable examples of Leeds, Halifax and Bradford.[23]

Yet, as in Doncaster, the Pontefract corps was never formed. Loyalist enthusiasm failed to transmute into participatory activity. Was this because of apathy? Doncaster and Pontefract had no recorded Constitutional Societies or radical activity at this time: did this translate into the lack of will to form volunteers to combat a threat that many did not appreciate, as it was not happening in their town? Perhaps. It is also possible that after a burst of initial enthusiasm, 'cooler heads' prevailed when those proposing forming a corps realised the time and money needed to do so. Both hypotheses could also be mutually supporting. It seems therefore that urban corps were formed in 1794 primarily in towns with a record of radicalism. We will come back to this in a later chapter.

The experience of problems in forming a Volunteer units was not just restricted to the former West Riding. Not every county was as ready and willing as the West Riding of Yorkshire to form Volunteer units. By New Year 1795 the principal towns of the West Riding had a Volunteer corps, yet in Shropshire no Volunteer units were formed under the legislation of 1794, other than the county Yeomanry and a single independent cavalry troop.

The same story is presented in Gloucestershire where the first formations were from 1797 and in Cheshire just one corps was formed in Stockport with contemporary initiatives at Macclesfield and Northwich being unsuccessful. In Lancashire the Rev. Ralph Fletcher formed the Bolton Infantry Volunteers, and a second unit was raised in Rochdale, tellingly both rapidly industrialising centres. In North Yorkshire, the first Volunteers appeared in Scarborough to defend the town and port. A meeting of the Lieutenancy on 3 April 1794 resolved to form two Volunteer companies of infantry at Scarborough and Whitby, for the purpose of manning the coastal batteries, under the orders of Major Commandant John Tindall. Tindall had been a captain in a previous Volunteer corps formed in the town in 1782–3. Whitby boasted furthermore an 'independent' company that was formed in 1794 under Captain Erasmus Gibson – whose brother (?) Francis commanded the artillery company – and was reported as parading on 5 November that year. Extracts from a company orderly book show that in the summer two parades were held each week, one in full uniform, but the other in 'plain clothes' with firearms only, suggesting that no form of undress was adopted. In July 1795 hair powder was left off, but hair was to be 'neatly clubb'd'. In October parade in full regiment also was to be with hair 'neatly tied' but well powdered. In September 1798 new clothing was adopted. Hair was now to be cut at the sides or plaited into a clubbed tail. In November 1798 each company was ordered to attend the batteries once every four weeks for exercise at the 'great guns'.[24] In East Yorkshire, a flurry of activity to guard the coast resulted from the 1794 Act. A meeting of the East Riding and Hull Committee for Internal Defence on 30 April 1794 resolved that a company of infantry should be raised for the defence of the fort on Bridlington Quay and its neighbourhood. A further meeting on 17 May authorised two further companies, the whole to be commanded by Colonel Pitts. Apparently three companies existed under Pitts, including an artillery company.[25] In Hunmanby a meeting of the East Riding and Hull Committee for Internal Defence on 17 May 1794 approved the formation of a company under the command of Captain Osbaldeston. The corps subsequently expanded to three companies.[26] The same committee authorised a company being formed in Hornsea.[27] The earliest formation in Hull witnessed the creation of separate companies, with no overall commander. A meeting on 22 May 1794 resolved that three companies of infantry and one of artillery were to be raised in and around the town. The date of the earliest commissions appears to be 21 June 1794. The three initial companies were 'The Hull Independent Volunteers', headed by Captain John Wray, 'The Dock Company Volunteers', commanded by Captain Joseph Outram, and a third company was under the command of Captain Osbourne. A fourth infantry company was formed at Cottingham in late 1794 under Captain George Knowsley.[28]

## Officers

Before a prospective corps could be issued arms, it had to be accepted by the Lord Lieutenant and officers' commissions gazetted. Officers tended to be those who called the meeting to form the corps and were often prominent members of society. In most cases the Lord Lieutenant was presented with a 'done deal': more often than not a corps would be fully organised, with a committee, rules and regulations in place, and officers appointed before the corps was proposed for approval by the Lord Lieutenant before formal acceptance by the Home Office. The Lord Lieutenant had the power to decline offers of service by corps and by individuals as officers. The Home Office was generally content to trust the judgement of the Lord Lieutenant, and merely 'rubber-stamped' his recommendations. The principal concern of the Lords Lieutenant was to ensure the officers were 'gentlemen'. In Leeds, officers were appointed at the end of April: they were democratically elected by the committee and members. Those elected Captains were George Beaumont, Thomas Cookson and Joseph Wilkinson, and Lieutenants were Thomas Close, Thomas Ilkin, Richard Pulian, Athertone Rawsthorne, Christopher Smith and John Williamson.[29] However, none of the commissions were confirmed until July:[30]

>   Captain Commandant: Thomas Lloyd
>       Captains: George Beaumont, Joseph Wilkinson, Thomas Cookson
>       Lieutenants: Christopher Smith, Richard Pulian, Thomas Ilkin, Athertone Rawsthorne, Thomas Close, Francis Ridsdale, John George Child, Henry Dunderdale.

Lloyd had commanded the Leeds Volunteers formed in 1779 and wound up in 1783. The Corps had been raised by 'Church and King' supporters to guard against Dissenters and French invasion: history was repeating itself as the men opposed to American liberty now roused themselves to fight against French and English liberty.

## Clothing

Once a corps had been accepted and officers appointed, it need to be clothed, equipped and trained. To clothe the men, subscription lists were opened and managed by the committee of the corps. In Halifax, the corp's first appearance in 'full and elegant' uniform was reported as on 17 August 1794. William Wilberforce, the MP for Yorkshire, was keen for the Halifax Volunteers to be on 'a respectable footing' and they were attired in scarlet coats faced with black silk velvet and silver lace, even extending to the grenadier company being attired in bearskins.[31] At a meeting held in Halifax on 23 August 1794, William Norris, secretary to the Committee reported a stagging £7,049 16s had been raised to clothe the corps from public donations.[32]

In Wakefield the subscription list was headed by a Tory cartel of Benjamin Kennett, Rev. Dr Bacon, John and Jeremiah Naylor, Henry Andrews, John Charnock, John Lee, Edward Ridsdale, Thomas Charnock, Thomas Hardy, Alan Johnson, Francis Ingram, William Steer and General Tottenham, who all gave £100. Other subscribers were small merchants and tradesmen, as well as wool-staplers: the Unitarian Harper Soulby gave £10 10s, so too did his co-religionists Samuel and Joseph Holdsworth and Joseph Burrell. We also note John Soulby and William Rideal who gave the same subscription of £10 10s each. Other Unitarians who contributed were Richard Burrell, who gave £21, W. and J. Holdsworth £12 12s, and John Clarkson £21, being secretary to the trustees and mill owner. In total £4,500 was raised.[33] We note £10 10s was received from the Wakefield Loyalist Club of St George.[34] Furthermore, William Dawson, a grenadier in the Royal Wakefield Volunteers, declared he had joined up 'in defence of religion, the laws and liberties of Great Britain against a democratic revolutionary system of government'.[35]

The Rev. Dr Bacon, wrote to the Home Secretary on 31 May informing him that three companies had been formed, noting that 'all men independent and respectable and will serve without pay'. He requested that the corps be allowed blue facings and take the title 'Royal Wakefield Volunteers', adding as a postscript 'our Lord Lieutenant is extremely unpopular indeed, and we cordially wish for another'. This was the Duke of Norfolk who along with Charles James Fox had toasted 'the sovereign people' and backed the call for political reform. The Duke of Norfolk was replaced by Earl Fitzwilliam as Lord Lieutenant: the earl was seen as more politically reliable than the reform-minded duke. The request for the title and facing colour was seemingly granted. The uniform was a red coat with blue collar, cuffs and lapels, white kerseymere waistcoat and breeches. Buttons were brass bearing a crown over the initials 'R.W.V'. In November 1794 the

Royal Wakefield Volunteers purchased flannel waistcoats with 'sleeves and collars and long in the waist' as well as worsted stockings. These flannel waistcoats were probably some form of undress drill jacket.

The Royal Wakefield Volunteers received new uniforms in 1797. The Committee resolved that:

> The allowance for cloathing to consist of a coat, waistcoat, breeches, roundhat and cocakde, is for serjeant £3 3s 9, drummer, £2s 9s 6d, corporal £1 11s 6d and private man, £1 9s.
>
> The accoutraments to consist of a belt, pouch and sling, are also allowed for each man furnished with a firelock. These articles are either supplied from the ordnance or an equivalent thereto is given in money by that department, at the option of the commandants.[36]

For the Sheffield Volunteers, the regimental rules and regulations found in Sheffield City Library state:

> I.
> THAT the Corps shall be formed into Six Companies, viz. – One Grenadier, One Light Infantry, and Four Battalion Companies, consisting of One Major Commandant, Five Captains, One Captain Lieutenant, Seven Lieutenants, Four Ensigns, One Adjutant, One Serjeant Major, Eighteen Serjeants, Eighteen Corporals, One Drum Major, Six Drummers, Four Fifers, and 282 Privates.
>
> II.
> That the Uniform Coat shall be Blue Cloth, with Cape, Cuffs and Facings of Scarlet Cloth. Wings and Shoulder Straps, ornamented with Gold Lace and Fringe, the Waistcoat and Breeches to be white Cassimere, the Buttons to be Gilt, and the Letters S.V. stamped on them.
>
> III.
> That the Grenadier Company wear Cocked Hats with Gilt S.V. Buttons and Loops, Black Cockades and Scarlet Feathers with white Tops, Hair Plaited and turned up behind with a Comb.
>
> IV.
> That the Four Battalion Companies, wear the same Kind of Hats, Cockades, Buttons and Loops, but without any Feathers, and to have their hair clubbed.
>
> V.
> That the Light Infantry Company wear Jackets, with the same Cape, Cuffs, Facings &c. and Helmets with Scarlet Fillets and Yellow Metal

Mountings, White Feathers with Scarlet Tops, and Black Fur laid over the Crowns, and to have their Hair also clubbed.

VI.
That a Band of Music consisting of Twelve Performers be attached to this Corps.

VII.
That the Uniform Coats for the said Band be Scarlet Cloth, with Blue Capes, Cuffs and Facings, Wings and Shoulder Straps ornamented with Silver Lace and Fringe, Waistcoats and Breeches of White Cassimere, Plated S.V. Buttons, Cocked Hats edged with White Eckle Feathers, Black Cockades, with Plated S.V. Buttons and Loops, Scarlet feathers with white Tops – the Hair to be clubbed.

VIII.
That the Fifers wear the same Kind of Coat, Waistcoat and Breeches as the Band, but to have Cocked hats with Green Cockades, Plated S.V. Buttons and Loops, and Yellow Feathers.

IX.
That the Drummers wear Scarlet jackets, with the same Facings and Ornaments as the Fifers, White Cassimere Waistcoats and Leather Breeches, Round Hats, with a Black Feather over the Crown, turned up on the left side, with a plated S.V. Button and Loop, Green Cockades and Yellow Feathers.

X.
That the whole Corps wear half Gaiters of Black Cloth, Black Velvet Stocks with White Neckings, plain Yellow knee Buckles, plain white Cotton or Thread stockings, and plain Shirts with Frills at the Breast.

Most Volunteer corps had their own unique design of uniform. Given the plethora of units that existed, it is impossible to give an exhaustive list: for those interested in the dress and appearance of these units, I heartily recommend the website of Richard Warren 'This reilluminated School of Mars'.

## Training
Volunteers met to train weekly. The Royal Wakefield Volunteers' orderly book in the John Goodchild Collection reports drill sergeants were to attend musters on Mondays, Wednesday and Saturdays from 06:30 to 08:00 and from 18:30 to 20:00. A forfeit of 6d was charged for

every missed drill session. On the first Monday of each month, between 17:00 and 20:00 a general field day was to be held, where every man was to attend in full uniform or pay a fine of 2s 6d. The drummers were to march around the town in full uniform to call the men to the muster. For those at work, this was a major commitment in terms of time and lost earnings. Many of the lower-class volunteers, especially in the summer on piece work, would have lost income to attend. We touch on this again in a later chapter. Training of the men of the Royal Wakefield Volunteers was handled by 'an old soldier', Captain David Parkhill. Parkhill was a veteran of the American Revolutionary Wars, and had been gazetted Captain on 17 January 1761 in the 41st Regiment of Foot. He had served as a Lieutenant at Minden in 1757. He served in the 12th Regiment of Foot during the America War and was invalided out on full pay. His son was Lieutenant-Colonel Parkhill of the 35th Regiment of Foot. By faith he was a fully paid-up member of Westgate Chapel, founded in 1661 as Presbyterian but by the mid-eighteenth century increasingly Unitarian in theology. In 1794, he is recorded as renting pews 31 and 32, paying £5 3s per year subscription. From January 1795 his attendance became sporadic, paying £1 5s 6d.[37] Parkhill was perhaps not unique in that 'old soldiers' came back to the colours.

Outside of this weekly commitment, the Volunteers were paid to attend a yearly training muster. Again for labourers and the less well off, this meant a loss of income, for others this may have been their first 'time away from home' and perhaps felt a sense of excitement in travelling to a new town. The notebooks of the orderly sergeant of the Loyal Sheffield Volunteers contains a vivid 'snapshot' of participating in the Volunteers.

The Volunteers were mobilised for ten days a year for training, often in a town local to their permanent locale. On 18 June 1799 'The commanding officer orders the regiment parade on Monday morning in undress, at half-past five O'clock in order to commence the march to Worksop'. The order further noted that the 'regiment have their hair clubbed close except the flank companies, which will have theirs plaited'. The regiment arrived in Worksop on 24 June. After time to sort out billets and a meal 'Evening parade at 8 O'clock. After orders the regiment will parade at 8 O'clock in the morning for exercise with 10 rounds of cartridge.' After the days exercises, on the evening of Tuesday 25 June the Colonel 'felt himself very remiss' following the parade 'to pass over in silence the steadiness which the regiment showed this morning under arms. He begs they will accept his warmest thanks.' The Colonel then ordered 'the regiment will parade at 6 O'clock in the morning that they may have the opportunity of seeing the cavalry inspected at 10 O'clock'. On Wednesday 26 June, the regiment paraded at 06:30 with 18 rounds per man, to train for the inspection on the Friday. The grenadier company was detached to 'join the Foresters under the command of Captain White'. On Thursday 27 June, the regiment was on parade at 09:00, each man being issued 20 rounds to practice 'the retreat of the defending army through a wood'. The evening parade was at 18:30 to 'enable such of the regiment as wish to go to the play'. Following the drill evolutions on Friday 28 June, the Colonel acknowledged the regiment's 'well deserved applause they received from the surrounding spectators' adding 'he makes no doubt but the conduct they have shown whilst at Worksop will endear them to the inhabitants of that town'. Lieutenant-Colonel Cooke seconded Lord Effingham, and wished to

> express his high approbation of the good-order and discipline of the Sheffield Independent Volunteers, which must arise from the great attention of their officers, and the strong disposition of the whole to attain that perfection which may better enable them in case of necessity to maintain that constitution for which our ancestors bled, and for the preservation of which they are now armed. Worksop June 29th 1799.[38]

## Men of the Volunteers

The experience of the men in Sheffield was repeated across the country, with units being marched to take up billets and conduct training outside of their own recruiting area. Upon joining the Volunteers, each man had to swear the following oath:

> I . . . do sincerely promise and swear, That I will faithfully and bear true allegiance to His Majesty King George, and that I will faithfully serve in the Royal Wakefield Independent Corps of Volunteers in support of the constitution of my country, as now established by law, and that I will willingly obey all such lawful Orders and Commands as shall be given by the Officers put over me in the said Corps for the Internal Defence of the Town and Neighbourhood of Wakefield. So help me God.[39]

We know a great deal about the men who stood forward to volunteer from the muster lists of the corps. Most recently, Professor K.B. Linch of Leeds University in his study of the men of Wellington's army and Volunteer forces, identifies that three main groups of occupations can be assessed to look at the makeup of the men who participated in volunteering. The groups comprised labourers (those who were employed and paid directly by others), artisans (those who had some degree of economic independence of various grades) and retailers (those who owned their own business). We also need to make note of merchants and gentlemen who we can class as professional. The ratio of professional to artisan and labouring men is what we look at in the following chapter. Urban gentlemen Volunteers and 'the sweepings of the street' formed the backbone of the Volunteer infantry, according to magistrates and vicar James Wilkinson of Sheffield.[40] Was the good reverend correct? As befitted corps organised around the former Reevesite associations, in the Bradford Volunteers formed in 1794, the allegiances of each new recruit were investigated 'minutely' and only those men who were 'unquestionably staunch in [their] political principles' to the Crown were accepted.[41] Likewise, in both Sheffield and Birmingham membership was contingent upon demonstrably loyalist politics.[42] In the 1790s, it was reckoned that the Sheffield Volunteers was composed:

> chiefly of journeymen manufacturers, many of them who severely feel the pressure of the times, and would be as likely to turn their arms against the magistrates, as to support them in any disturbance that may be excited on the pretence of the high price of provisions.[43]

In Leeds, the membership list of the Loyal Leeds Volunteers in 1802 reveals a mix of independent gentlemen and trades: of the 204 privates and 13 sergeants where names and professions are recorded, 1 per cent were labourers, 5.1 per cent low artisans, 11.73 per cent medium artisans such as butchers and shopkeepers and 14.8 per cent high artisans, very much skilled tradesmen like cloth dressers, druggists etc.[44] Tellingly we find only seven men directly engaged in the woollen trade:

> Burrow Copley, clothier, Hunslet; William Crabtree, cloth dresser, Bowman Lane; Henry Higgins, cloth glosser, Ebenezer Street; John Kershaw, cloth dresser, Meadow Lane; ? Littlewood, cloth dresser, Briggate; Joseph Moxon, cloth dresser, Meadow Lane; James Taylor, cloth glosser, Ebenezer Street.

We also record: 'Jeremiah Chadwick, dyer, Bowman Lane; James Motley, wool-stapler; Luke Wray, dyer, Swinegate; William Woodhead, wool-stapler.' Therefore, from our 217 other ranks, 3.2 per cent were involved directly in the production and finishing of cloth, and another four men involved in woollens, or 5 per cent of all members were engaged in the cloth trade, which given that Leeds' wealth was based on the woollen trade is remarkably small. We note 15 men, or 6.9 per cent were innkeepers. The cloth dressers, better known as croppers, were amongst the most active working-class agitators of the period: Whig appeals to the croppers and clothiers directly affected the 1806 and 1807 general elections. The minimal involvement of those working in the woollen trade in the Volunteers may be significant. We are not seeing the woollen trade rallying to support the mechanism of oppression. Indeed, many croppers and clothiers were angry at soldiers being used to defend illegal machines, which implies the Volunteers were not a unifying force in Leeds across the social divisions in the town.

Discounting the NCOs, the Loyal Leeds Volunteers had 26 identifiable voters out of 204 men, or just 12 per cent were voters, with six voting for the Whigs. From this data, it seems unequivocable that the Loyal Leeds were very much Tory. We are seeing largely Tory artisans, merchants and gentlemen: exactly the power base that the anti-war liberals actively campaigned against and sought to disenfranchise. Weaving and spinning from the sixteenth century until well into the nineteenth century in the West Riding was a rural-based cottage industry. Certain processes – usually the most highly skilled and the most remunerative – remained centred in urban areas. Cloth finishing and dyeing was once such skilled activity and was centred in Wakefield for a large proportion of the West Riding in the Calder and Aire valleys. It was to these highly skilled artisans that the 1780 and 1783 Yorkshire Association petitions had been distributed, and again in 1800, and with spectacular results in the 1806 and 1807 general elections. If the 217 recorded names, is reflective of the Corps as a whole, then the Tory Anglican Borough of Leeds and its magistrates was supported by a Volunteer corps in the 1790s that was representative not of the town as a whole, but largely of its own supporters. 'Church and King' supporters rallied to the flag and volunteered, while the Whigs, anti-war liberals and importantly, the working-class radicals were either excluded or as a collective via their institutions and combinations – which were nascent trade unions and very much illegal – did not engage with the Volunteers.

Amongst the 467 men of the Loyal Sheffield Volunteers recorded in the muster list preserved in Sheffield City Library, we find very few professionals: one man was a writer, another was an attorney at law, we find 173 were skilled artisans, the remainder being labourers. This was a very working-class unit. Sheffield at the time did not have the same middle-class element that Leeds and Wakefield boasted at this period. This is not to say that Sheffield lacked a middle class: it most certainly had one that flocked to the theatre in the town, but it was dominated by the likes of Samuel Shore, the extended Hunter family and other notables who were by and large anti-war liberals and religious Dissenters. Shore and the Hunters were Unitarians at Upper Chapel. We see in Sheffield the working men mobilised in opposition to the radicalised working men of the Sheffield Constitutional Society. It is perhaps significant in this regard that no man was a voter.

In comparison, of the 167 names enrolled in 1795 into the Royal Wakefield Volunteers, we find that all members were professional. Not a single labourer was enrolled in the corps. We find four gentlemen under arms, a schoolteacher, Samuel Thwaite, and a hairdresser and perfumier Thomas Warterworth, as well as mill owners like Joseph Chambers and cloth manufacturers like Luke Race. We see that 20 per cent were low artisans, 30 per cent medium artisans – wheelwrights, blacksmiths, harness makers, basket manufacturers – and 37.1 per cent high artisans such as clockmakers like John Day or John Potter, a druggist and chemist, shopkeepers, drapers etc, and 10 per cent professionals like John Whitworth who was a magistrate's clerk, Henry Lumb a lawyer, Robert Whitworth agent for the Phoenix Fire Insurance Company and 3 per cent were gentlemen. We note one high artisan was William Puckrin, a builder, who with his father erected the large house at the eastern end of St John's North Wakefield. Furthermore, we note that he along with his father John built seven other houses on the street through a building society they ran, 'The Union Society'. In 1827 William would build St Austin's Catholic Church in Wakefield. When we look for political and religious ties we find:[45]

Michael Bentley – Tory, cloth merchant, Anglican
John Statter – Tory, cloth draper, Anglican
Samuel Oates – Whig, husbandman, Unitarian
Thomas Foljambe – Tory, gentleman and notary, Anglican
Robert Webster – Tory, carpenter, Anglican
Charles Tunnacliffe – Tory, plasterer, Anglican
Joseph Penney – Tory, shoemaker, Anglican
Thomas Glover – Tory, cloth dresser, Anglican
Joseph Holdsworth – Tory, cloth merchant, Methodist
Joseph Scott – Tory, cloth dresser, Methodist
William Holdsworth – Whig, merchant, Unitarian
William Dawson – Tory, gentleman, Anglican

We see the two Whig voters were Unitarian. Volunteering allowed new bonds of patronage to be developed between merchants and traders who may not have previously associated due to religious differences. Amongst the NCOs we find Sergeant William Rideal:

he paid pew rent at Westgate Chapel where his four children were baptised; likewise, Benjamin Willoughby and John Booth listed as bandsmen and or drummers were Westgate Chapel men. William Rideal's father, Titus, had invested in Leeds' White Cloth Hall in 1772 and was manager of James Milnes & Co, cloth merchants, by 1779.[46] Indeed, Titus rented a large mansion on Westgate in Wakefield from the Milnes family.[47] By the 1790s William Rideal was in business as Messrs Drake & Rideal. The concern was described as 'Mercers and Drapers' of Wakefield and Pontefract. The concern had purchased the business of Mr Lazenby of Pontefract in June 1794. John Drake was the buyer for the concern, and bought goods in London according to an advert placed in the *Leeds Intelligencer* of Monday 16 June 1794. William Rideal was declared bankrupt on 17 December 1800 due to unfavourable trading conditions occasioned by the war he supported.[48] A fellow sergeant in the same corps was John Halliley: from Earls Heaton, Dewsbury, his father John Halliley senior had established blanket manufacturers Halliley, Son & Brooke. As business owners, Rideal and Halliley had a stake in the status quo: as local businessmen, they had a lot to lose from a French invasion, and his obvious support for the Volunteers brought him to attention of loyalist inhabitants and other men of business: public displays of patriotism was a good way of forging new alliances across political-religious grounds to further one's own prospects.

Overall, in Leeds and Wakefield we are seeing a cross section of shopkeepers and professionals across the social and religious spectrum of the town. Indeed, from 1798 the corps only recruited men who were respectable free householders, or those recommended to the committee by two current members, exactly the same recruitment base as the Armed Association.[49] The Royal Wakefield Volunteers of the 1790s were solidly middle-class, property-owning professionals who owned their own businesses, and were markedly different to Bradford and Rotherham in composition. When we look at reports about the men as we progress towards the end of the 1790s we find two men had died in May 1799, and in June and July, eight men were discharged for disorderly conduct, nine were discharged from May to June 1800 for not attending musters and as the food rioting escalated again in summer 1800, eighteen men were discharged. As we progress into 1801, twelve men were discharged for not attending musters and bad conduct. Clearly the corps had faced internal disciplinary issues when called out to face the food rioters: it was not totally immune from the underlying societal grievances of the time. The corps never mutinied, but it is obvious that it was not a happy time for the men.

How reflective of national trends were Leeds, Sheffield and Wakefield? We can compare the Leeds, Wakefield and other corps formed in the same period after Austin Gee:[50]

The table overleaf clearly shows that in urban centres, professionals, skilled workers and shopkeepers made up the bulk of the Volunteers. As could be expected in largely rural Buckinghamshire, the Volunteers were mostly agricultural labourers. Bristol, with its wealthy middle class, outstripped Leeds and Wakefield in the percentage of gentlemen and professionals such as clerks who joined up to defend hearth and home. By and large the urban corps was a mobilisation of the possessing classes, seeking to protect their business and property from both the French and more importantly from the working-class radicals and Jacobins.

| Unit | % Labourer | % Low Artisan | % Medium Artisan | % High Artisan | % Professional | % Gentlemen | No recorded trade |
|---|---|---|---|---|---|---|---|
| Aylesbury | 37.9 | | 18.1 | 33 | 8.1 | 2.9 | 0.5 |
| Bristol Volunteer Infantry | 0.4 | | 36.1 | 23 | 42.7 | 11.5 | 10 |
| Borough of Buckingham | 45.6 | | 10.5 | 27 | 8.6 | 1.4 | 6.8 |
| Dinton | 60 | | 13.3 | | 0 | 0 | |
| Leeds | 2 | 10.2 | 31.73 | 26.57 | 24.3 | 5 | |
| Sheffield | 62.5 | 6.9 | 30 | | 6.3 | | |
| Princess Risborough | 51.8 | | 13.9 | 22.6 | 8.6 | 3.6 | |
| Royal Wakefield Volunteers | - | 16 | 34 | 37.1 | 10 | 3 | |
| Winchcombe and Sudeley Loyal Volunteer Infantry | 35.7 | | 21.4 | 29.5 | 5.8 | 7.1 | |

Chapter 3

# THE COUNTY YEOMANRY

As well as needing infantry and artillery for home defence, if an army was to be built on the cheap, cavalry was needed, thus the county Yeomanry came into being. The formation of the Yeomanry was markedly similar to that of the Volunteer infantry, largely thanks to the activities and funding from the local 'great and good', and offered a similar opportunity for self-aggrandizement through adoption of military rank and dress.

Although the earliest Volunteer infantry corps were formed in coastal areas, by the summer of 1794 counties across the country were busy forming Yeomanry regiments. It did not take long for the movement to develop national coverage and stretch inland. Within the first two years of the force's existence, approximately one-third of its strength was found in Yorkshire, the Midlands and Gloucestershire.

In North Yorkshire, a meeting of 12 June 1794, chaired by Lord Fauconberg, the Lord Lieutenant of the North Riding, resolved to raise an unspecified number of troops of Volunteer cavalry, 'to consist of the Gentlemen and Yeomen', the government to provide arms and accoutrements. A second meeting was held on 18 July, chaired by Lord Morpeth, and resolved that four troops should be formed. These were commanded by Captains Henry, Lord Morpeth, Charles Duncombe Thomas Core (Coore) and John Wharton. Their commissions were all dated 18 July, the day of the meeting on which their appointments were proposed. Though these troops were technically independent and do not appear to have been constituted as a regiment, in the West Riding a Northern and Southern Regiment were formed, the density of troops again representing the primary objective of the Yeomanry being to aid the magistrates in local policing rather than against invasion.

The Warwickshire corps of Yeomanry cavalry originated at a meeting in June 1794, at which four troops were proposed, their officers' commissions being dated 16 July: 1st Packington, Captain Heneage, Earl of Aylesford; 2nd Aston, Captain Heneage Legge; 3rd Rugby, Captain Simon Adams; 4th Kineton, Captain Evelyn Shirley. In 1797 these four troops were constituted as a regiment under the command of Lord Aylesford, his colonel's commission dated 9 November.

In Gloucestershire, a troop was organised at a meeting of 30 July 1795, and raised under Captain Powell Snell, who was commissioned on 15 August. The 1st Gloucester Troop was brigaded with the Cotswold Troop to form a squadron. The squadron was battalioned with the Wotton – formed in December 1796 – and the City of Gloucester Troops, under Snell. The Cotswold Troop was formed on 4 January 1797. The City of Gloucester was formed 7 March 1797 under the orders of Captain Robert Morris, the combined troops becoming the Royal Gloucester Yeomanry soon after.[1]

We now look at a case study of a typical Yeomanry regiment.

## The West Riding

One of the first meetings to discuss the formation of a body of country Yeomanry was held on 30 April 1794. It was now that the West Riding magistrates met in convocation where they resolved that despite the formation of the Volunteers in the urban centres of Leeds, Bradford and Halifax, more troops were needed for the defence of the West Riding, and organised a meeting in the Moot Hall, Pontefract, on 21 May 1794. The magistrates' call to arms was headed by Bacon Franck, George Armytage, Henry Duncombe, Rev. James Wilkson, Robert Athorpe, Henry Wickham and John Blaydes of Leeds: notable by his absence from the magistrate's bench was Pemberton Milnes, Whig, Unitarian and leader of the Dissenting Whig faction in the county.[2] The Lord Lieutenant, the Duke of Norfolk, presided over the meeting which agreed:

> that the Gentlemen, Yeoman and substantial inhabitants of the Riding, not resident in or near the Market Towns where Corps of Infantry may have been or shall be formed, be invited to enrol themselves into a Corps of Cavalry, each person to furnish his own horse . . . That a subscription be opened for the purpose of providing cloathing and for such other purposes as may be thought necessary for the use and benefit of such Corps.

29

That a general committee be appointed for the purpose of carrying these resolutions into effect, with power to direct application of the subscriptions and to appoint sub-committees, with such powers and authorities as the said general committee may think proper.

That the said General Committee do consist of all subscribers of Fifty pounds or upwards and any seven or more to be a Quorum.[3]

The committee formed in pursuance of forming the Yeomanry resolved furthermore that:

1. That Leeds, Bradford, Halifax, Wakefield and Sheffield, having already formed Corps of infantry, it is the opinion of this committee, that a Corps of Five Hundred Cavalry be raised within this Riding, who are hereafter to be formed into Troops; Regarding being had, as much as possible, to the respective places of residence of the persons comprising such corps. That said troops to be trained and exercised not oftener than once a week; it being the intention that the service should interfere as little as possible with each individual's private occupation, except in the case of [illegible] Commotion.[4]

In the subscription list opened for the West Riding Yeomanry Cavalry raised in Pontefract, we find conspicuous displays of wealth, and therefore loyalism, from the nobility of the Riding:[5]

£1,000, Earl Fitzwilliam.
£300, Godfrey Wentworth.
£200, Roland Wynn.

We also find the Unitarian 'merchant princes' giving money to the cause in a display of ostentatious loyalism: £1,000 came from James Milnes, £50 from Richard Slater Milnes, £50 from William Oates, and £25 from John Milnes.[6] By and large the Yeomanry was funded by the rural elites and 'squirearchy': many urban merchants had evolved into country squires. James Milnes had town houses in Wakefield and London and a country mansion; Richard Slater Milnes had likewise York and London residences in addition to Fryston Hall. The merchants evolved into landowners of the Riding. The squirearchy was not as socially conservative as we would expect: men like Thomas Lumb as well as the Milnes were newcomers to this rural elite. This ostentatious display of wealth did not mean support for the war or the Yeomanry. Both Richard and James Milnes had been named in the Treason Trials, and this display of wealth helped display their loyalism. Both men were committed anti-war liberals, and sought to mobilise public opinion in 1797, 1801 and 1803 for peace with France.

Two regiments were formed on 13 August: the 1st or Southern Corps of West Riding Yeomanry Cavalry at Pontefract and the 2nd or Northern Regiment in Knaresborough. As with the Volunteer infantry, the formation of the Yeomanry was not without its problems. Magistrate Bacon Frank explained to Fitzwilliam in June 1794 that at a meeting in Doncaster, just three men enrolled, and the public opinion in the town was against the cavalry, in case the men were embodied into the regular army and forced to serve overseas or sent to crush riots outside the county. The Yeomanry was expensive, and the public mood was against forming Volunteer units wherever the magistrates travelled in the county.[7]

On 1 October 1801, with the signing of peace preliminaries with France, Volunteers and Yeomanry were to be stood down, and all but two troops stood down. The King issued a letter of thanks on 10 October 1801.[8] It was hoped that with peace, Volunteers would remain under arms. In the West Riding, the 1st and 2nd Regiments of Yeomanry Cavalry were wound down on 27 April 1802.[9] The Harewood Troop, commanded by Joshua Field, renewed their service three days later.[10] Likewise, the Skyrac Troop never stood down.[11] The Captain commanding the Barnsley Troop, Walter Spencer-Stanhope, was critical of the continuation of service. He spoke in the House of Commons on 4 May 1802, of the administration's intention to accept of any services offered by existing Yeomanry and Volunteer corps, thinking such an armed force in peacetime 'alike unnecessary as *unconstitutional*'. If the intention were to combat Jacobinism, he did not wish to 'dragoon the people in this way with sword and helmet' and objected to the Yeomanry protecting the farmer against the manufacturer 'and thereby inadvertently protecting his monopoly' at a time of national food crisis.[12] Parliament passed an Act on 22 June which officially sanctioned the retention of the Yeomanry and Volunteers, and would be exempt from being balloted for the Militia if they remained under arms. This was disseminated to Lords Lieutenant in a circular of 2 July 1802.[13]

Under this Act, three troops from the Northern Regiment offered to renew their services and were accepted, comprising the Knaresborough Troop under Captain Robert Harvey, the Tadcaster Troop under Lord Hawke, and the Aberford Troop under Lieutenant Bainbridge.[14] Four further troops were added to these in October, one of which was from Ripon. By the end of October the Barnsley, Doncaster and Pontefract Troops were re-activated following a meeting with Earl Fitzwilliam on the 24th.[15] The Sheffield and Rotherham Troops were active again by June 1803, when the officers were entertained by Earl Fitzwilliam at the Angel Inn, Sheffield.[16]

## Uniforms

We are fortunate that a considerable amount of archive material exists concerning the dress of the West Riding Yeomanry: I am sure other archives across the country hold similarly detailed records. With regiments providing their own uniforms, things could go horribly wrong with the procurement process. The first document relating to the dress of the regiment is from early summer 1794. Prices were fixed on 10 July 1794:[17]

> Buff leather breeches 25s
> Boots 24s a pair
> Saddle and bridle £6 6s

The uniform was to comprise a coat and waistcoat costing £3 3s, leather breeches at £1 7s, knee boots with cuffs cost £1 2s, and a hat with bearskin crest and plume costing £1. The whole cost was £6 12s: each man had to provide his own saddle, and was allowed £1 5s towards this, making an allowance of £7 17s.[18] The privates' clothing was to be provided by the general subscription fund, but the officers and sergeants had to buy their own uniform and equipment.[19] By March 1795, the situation of the clothing of the regiment was deplorable. Magistrate Bacon Frank reported to Earl Fitzwilliam that: 'the clothing of the Cavalry has proved so exceedingly bad and in many instances the coats is so much run up with being wet that it is almost impossible for the Volunteers to get them on, it was absolutely necessary to new cloath the cavalry'.[20]

Clearly something had gone terribly wrong with quality control of the cloth! Henceforth, it was agreed the Yeomanry were to 'be cloathed exactly as the light horse have, coats with short skirts'. Another issue arose over supply of arms. The regiment had made pistol holsters to the army regulation, to be 9in long, yet the Board of Ordnance supplied pistols with 12in barrels![21]

By spring 1795 the Rotherham Troops were wearing:

> a helmet, scarlet jacket and waistcoat with buff silk twist button holes, but without any epaulettes or other adornments for the shoulders (except for our officers who are to have a plated fish scale epaulettes with silver bullions).

The Troops requested they be authorised to wear fish-scale epaulettes and to change their buff leather breeches and equipment to whitened leather, and to adapt the cloaks to have sleeves. Lieutenant Colonel Bryan Cooke, as second-in-command of the regiment, on receiving the request from Rotherham, raised some concerns with Earl Fitzwilliam, the Colonel Commandant. In reply, the Earl instructed Pontefract banker and agent to the Yeomanry Thomas Tew to respond. Tew noted that Rotherham were mistaken, in that the uniform was a scarlet coat 'turned up green', with buff waistcoat, and buff silk twist trimming, and that the 'trumpeters coats & jackets were buff ornamented with trimmings at a considerable expense'. Tew also noted that fish-scale epaulettes for the troopers had been agreed in the previous year, a pattern produced and the price set as 12s, but the considerable expense of fish-scale epaulettes to the regiment as a whole had seen the idea dropped. If the men wanted such epaulettes they had to pay for them themselves and not expect the regiment to pay for them. Tew was concerned however that only the more affluent troops could afford such extravagances. Sleeved cloaks were disallowed originally 'on account of the greater difficulty in folding them up', but the committee felt sleeves could be added at no great cost. In due course, all the buff-coloured breeches and buff equipment were to be 'whitened' across the regiment as a whole as long as 'they were kept clean'. Hats, Magistrate Frank informed Earl Fitzwilliam, had not yet been agreed upon, but were to have bearskin crests and feathers and to cost £1. A coat and waistcoat cost £3 3s. The jacket and waistcoat were to be made from superfine English scarlet broadcloth, ornamented with buff silk twist, have silver-plated buttons, and cost £3 14s 6d.

A month later, the regiment's general committee met to agree to new terms for the dress of the regiment. It was resolved on 6 May 1795 that:

1. The headpiece of the bridle was to be reinforced with a piece of chain to protect the horse from sword blows
2. The contract with Joseph Rhodes of Leeds for providing clothing to the entire regiment was to be annulled. Troop commanders were empowered to produce new clothing locally in numbers required.
3. The helmet proposed by Hawkes of London was approved, to which was fitted the bearskin crests from the old hats. The motto on the silver plate to read 'Forward Pro Patria' with the initials YWRC engraved. Scarlet plumes were adopted.
4. Sleeves were added to the cloak.

5. Buff silk twist and trimmings to be replaced with white. Trumpeters to wear white coats and jackets in consequence.
6. Silver plated fish-scale epaulettes were adopted. Each epaulette consisted of 15 scales on green backing with white silk twist, to be provided according to the pattern of Wrightson of Doncaster, and supplied by the same at 10s a pair.
7. Officers were allowed epaulettes provided by Hawksley of Sheffield to cost no more than 9 guineas a pair.
8. Wrightson & Firth of Doncaster were the favoured contractor of jackets and waistcoats, costing £3 14s 6d excluding epaulettes.

A year later, the issue of whitening the belts and breeches was still a cause of concern or consternation within the regiment. The Home Office had been consulted on the issue of whitening belts, trumpeters' pay and providing allowances to provide new uniforms for the men: the government replied that the clothing allowance allowed for volunteers was not applicable for the Yeomanry as 'the gentlemen comprising the Yeomanry cavalry were in a situation above being cloathed by the government'. A new subscription was needed to buy replacement clothing, but the government did agree to the regiment whitening its belts. In 1798 when the clothing again needed replacement, it was resolved to adopt white lace, and adopt the uniform of the 10th Light Dragoons, but in scarlet with green facings, and requested a pattern to be supplied which would be copied. Cloth was to have been supplied by Milnes, Heywood & Co of Wakefield, but as Mr Heywood gave a lead time of three weeks to complete the order, Captain Francis Ferrand Foljambe, commanding the Rotherham Troop, urged that a Leeds manufacturer could supply the cloth immediately. Foljambe also stressed that the regiment was to be dressed like the regulars, and the officers' distinctions to be the same, though he urged the use of the existing epaulettes as the 'cheapest convenience'. Foljambe noted that the Leeds Volunteers dressed their men in cloth made in the West of England, as it was superior to cloth made in Yorkshire, and hoped that their 'brother volunteer have the finishing of it' identified as Thomas Staniforth. He ran a cloth-finishing concern. Clearly Foljambe ordered 'loom finished cloth' which he hoped that Staniforth would finish at minimal or no cost. We note Staniforth was the son of a major slave trader, who provided cloth for the two Rotherham Troops. Lieutenant-Colonel Bryan Cooke, on learning that the cloth for the regiment was to come not from Yorkshire, and was of a different colour to that used in the regiment went apoplectic at Foljambe for acting on his own initiative. In August Cooke ordered that the belts, breeches and lining of cloaks was to be white, and the trimmings of the new uniforms was again to be white: it had taken nearly four years to get the change sanctioned! New breeches costing £1 4s and boots costing £1 6sd were to be provided from the government allowance. Rather than boots and breeches, Lord Ribblesdale requested pantaloons and half boots were adopted as they were 'not only more comfortable to the dragoon, have a more military appearance and cannot be as often to marked and paired as boots & breeches'. In civilian fashion, tight-cut pantaloons were increasingly 'à la mode', and we see here the officers seeking to copy the latest trends. In another letter, Bryan Cooke commented that in 1795 the regiment had changed from coats to 'Jackets and Shells' bought from the central committee's funds, and requested from the War Office, 36s bounty per man for new clothing as the committee lacked funds to replace all the clothing in the regiment and to purchase new jackets, breeches, boots and to make repairs of the saddles and harness. Cooke reported that a jacket cost £2 14s 6, breeches £1 6s and boots £1 4s, and repairing epaulettes, and accoutrements would cost 15s 6, making exactly £6 per man. Fitzwilliam wrote to Lord Windham stating that the regiment needed new boots and breeches as they had not been renewed in 1795, and had been purchased in 1794 and added 'All the articles of cloathing, helmets excepted, were on inquiry found unfit for further service'. No new uniforms had been issued in bulk since 1795. The government allowed '£4 a man which is pitiable', which the Earl noted was far less than the regulars who received £9 for their clothing allowances, and £3 in the infantry. Clearly the Earl felt that War Office was trying to build the Yeomanry 'on the cheap' using the units' own funds rather than spending its own money. Fitzwilliam was perfectly correct: the Yeomen were to pay for the privilege of serving. For their existing men, troop commanders submitted returns of required clothing and equipment. Captain Chaloner commanding the Agbrigg and Morley Troop reported he required 15 jackets and shells, 50 black stocks, 9 cloaks, 50 pairs of leather breeches, 50 pairs of boots, 5 saddles and bridles, 8 saddle bags and 'horse collars', 50 pairs of gloves, 2 helmets for the sum of £272 8s. Major Benjamin Ferrand reported he needed '6 suits of regimentals, arms and accoutrements, 47 prs of boots, 47 prs of breeches, 12 swords and 1 saddle'. Bryan Cooke noted he needed to clothe 19 recruits, '1 farriers regimentals, Churns, Caps etc' as well as 47 men needing new clothing. Captain Harvey reported that he could not completely renovate the clothing of his troop for under £6 per man.

The farriers were to wear blue coats faced green, with bearskin caps, aprons, and to carry a hatchet from the saddle. The bearskins were provided by Mr Lempiere of London. Lempiere also supplied white goatskin housings for all the officers 'to ride upon' as it was felt it was 'essential to distinguish an officer readily in the field'. We assume these are a form of schabraque. The aprons, holster caps, saddles, cloaks for the farriers were all came from the regimental store or were made locally. New clothing was being produced by January 1799, as a sum of £1,534 having been allocated by government, which was far below the sum needed. Robert Harvey, commanding the Doncaster Troop, requested a pattern jacket and noted that his men desired to adopt chain epaulettes as the old ones were not fit for service. The officers, he reported, would provide their own clothing and sought permission for the officers to adopt silver lace trimmings. By summer 1800, due to lack of funds, the regiment presented 'a Motley crew' as old and new issue clothing was in use side by side. As late as summer 1800, the cost of changing trimmings from buff to white was still an ongoing problem! When re-formed in 1803, the regiment was dressed as hussars, in a blue dolman with blue pantalons, the cloth being provided by Milnes, Heywood & Co of Wakefield. The Rotherham Troops were armed with 300 sabres, and the same number of pistols, carbines, bayonets, sword belts, sword knots, carbine belts, cartouche boxes and belts.[22]

Their sister regiment had better luck in organising its uniforms. On 26 August 1794, the general committee of the Northern Regiment agreed that the epaulettes and clothing were to be supplied by Robert Rhodes of York, and cloaks were supplied by Captain John Pate Neville who 'agreed to buy up at the Leeds market the whole quantity of cloth necessary', the committee ordering that troop commanders were to buy from Neville the required amounts of cloth, and to engage local tailors to cut out the uniform according to the regimental pattern and for seamstresses to sew them up. The tailor was allowed 4s for buttons and making each cloak. The first uniforms were finished by Rhodes by the end of August and on 3 September 1794 were sent by carrier from York to Otley via Skipton, Keighley and Bingley. To speed up production, it was agreed on 10 September that each troop was to have its own tailor, who was to be supplied with authorised sealed patterns. Thus, for the Craven Legion, we find that uniforms were also provided by a Mr Robinson and also a Mr Holmes, both of Skipton who 'made up uniforms according to the specifications . . . the men's jackets had silver lace shoulder straps and fringe, the officers' rich epaulets'. The round hats were supplied from Messrs Hotham and Wilkinson of York, who were contracted to supply the hats complete with bearskin crest, feather plume and cockade at £1 12s. Produced in September were 'uniform jackets of blue cloth with scarlet cape to cost no more than 15s' which we assume were stable coats. Trumpeters wore reversed colours, so buff with scarlet collar and cuffs 'ornamented with trimmings at a considerable expense . . . ' and had been allowed to ride grey horses, purchased by the corps as trumpeters' mounts. Saddles and equipment came from Joshua Dawson of Otley.[23] In March 1795, it seems both regiments were re-dressed after the fashion of the Light Dragoons but in scarlet faced green, and the round hats were replaced with Tarleton helmets. May 1795 the contract with Rhodes was annulled by the general committee and new contracted entered into with Messrs Wrightson and Firth of Doncaster to provide 'A jacket and waistcoat ornamented with buff silk cord, best plated buttons, and of the very best superfine scarlet cloth manufactured in England, and shrunk, for £3 14s 6d exclusive of epaulets'. The same concern provided fish-scale epaulettes comprising 15 scales backed onto green broadcloth edged round in twist for 6s a pair, officers' epaulettes being provided by Hawksley & Co at 2 guineas a pair. New helmets were supplied from Thomas Hawkes of London, the bearskin crests from the round hats being re-used on the new helmets: Hawkes sent a consignment of 53 helmets and plumes to Major Ferrand of the 2nd regiment in August 1795.

The trumpeters' clothing changed in 1797 to entirely buff, the parade coat being dispensed with, the new buff jackets being supplied by Messrs Drake and Rideal of Wakefield. In 1799 new jackets were supplied by Messrs Hardwick of Leeds at £2 14s 6d, boots cost £1 5s, leather breeches £1 5s and horse furniture £6. Rather than boots and breeches, Lord Ribblesdale had adopted pantaloons and half boots.

In 1801 new clothing was issued which comprised an 'Austrian style jacket' in scarlet broadcloth, with green collar and cuffs, supplied by Messrs Wrightson of Doncaster costing £2 14s 6d being made from 'the best West of England Cloth, costing at Gloucester £1 2s 6d'. The Tarleton turban was changed to green and a white plume tipped red was worn. The farriers, added to the regiment in that year wore blue jackets with green collars and cuffs, and were also allowed 'fur caps, aprons, holsters and green cloaks'. When reformed in 1803, the 1st regiment wore blue dolmans and pantaloons, and were clothed as hussars.

For the 2nd regiment research by my twin Anthony Leslie Dawson presents a full breakdown of the clothing of the Corps as it was adopted 18 May 1803 through to 1808, stating that the uniform switched from scarlet to blue and had mustard-yellow facings. A Tarleton with blue turban and white over red plume was worn for full dress, and in undress a blue folding forage cap. The regiment was dressed as hussars, and adopted a dolman with 21 rows of frogging to the front, with three vertical rows of buttons. Trumpets were adorned with white dolmans and farriers blue. The stable coats were made from white kersey, closed with 16 white metal buttons. In marching overalls, blue overalls strapped with black leather and opening on the side seams were worn, replaced in 1805 by white canvas overalls. Officers and men alike were to provide black tail bags made from silk to cover the queue which were to be decorated with a black velvet bow. In the same year officers were authorised to wear a sabretache, with scarlet superfine broadcloth facing, 'edged all round in silver French check lace' and a silver white rose at the centre.[24] Again, Richard Warren's website provides copious details for those interested in the uniform side of the Yeomanry.

## Men of the Yeomanry

The cavalry required men with a different degree of 'world experience' to the infantry. They had to be able to ride, and care for their horse. For merchants, farmers and gentlemen alike the horse was the means of transport and power: pulling a plough, a wagon, drawing a handsome phaeton or providing a riding horse. Horses were more than just a part of everyday life in Regency England, they were fashion statements and sporting trends. Fox hunting and racing were the pursuit of rural and urban elites. For the Yeomanry, as well as the independent cavalry, the hunting field did however have one benefit for the military. Cavalry regiments, officered by huntsmen, tended to mount their regiments on hunters – good sturdy horses, often 'good doers', that is, horses that could manage on sparse or few rations of hard feed like oats and needed only grass and hay to be 'fit and active'. The hunting field was and still is an excellent schooling ground for the rider and horse. But with racing becoming increasingly fashionable, late eighteenth-century society went Thoroughbred mad, and in the military away went the old-fashioned hunters and middleweights, and in came lightweights. As well as keeping up with fashion, hunting changed during the middle decades of the eighteenth century. By 1780, hunting with hounds bred for speed, the foxhound, had become the norm, and the huntsmen needed a horse that could keep pace with them, so many hunters became Thoroughbreds or Thoroughbred crosses. The horse was indispensable to both everyday life and the economy during the late eighteenth and early nineteenth century. The demand for the horse in the military, however, with the prolonged wars with France, inflated the price of horseflesh to such an extent that by 1800 the steam engine and locomotive was developed to provide a replacement.

The men had to provide themselves with a uniform and a mount, which in theory meant labourers were unable to join as they could not afford a horse. It was reckoned a good horse for the Yeomanry would cost £17–£25, equivalent of a year's wage for a labourer. They were therefore socially exclusive units. The Duke of Richmond described the Sussex Yeomanry as the 'younger, brothers, sons and servants of [the] Farmers'[25] while the Marquess of Buckingham characterised them as the 'young idle gentlemen of the country, foxhunters and sportsmen'.[26] In Oldham the members of Yeomanry were the 'principal Inhabitants' – factory owners and churchwardens, and thus overall, it seems, tended to represent the interests of industrial or agrarian capital depending on where they were formed. The Yeomanry therefore were understandably reliable when it came to resisting crowds attempting to force down prices or to seize stocks of grain and were frequently praised for their 'readiness to give their assistance'.[27] Yet in more rural areas, we don't see this pattern emerging. For example, of the sixty-two men of the 1st Craven Troop, we find just J. Hall of Settle, a surgeon, and James Wilson a farrier of Gisburn, with trades other tenant farmer. Of the men forming the 2nd Craven Troop in 1794, we find few professional men beyond tenant farmers who made up the fifty-eight troopers:[28]

> Jonathan Anderton, enrolled 7 June 1794, physician in Keighley.
> James Barber, enrolled 7 June 1794, resigned 1799, maltster, Bingley.
> David Binns, enrolled 7 June 1794, weaver.
> Francis Butterfield, enrolled 18 September 1797, yeoman, Bingley.
> Charles Hartley, enrolled 7 June 1794, cotton spinner, Bingley.
> John Heelis, enrolled 7 June 1794, land agent, Skipton.
> Christopher Scott, enrolled 7 June 1794, maltster, Bingley.

Evidently, the troop was primarily rural farmers, rather than urban merchants and industrialists, which is as one would suppose. Indeed, not every man could afford a horse. When we look at the sixty-two men on the muster roll of the 1st Craven Troop for 1794, nine men could not provide a horse: three horses with full equipment were provided by Stephen Carr of Gisburn, and a horse apiece by J. Slinger of Settle, Thomas Wilkinson, John Robinson of Downham, John Holmes of Gisburn, Anthony Lister and Lord Ribblesdale himself.[29]

In comparison, the Buckinghamshire Yeomanry offer some interesting details. When we look at the 1798 muster list, we find a preponderance of farmers and their sons, but also a substantial secondary intake of professional men and tradesmen as well as a steady number of skilled craftsmen. We find no labourers, and out of the ninety-six men in the Burnham and Stoke Hundreds, thirty-three were voters. Of these ninety-six men, fourteen were gentry, seventeen were farmers, twenty were professionals such as clerks, twenty-one were tradesmen – including the landlords of the Crown Inn at Slough, the Christopher at Eton, the Turk's Head at Eton, the Crown at Windsor, and the Three Tuns at Salthill, as well as premises in Stoke Green – seven were artisans and five were servants. Of 110 men serving with the Aylesbury Troop in 1800, there were substantially more farmers – some 54 men – no doubt representing the greater significance of agriculture in the Vale. Just eight were considered to be gentry and again no labourers were amongst the ranks.[30] In Devizes, the troop was dominated by farmers, and had a similar recruitment based to Aylesbury and Buckingham, the West Riding Troops being conspicuous by their almost total reliance on tenant farmers. Yet we have to admit that the Yeomanry cavalry presented a split personality: on the one hand it had aspirations to a military role, on the other, it was a social organisation which was embedded within the middle class in the Home Counties at least. The data is perhaps better to understand in table form:

| Unit | % Farmers | % Low Artisan | % Medium Artisan | % High Artisan | % Professional | % Gentlemen | No recorded trade |
|---|---|---|---|---|---|---|---|
| Aylesbury | 49 | | | 21.9 | 21.9 | 7.2 | |
| Buckingham | 17 | 5.2 | 7.2 | 21.8 | 20.3 | 14.5 | |
| 1st Craven Troop | 96.8 | | | 1.6 | 1.6 | | |
| 2nd Craven Troop | 88.1 | | | 6.8 | 3.4 | 1.7 | |
| Devizes | 59.3 | | 7.4 | 22.2 | 14 | 7.4 | |

Turning these huntsmen into soldiers was not an easy task. Not every yeoman was a good rider. When the Northern Regiment of West Riding Yeomanry Cavalry passed in review on 7 November 1794, the inspecting officer remarked 'not half ride their own horses and most of them very indifferent'.[31] Aware of this, the government paid for each troop to appoint a sergeant and corporal, whose duty was to turn civilians into soldiers. Quite often these men had been serving soldiers. The sergeants were considered on permanent duty and paid 1s 63/4d a day. In the infantry Volunteers, each corps was allowed a drill sergeant and drum-major.[32]

# Chapter 4

# THE PROVISIONAL CAVALRY

The Yeomanry proved essential in riot control alongside the regulars during the crisis of 1795 that lingered into 1796 as the author has described elsewhere in *Fighting Napoleon at Home*, also published by Frontline. Without going into too much detail, the Yeomanry – acting like the modern-day mounted police at Orgreave during the Miners' Strike in the 1980s – had galloped into action in the West Riding as well as the Midlands, often wounding, maiming and killing the starving poor, who when faced with the bleak prospect of starvation had 'taken matters into their own hands' to survive. The infantry contingents had seen action – the Royal Wakefield Volunteers for example – but their slow rate of movement after mobilisation was their Achilles heel. Men not used to long marches or long hours under arms, particularly in the more middle-class units, hardly made good or effective soldiers. Men used to riding for hours on end hunting or for their day-to-day existence could suffer the fatigues of long marches far better. Looking at the seventy-six food riots recorded by the Home Office that took place in the Midlands and elsewhere that required intervention by armed forces, twenty had been put down by the Yeomanry, thirty-nine by the regular cavalry, and seventeen by Volunteer infantry. The county Yeomanry had proved its worth.[1] Seventy-two per cent of deployments in the West Midlands were of mounted units. Looking at the West Riding, the Yeomanry was pivotal in riot suppression in Wakefield,[2] Pontefract,[3] Rotherham, Knottingley[4] and Sheffield. The Yeomanry had also been deployed at Grassington when Thomas Lister's troopers charged into the marketplace, and 'took 14 prisoners'. Lister does not report any fatalities, but took great pride in reporting the conduct of his men in supressing the common people.[5] The Skyrac Troop of Yeomanry was called out in May 1796, again against food protestors.[6] Volunteer infantry had been deployed in Knottingley,[7] Rotherham[8] and Halifax.[9] Earl Fitzwilliam later wrote on 9 August:

> . . . the Volunteer corps have shewn their readiness to act in support of Law and Order, in a manner that must give great satisfaction to all those, who wish to see them maintain'd . . . in the manner, in which it has ended, I trust it will be productive of good, and tend much to the future quiet of the place.[10]

During a food riot in Barrow-upon-Soar, the Leicester Yeomanry Cavalry shot dead several individuals.[11] Looking at the Home Office statistics of the seventy-six military interventions in the food riots of 1795, we note six civilians were killed by the Volunteers and Yeomanry, most notably in August 1795 when sixteen Volunteers in Rochdale opened fired, killing two men.[12] Two rioters were shot dead by the regular soldiery during disturbances in Birmingham.[13] The 5th Dragoon Guards were involved in three major clashes with civilians in 1795 alone, the last of which, at Stratford-upon-Avon, resulted in a civilian fatality.[14]

If the nation was to be defended from home-grown dissidents, and with the possibility of ever more regulars being drawn off to Flanders, the cavalry force for home defence had to be massively expanded. The Yeomanry was seen as 'invaluable' in terms of preventing rural disorder by the Lords Lieutenant of Northamptonshire and Buckinghamshire.[15] In Derbyshire the Yeomanry was paraded in several locations where there were fears of disorder, and the measure proved effective in curbing riots before they happened.[16] The same was true in Norfolk and Essex, where local authorities also praised the Yeomanry's presence as minimising overt acts of protest.[17]

However, the Yeomanry was too weak, just 4,000 men spread piecemeal across the country,[18] and too ad hoc inasmuch as not every county had formed a body of Yeomanry. Therefore, other means of recruitment – some would say coercion – was needed to provide more mounted troops. The infantry Volunteers had proven too slow to muster to be of the same utility as the Yeomanry. For example, during a food riot in Yaxley, Earl Fitzwilliam's troop of Gentlemen Cavalry were assembled at Peterborough and within 25 minutes had travelled five miles to the scene of the disturbance.[19] Therefore, the Crown believed it needed to massively expand the number of mounted troops available for home defence. To do so, legislation to enable a provisional force of cavalry, to be embodied in the manner of the Militia, was passed in November 1796. Under the Provisional Cavalry Act anyone who owned ten or more horses could be required to provide one man on a horse for the county's regiment; those owning fewer were grouped to the same purpose. Unlike the Yeomanry cavalry, who were paid only when called up, troopers of the Provisional Cavalry received a wage. Upon being balloted, the new trooper had to take the following oath:

> I, A. B. do sincerely promise and swear that I will be faithful and bear true allegiance to His Majesty King George, and I do swear that I am a Protestant; and that I will faithfully serve in the corps in which I am enrolled, within the Kingdom of Great Britain for the defence of the same during the continuance of the Act.[20]

Men who were balloted aged over 50 were exempt from service, likewise those considered infirm, and therefore had to provide a substitute, fully clothed, equipped and mounted.[21]

In late November 1796 Lords Lieutenant of counties received a letter from the Home Secretary, the Duke of Portland, outlining their responsibilities under the legislation. A quota was established for each county that it was expected to keep. However, the Provisional Cavalry was unpopular, being a drain on county funds and effectively conscripting members of the landowning class.

With the publication of the Provisional Cavalry Act a meeting was held in Leeds on 24 November 1796 to enact the survey of horses in the West Riding and men fit for duty under the Act.[22] A meeting of the Lieutenancy on 26 November 1796 resolved to form a regiment of six troops, trained as light cavalry and commanded by Colonel Sir John Fleming Leicester, commissioned on 17 January 1797. A meeting of the Lieutenancy of Gloucestershire was held on 10 February 1797, which agreed to the formation of a troop of Provisional Cavalry with enrolments being held on 14 February 1797.[23] In East Yorkshire, five troops, under the command of the Duke of Leeds, were formed: he was both colonel and Lord Lieutenant. The regiment was first assembled at Beverley on 17 March 1797.[24] Across the country border into the North Riding, the Riding's Deputy Lieutenants met in January 1797 to consider raising Provisional Cavalry among other matters, and on the 30th adopted the government estimate of £2 9s 6d for the clothing allowance, and their own estimate of £4 17s 0d for the horse furniture. By the end of June 1797, progress was extremely patchy; some of the companies had men who had enrolled as volunteers, others were raised men by ballot.[25]

However, the formation of the Provisional Cavalry was not universally popular: moves were made in 1797–8 to organise a regiment in Shropshire under Major Hill, but were offset by a persistent consensus in favour of raising additional Yeomanry troops as a substitute, as conceded by legislation.[26] The Pontefract and Doncaster Troops of the West Riding Yeomanry met in January 1797, resolved not to change their enlistment terms as volunteers and preferred to remain as Yeomanry, refusing to be balloted for the new corps.[27] Despite this, two regiments appear to have been organised, a First (or Southern?) under Colonel William Wrightson, covering Doncaster, Rotherham and Sheffield, and a Second or Western Regiment under Colonel Sir John Lister Kaye, presumably covering Bradford, Leeds, Wakefield, and Halifax.[28] The officers of the West Riding Provisional Cavalry were appointed on 9 May 1797: Alexander Hart was named Lieutenant-Colonel, William Tancred and Edward Dyrne Brisco of Wakefield were named captains, as was James Collins of Knaresborough, the lieutenants being Thomas Boothroyd, gentleman of Halifax, Ralph Walker, gentleman, of Wakefield, and Charles Brown, gentleman, of Leeds. John Wilson of Headingly was named cornet.[29] Once the men had been balloted, they needed to cloth themselves, and at meeting of the Deputy Lieutenants of the West Riding held in Leeds on 6 February 1797 resolved that:[30]

> For providing clothing for a cavalry man according to pattern. £2 9s 6d
> Horse furniture. £4
> Extra expense of a horse per annum. £6

The pattern would have been identical to that of other corps: a dark green jacket, with white braid to the edges, red collar and cuffs edged in white, possibly green pantaloons and half boots. The headdress was clearly not a Tarleton helmet as these, based on extant items and portraits, were for officers only.

Substitutes for balloted men were allowed for £7s and £15 for a horse, where a substitute could not provide his own. For clothing and equipment, local businesses provided their services. For example, Joseph Green, saddler of Bradford, provided the corp's harness, tack etc.[31] So too did William Smith, a saddler trading near the White Hart Inn.[32] R. Cundall of Leeds announced that he was able to provide horse furniture, pistol holsters and cartouche boxes of the pattern agreed at the general meeting in Leeds.[33] Joshua Dawson of Otley advertised:

that he makes the horse furniture &c on the following terms, viz:

Strong regimental saddle, with brass cantle; broad linen white girth and loups; stirrups, leathers and ions; holsters or half covers with cartouche case; black bearskin flounce; pad with straps, crupper, breastplate, leather surcingle, bridle and every other article to complete the horse furniture, at three pounds eighteen shillings.

Those gentlemen who wish to have furniture of a superior kind, may have it made as follows for six guineas.

Saddle with hogskin seat; silver head and cantle, superfine broad woollen girths; stirrups leathers and irons highly polished; superior black bearskin flounces; pad with crupper, breastplate, surcingle and bridle with bits well finished – the rings, buckles, dees, staples &C of this furniture all plated.[34]

The West Riding Deputy-Lieutenants agreed to raise a subscription to defray the costs of the expenses of the Acts to raise the Provisional Cavalry. The meeting, held in Leeds on 27 May 1797, stated that:

no persons whatsoever, whether serving as officers in the Militia or Volunteer Corps, or Volunteers serving in the Militia or Volunteer Corps, Clergymen keeping only one horse, dissenting teachers, quakers or any others, are entitled to any exemption from such assessment; but on the contrary, the owners of all the horses affected to the Duty upon Horses in April 1796, must be affected for every horse then entered, even the very horses sent to serve in the Provisional Cavalry.[35]

The third muster of the Provisional Cavalry was held in York on 26 June for the City and Ainsty of York, for the wapentake of Claro at Knaresborough on 38 June, for Staincliffe and Ewecross at Skipton on 28 June, for Morley at Halifax on 29 June, Skyrac and the Borough of Leeds on 30 June, for Agbrigg at Wakefield on 1 July, Staincross at Barnsley on 3 July, Strafforth and Tickhill at Doncaster on Monday 3 July, Osgoldcross at Pontefract on 5 July and Barkston Ash at Sherburn on Thursday 6 July.[36] Musters were held throughout April 1798, the first since October the previous year to mark the King's birthday.[37]

The Provisional Cavalry levies of 1797 failed to provide the minimum numbers that Dundas had set. In March of that year Colonel Mark Wood decried the Provisional Cavalry in a Parliamentary speech as an 'unpopular measure . . . so little calculated to afford any adequate degree of security to the public'. Dundas described his intentions for the various cavalry units in case of an invasion. The regular cavalry was to attack the enemy, the Yeomanry to preserve the peace in civilian areas and the Provisional Cavalry to drive away cattle and carry out similar duties of a 'hussar nature'.[38] Despite the unpopularity of the Act, the *Leeds Intelligencer* reported the resolution of a meeting held in Leeds on 25 March 1798:

> Notice is hereby given, that the list of all persons charged within the Wapentake of Skyrac (including the borough of Leeds) to the duties upon horses kept for the purpose of riding or drawing carriages with their respective places of residences as described in the schedule delivered into the Deputy Lieutenants by the surveyor of the said Duties, of the persons so charged to the same duties, since the former schedule was delivered to him in December, 1796: and also the several classes in which such persons are placed for the purpose of standing their chances in relation to the ballot to be made of every class, pursuant to the directions of the late Acts of Parliament for enabling His Majesty to raise a provisional force of cavalry are deposited with Thomas Bolland, of Leeds Clerk of the Sub-Division Meeting.[39]

Notice was given of the ballot in Staincross on 20 April.[40] One of the men selected by the ballot in Agbrigg was No. 10 Thomas Omeroyd, Class Number 133, who was balloted on 4 May 1798. He was enrolled on 17 May.[41] At a meeting held in the Moot Hall in Wakefield on 23 March 1798, rather than having independent troops in each wapentake, a single, cohesive regiment for the West Riding was ordered to be formed.[42] It lasted barely a year as beginning in May 1799, the Provisional Cavalry, bar the six embodied regiments which were transmuted to Fencibles, were absorbed into the Yeomanry. The men were, in some cases, ostracised for their lower social status.[43] For example, in Buckinghamshire, the Yeomanry and Provisional Cavalry were at loggerheads. The Yeomen objected to exercising with men of 'inferior description'. Edward Horwood of Buckland resigned in November 1797, complaining about the 'uncivil' behaviour of the Provisional Cavalrymen. He further considered that their admission had broken the articles under which he had enlisted in the Yeomanry. When we look at the muster list for the Provisional Cavalry here in Buckinghamshire, we find of the 171 troopers, just 39 were riding their own horses and three troopers provided 26 troop horses between them. Four of the troopers were considered 'poor' and were all urban shopkeepers or artisans rather than the rural farmers that made up the Yeomanry.[44]

46

## Independent Cavalry

So unpopular was the Provisional Cavalry, that in order to circumvent the Act, volunteer cavalry units were specifically raised. In the West Riding, a public meeting to raise such a body of volunteer cavalry was held in the Old King's Arms Inn in Leeds on 23 November 1796:

Resolved,

That a troop of Volunteer Cavalry, attached to the Corps of Leeds Volunteer Infantry and acting under the Command of Colonel Lloyd, may prove an useful and exemplary institution at this juncture.

We whose names are hereunto subscribed, do engage to enrol ourselves to serve in the said troop.

William Blackburn, Matthew Shirtcliffe, Edward Armitage, John Shepperd, Richard Mathewman, Edward Wilks, James Rhodes, Abraham Walker, Joseph Harrison, William Walker, John Brown, Charles Coupland, Eli Musgrave, John Turton, T Read, Richard Paley, Walter Beaumont, James Nicholson, John Nicholson, Edward Atkinson, Peter Rhodes, Edmund Maude, Thomas Micklethwaite, James Sowden, Edward Reeve, William Close, Edward Oates, William Tetley, John Warham, David Rimmington, John Mickelthwaite, John Vincent, Joshua Walker, William Hett.

Such Gentlemen as intend to serve in the said Troop are requested to add their names immediately.

William Cookson, chairman[45]

Wade Brown enlisted in January 1797.[46] By the middle of the month the following men had enlisted: Jeremiah Barlow, Simon Spence, John Plowes Jnr, Abraham Thompson, Richard Thompson, William Carr, James Hirst, Isaac Rimington, William Stirk.[47] At a meeting of 16 January 1797, the committee resolved:

having declined to concur in the resolutions agreed to at a meeting of the inhabitants of this Town, held in the White Cloth Hall Yard on Friday last,

The inhabitants of this Borough are therefore requested to meet THIS DAY at the Moot Hall at Eleven O'clock in the forenoon to consider the most measures for carrying into effect the first resolution agreed to at such meeting, viz 'that it would be highly credible and advantageous for this District to raise its quota of cavalry under the Denomination of Volunteers' By order of the Mayor, Lucas Nicholson, Town Clerk.

The following Gentlemen have offered their services for this purpose:

Wade Brown, John Cookson, William Clapham, John Lee, Lucas Nicholson, R R Bramley, Thomas Hainsworth, John Hey, James

Nicholson, E Atkinson, Thomas Benyon, William Sheepshanks, Joseph Stead, Joshua Burton, Thomas Clouth, William Stirk, Joseph Ogden

And each of the following Gentlemen have offered to provide a man and a horse,

William Thompson, George Bischoff, Benjamin Gott, Richard Wormald, John Calverley, John Brooke, Richard Paley, Thomas Wright,

Several other gentlemen have offered to find horses.[48]

The men were sworn in to the new corps at the end of January 1797 and an advertisement was placed to recruit a drill sergeant. Interesting to note, Thomas Hainsworth was a cloth merchant and trustee of Mill Hill Unitarian Chapel, as was George Bischoff, who was likewise a wealthy cloth merchant and trustee at Call Lane Unitarian Chapel, who served, it seems, quite happily alongside hardline Anglican Tories like Benjamin Gott and Wade Brown, suggesting religious and political differences were set aside for the 'greater good' and above all else, civic pride in Leeds. The Duke of Norfolk, had received from the Duke of Portland an address stating:

I have received his Majesty's Commands to inform your grace, that his Majesty highly approves of this additional mark of the zeal and loyalty of the inhabitants of the town of Leeds; and he is please to secede to their proposal for raising a troop of cavalry in that Town.[49]

Officers of the Leeds Independent Cavalry were appointed in February 1797: William Blackburn was named Captain Commandant, James Rhodes Lieutenant, and William Walker Cornet.[50] A few months later in May, James Rhodes was Captain Commandant, William Walker was Lieutenant and David Rimington was made Cornet.[51] The corps was wound down in 1811.

Leeds was not alone in taking this action. According to Richard Warren, the de facto expert on Volunteer soldiers of the period, in Gloucestershire, the 'Bristol Light Horse Volunteers' was formed in 1797 under the command of Captain William B. Elwyne (Elwyn), who received his commission on 1 April 1797. A second Bristol troop was formed in November 1797 commanded by Captain Timothy Powell. The Staincross Gentlemen Yeomanry were raised, paid for and commanded by Godfrey Wentworth of Woolley Hall. They were 'to act in case the Volunteers were called away on active service', and it was 'the duty of every man to stand forward in defence of his country'. Wentworth's tenants were to be encouraged to enrol.[52]

Chapter 5

# INVASION SCARE

The legislation of 1794 had not resulted in the formation of a body of Volunteers in every county, let alone town, in the country. All that was to change with the arrival of the French fleet off Ireland on Christmas Day 1796, followed by an abortive landing in Fishguard by the French described in detail in the author's companion book *French Invasions of Britain and Ireland 1792 to 1815*, also available from Frontline. Across the country, thousands sought to enrol as Volunteers. The Crown was acutely aware of the shortage of manpower in some counties. In Staffordshire for example, no volunteer units of cavalry or infantry, other than the county Yeomanry, had been formed with the legislation of 1794.

Again, the West Riding will be used as an example thanks to the wealth of archive documents. As we noted earlier, eight corps of Volunteers were formed in immediate response to the legislation of 1794. The invasion scare of 1797 does not seem to have stimulated a general revival of the volunteering spirit across the Riding which witnessed only a single Volunteer corps being formed. Perhaps this is explained by the fact that most urban centres already had a volunteer unit, and moreover, the 'Country Gentlemen' were busying themselves in organising a county-wide meeting to demand a general election to oust William Pitt and replace him with Charles James Fox and the Whig party. For men like Rev Wyvill, Charles Grey, and a plethora of MPs, Dissenting clergy and members of the House of Lords, peace was the panacea to a faltering economy, rising levels of social unrest and to turn back the repressive legislation of the Sedition Acts and the Gagging Acts of 1795.

The Pontefract Volunteers had been envisioned in 1795. Their nominal commander, Teesdale Cockell, a veteran soldier from the American War of Independence, found it almost impossible to

49

form a corps due to a series of disputes with the local magistrates. Cockell refused to command the corps because, in his view, it would have consisted of a 'few gentlemen and tradesmen, whose chief inducements appear'd to be center'd on the richness of their uniform'.[1] Due to the impasse between the Borough and Cockell nothing happened regarding the formation of the corps until 21 August 1797 when:

> The committee appointed for the management, affairs and expenditure of the money raised by subscription for the clothing and training to the use of arms, a Body of Volunteer Infantry, for the Defence of the Town and its Vicinity, to serve without pay (Government having engaged to find them arms and accoutrements), present their respectful compliments to the families in the neighbourhood, and beg leave to inform them, that Corps is now formed, consisting of two companies, of sixty men each.
>
> The loyal inhabitants of Pontefract have most liberally subscribed, and many of the tradesmen from a spirited principle of loyalty, have been extremely generous and spirited – printed lists of the subscriber's names will be sent to every subscriber when the whole is finished.
>
> We hope the families in the neighbourhood will be equally zealous with the inhabitants of Pontefract, in giving their support to the Corps that may one day render essential service. It is unnecessary to say that the present times are pregnant with the most serious Alarms, that a Diabolical Revolutionary Faction is eagerly endeavouring to realise in this yet happy country, the same tragical scenes that have deluged France with the blood of her best and noblest inhabitants.
>
> To those possessing affluent fortunes, what can be more desirous than seeing a Loyal battalion ready to come forward of their lives and property against all attempts of those Jacobinical plunderers.
>
> Should a peace take place, the necessity of those useful Loyal Associations will become more needful and with proper care in the formation of them, will ever prove a rock of defence against the evil designs of Republican Jacobins, and present a rallying point of security to the Loyal and Peaceable state.[2]

The *London Gazette* informs us that on 31 August 1797 Teesdale Cockell was named Major Commandant, John Perfect Esq. was promoted to Captain from Lieutenant, Ensigns Robert Seaton and George Alderson were made First Lieutenants, and John Willott and George Pyemont were promoted from Ensign to Second Lieutenant.[3]

When finally raised, according to Cockell the corps was formed by 'Loyal Mechanics, Husbandmen, & middling Trade's people . . . [and] promises an effective corps of 150 men'.[4] Cockell, in order to increase the efficiency of this new command and no doubt to set his stamp as it were on his unit, threatened to expel any member who would not agree serve anywhere in Britain. As could be reasonably expected, and was perhaps Cockell's intention, this brought him into conflict with the 'men of consequence' in the unit. Thanks to this, he had the excuse to expel the middle-class members of the corps after they challenged his authority. Cockell was a social inferior to the leading men of the Borough: he had to command using his rank as well as social influence via Earl Fitzwilliam. In order to cement his position in the town and over the corps, he had to expel those from his corps that 'looked down upon him' and challenged his right to command. Understandably, the leading men of the Borough formed an alliance with the magistrates, who 'took every opportunity to discredit him and the Volunteers'. When a Volunteer was arrested for stealing a chicken during the famine of 1799–1800, he threatened the two peace officers who arrested him. The magistrates used this episode in their propaganda campaign against Cockell, and greatly exaggerated the event, causing much alarm in the town about the loyalty of the Volunteers and Cockell himself of course. Cockell had no option but to write and explain to Hobart (the Home Secretary) about the situation he faced in Pontefract and explained in great detail the precautions he had taken to prevent any similar episode occurring in the future.[5] About the composition of the unit, Cockell reported to Fitzwilliam that the corps was recruited from the 2nd Earl of Mexborough's tenants along with his brother's tenants, as well as from the tenants' servants.[6] The corps seems, despite being based in an urban area, to have had a largely rural, agricultural membership. What degree of coercion existed between landlord and tenant to enlist is not known.

The corps comprised at first two companies, increasing to a full battalion five companies strong in 1798. This increase subsumed the proposed Pontefract Armed Association.[7] Cockell was named Lieutenant-Colonel on 1 September 1798, Henry Saville was named Major, Hon Charles Saville Captain, John Willott First Lieutenant, and George Pyemont First Lieutenant.[8] The Hon Charles Saville and Henry Saville were the sons of John Saville, the Earl of Mexborough. Richard Wilkinson, gentleman, was named Lieutenant in August 1799.[9] Cockell's son was Lieutenant-Colonel of the newly-raised 105th Regiment of Foot.[10] The unit's second-in-command, William Sotherton, had been MP for Pontefract 1784–96. He was a native of Darrington, and was cousin to Bacon Frank, the West Riding magistrate. Elected on the 'householder' or Tory interest in 1784 he is never recorded as speaking or voting in the House. He died aged 51 on 31 January 1806.[11]

Like Cockell, he had served in the American War and was a professional soldier. Sotherton's brother Robert was also an MP. William Sotherton began his military career at the age of 15 on 6 June 1770 as a Cornet in the Royal Regiment of Horse Guards; he joined the 62nd Regiment of Foot in spring 1766 and served in America with the rank of Captain. Taken prisoner in 1777, he was released by 1780, was in England in 1781, and was made Captain of Grenadiers in September 1782. He purchased the rank of Major in 1789, and went on half-pay as a Captain in the 95th Regiment of Foot a year later. He was appointed Lieutenant-Colonel of the First West York Supplementary Regiment (Third West York Militia) on 25 February 1797 and subsequently Lieutenant-Colonel of the Pontefract Volunteers on 9 August 1803.[12] In recruiting men to the Corps, Cockell sought to exclude the petit-bourgeoise, and also the working man. In a letter of 21 April 1801, he reported to Earl Fitzwilliam that:

in consequence of a Ruffian having got into the Battalion and endeavouring to commit murder. As soon as we were informed of it, I instantly made a rule never to receive a recruit without two good Volunteers vouching for their character. At the same time, I discharged several of doubtful Charracter.[13]

Clearly Cockell's desire to recruit as many men as possible had led to an insufficient vetting process.

Pontefract was not unique in forming its Volunteers during 1797. In the wake of the abortive landing in Fishguard, across the Pennines from Pontefract, the townsfolk of Preston roused themselves to form 'The Royal Preston Volunteers', initially of two companies on 23 March 1797. A third and fourth company were added on 23 February and 10 May 1798 respectively. The committee's minute book provides a good deal of information; for example, a meeting of 20 March resolved that members should '. . . at their own Expence find and provide for themselves Regimental Cloathing . . . '. On 16 May 1797 the corps' committee decided that (rather eccentrically) it had 'thought it most adviseable to divide it into two Companies of equal numbers viz a Grenadier, and a Light Infantry'. On the 18th the men were measured and allotted accordingly to a company. Patterns of the uniforms were available to view on this occasion and the uniform resolutions, as below, were distributed in printed form:

The uniform of the Grenadiers to be a scarlet Coat with blue facings and lined with white shalloon but the turned laps with white kerseymere, a blue wing edged with a little Gold Fringe on each Shoulder and a yellow Button with the Letters R: P: V: embossed thereon. White Kerseymere Waistcoat single breasted, light mixed pantaloons edged in the Seams with Scarlet, and black Cloth Gaiters, a black velvet Stock, a smart cocked hat with a black cockade and black Feather. The uniform of the Light Company to be a scarlett jacket with blue facings, the wings as also the Waistcoat, Pantaloons Gaiters and Stock to be the same as the other Company, the Hat to be round, small in the Rim and turned up on the left side with a Handsome black cockade and <u>black Feather</u>.×

× Upon a consultation of the Officers of the Light Infantry Company this was altered to a green Feather.[14]

The 'Rules and Regulations' of June 1797 required each man to appear on field days 'neat and soldier like, in full uniform, with his hair short clubbed, a black Silk Rose thereon, and powdered'. In 1798 the corps purchased clothing for the band and for the drummers, the committee resolving 'that it is left to the Determination of the Officers what uniform shall be given to the Band and they are hereby authorised to see them cloathed so as such cloathing do not exceed the Sum of twenty eight pounds'.[15]

In Cheshire, the 'Loyal Chester Volunteers' were raised during 1797, with the date of the earliest commissions being 25 April 1797.[16] Henry Delves Broughton of Doddington Hall founded his own unit of Volunteers, aptly named after his residence, with the first commissions granted on 16 August 1797.[17] As with Pontefract, in Macclesfield a resolution to form a corps of infantry or cavalry had been passed at a meeting on 25 June 1794, which was approved by the Lieutenancy.[18] A committee was appointed and a clothing subscription opened, but no infantry corps was actually formed until 1797, when prompted by the threat of invasion.[19] The Loyal Macclesfield Volunteers, one company strong, was commanded Captain Jasper Hulley, who was granted his commission on 21 June 1797.

The invasion force that landed in Fishguard had originally been planned to land in Bristol and burn the town before marching to Chester. The French through their effective spy network knew Bristol was undefended by Volunteers. All this was to change when the 'Bristol Associated Volunteer Corps' came into being at New Year 1797. Originally proposed in June 1794, as with many other outpourings of loyalist fervour, the idea lay dormant for three years. A report of 18 February 1797 indicates that the corps was at first envisaged as a military association, with the stated aims of defending the town as well as guarding French prisoners at Stapleton, if required. Other resolutions passed included a request to government to provide 'Field Pieces' along with infantry arms and accoutrements.[20] Turning back to the West Riding, independent corps were formed into 1798. Originally proposed in June 1794, nothing came of the plan till May 1798. The new corps was to be raised within the wapentakes of Osgoldcross, Barkston Ash, and Skyrac: the 'Barkston Ash and Skyrac Volunteers' were commanded by Thomas Gascoigne, a recusant Catholic.[21] We look at the problems he faced in forming the corps in a later chapter.

Very few new Volunteer corps were raised: the majority of the later corps being raised were under the provisions of the Armed Association Act as our next chapter demonstrates.

Chapter 6

# 1798 ARMED ASSOCIATIONS

The abortive Irish invasion of 1796, the French landing at Fishguard and the naval mutinies of 1797 scared the nation and terrified William Pitt.[1] To make matters worse, Britain was losing the war: when young General Bonaparte dictated terms to Austria with the Treaty of Campo Formio, Britain found herself facing the direct threat of invasion in the shape of the menacingly-named *Armée d'Angleterre* massing on the coasts of northern France, and the reality that hundreds of thousands of British subjects would aid the French. As tensions rose, in Wakefield the Rev. Munkhouse preached on 19 December 1797:

> No man who is willing to serve his Country can have to lament a total absence of the means, nor need he look far for an opportunity, (if he be well disposed,) of displaying his Patriotism. Those among us, who would throw down our strong holds and set open the floodgates of innovation . . . must be vigorously opposed. No favour should be shewn to them which may be thought incompatible with the safety and prosperity of the State . . . The virtues of vigilance, energy, and perseverance, which are so conspicuous in the behaviour of the unruly, ought to be adopted and sanctified by the friends of religious and civil liberty, and brought into the service of better masters . . . little thanks will be due to him (whoever he may be) from his King and Country, in never having opened his mouth, nor lifted up his hands, no nor so much as his heart, against the enemies' not of Britons only, but of all men connected together by the bonds of unsuspicious intercourse, and social order.[2]

The extent of Pitt's hysteria was all too real. The French had attempted to land in Ireland and Wales, and when James O'Coigly was arrested on his way from Dublin to France carrying a letter from the 'Secret Committee of England' to the French Directory, inviting Napoleon

Bonaparte to invade Britain, drove the message home to Pitt that *'La Patrie En Danger'*.[3] Informants for the Manchester Bench reported to Richard Ford at the Home Office that for the past 18 months emissaries from the Irish rebels had been recruiting in London, Birmingham, Manchester and Sheffield preparatory to an insurrection.[4] From Nottingham came reports that two shopkeepers had stated that if there was an invasion by the French, they would support them.[5] Yet not everyone was convinced of the need to raise additional forces. Rev. Christopher Wyvill believed that 'the ministers magnify the danger'.[6]

The French *émigré* Prince Boullion reported to the Crown at the end of 1797 that 'clandestine projects against Ireland' were being planned.[7] A spy working for the Home Office confirmed the Crown's worst fears when he reported that the French would land on the Yorkshire coast as a diversion for the main attack which would be on Ireland.[8]

If the French were coming, argued Pitt, the Volunteers would need to march to the coast to act as auxiliaries to the regulars, and thus leave the towns and cities unguarded against riot and insurrection. The food riots of 1795 had shown the importance of the need for the magistrates to be able to call on troops to put them down. If the Volunteers were to leave their local area, William Pitt quite correctly realised that a new secondary – and very much auxiliary – line of defence was needed: the Armed Associations were born.

In its scramble for manpower, the British government not only set in motion the first ever national census (if you are out to get soldiers, you need to know the size of your population) but also more specifically with the Defence of the Realm Act of 1798 sought to more than double the Volunteer force. In the four months between April and July 1798, the number of Volunteers increased from 54,000 to 116,000. The Act of 1798 extended the powers of the Lords Lieutenant in a time of national defence. Plans from the time of the Spanish Armada were resurrected. An Alien Bill was passed and habeas corpus suspended again.

Under the Act, all householders were encouraged to enrol in classes of fifty men commanded by a captain. The newly-raised companies were to be organised by the Lords Lieutenant. The associations were to consist of 'none but the known and respectable householders', the captains having to own or rent land valued at over £1,000, and have an income of £50 or more, or be sons of men with these qualifications. The £50 threshold was the minimum threshold also for the 1799 income tax and to vote. The measure meant that the officers at least were middle class, although the comparatively low level of the £50 threshold meant that wealthy tradesmen and artisans could become officers.[9] The 'Armed Associations' were not expected to serve beyond a few miles from the towns in which they were raised, and undertook to serve without pay and provide their own uniforms. The Associations were not subject to military discipline, except their own rules and regulations, and the officers were not to take rank in the army. Dundas issued a circular at the start of April 1798 for the formation of Armed Associations to Lords Lieutenant.[10] He ordered that:

> no Volunteer to be admitted into the armed association, whose habitual occupation and place of residence is not within the division of the county to which the association may extend. Those who prefer cavalry may be received into the nearest troop, or formed in separate troops, of not less than 40 or more than 80 men. The officers to be recommended by the lord lieutenant, and entitled to Yeomanry cavalry allowance and assistance. To be trained for six hours, once a week, and, in case of invasion, serve within the military district to which they belong.
>
> The armed infantry to consist of companies, from 60 to 120 men, armed as the Volunteer corps of towns, or a certain proportion with pikes, with uniform clothing, or a fair allowance for the same, and to be commanded by proper officers, resident, and having not less than 50l. income in land within the county, or renting land in the same to the amount of 100l. The sons of persons so qualified, or persons having previously held some military commission, rendering them eligible for such a situation, are exempted from these restrictions. Persons accustomed to military service, on half pay or not, will be preferred, and allowed full pay. To be trained six hours once a week, and serve within the limits above.
>
> Every man of the Volunteer corps, who thinks proper to claim it, will be entitled to 1 s. per week, paid by government. A depot for the arms to be provided at a safe place within the county. None but known and respectable housekeepers, or persons who can bring at least two such housekeepers to answer for their good behaviour, will be admitted.[11]

The intention of government was that the Armed Associations were to be filled out with men from the middle and upper classes from the age of 15 to 60, the infantry to be armed with muskets and pikes, the cavalry with swords and pistols. Quakers were exempt from service. This was in essence the enabling measure of an Act taken the year before:

> PLAN of the General Association of the inhabitants of the parish of to serve without pay for the protection thereof, in case of any emergency, at the requisition of the civil power, to be submitted to the confirmation of the vestry to be called for that purpose.
>
> 1-A General Association shall be formed, which Association shall be composed of householders and such other inmates as shall be

recommended by two householders at the least, being themselves members of the Association, and approved, if judged necessary, by a committee of the Association to be chosen at a general meeting.

2-That the members of the Association shall put down their names and places of abode in a book, to be provided and kept in the vestry for that purpose.

3-The parish to be divided into districts; the inhabitants of each district, who enrol themselves, to be divided into classes of 50 each, to be commanded by an inhabitant of that district, who shall be considered as captain of the class, and act as such, under a commission from His Majesty. This officer to be recommended by a committee of the Association to the Lord Lieutenant. Each class shall carry a flag to distinguish it, and the person who is to carry it shall be nominated by the captain of each class.

4-The majority in any class shall be empowered to reject from that class any individual, whether householder or inmate, who shall appear to them to be an unfit member thereof.

5-In case of alarm and at the requisition of the civil power, the class to be assembled at a rendezvous, which shall be previously appointed by the captain.

6-Places of general rendezvous for all classes shall be appointed by the committee of the Association.

7-All persons enrolling themselves to furnish their own arms; which arms shall be either firelocks and bayonets, pikes, or any other arms which shall be approved of by the committee.

8-A list of the members in each class to be made, and a copy lodged with each member in that class, together with a copy of such instructions, signed by the captain of the class, as may be found necessary for their more speedily collecting together, in case of alarm, and for regulating the proper quantity of ammunition which each member furnished with a firelock shall constantly be provided with.

9-No member of the Association to be required to meet to exercise, but each class may be mustered with their arms, by its captain, at such convenient and stated times as shall be agreed upon; those who furnish themselves with firelocks will, at their request, be allowed a sergeant or corporal by Government, to teach them the use of firearms, in order that they may more conveniently act together, either in separate classes or jointly with others in the same class, as shall be agreed upon by the members of the association. – This was to be determined by each parish to suit the convenience of members.

10-A hat and feathers, or some other mark of distinction, to be adopted; or those provided with firelocks, if formed into classes by themselves, to have a uniform if they chuse it.

11-Not to go out of the parish except of their own accord.

12-No person who is engaged in any military corps, or other Association, to be appointed as captain; but such persons may enrol themselves and only engage to join this Association when not called away by other duties.[12]

Officers had no legal qualifications placed upon them, other than they had to be Protestant. As officers held their commission from the Lord Lieutenant they were under fewer legal restraints than if commissioned by the crown. The officers' commissions clearly gave their remit:

> George III. by the Grace of God of the United Kingdom and Ireland, King, Defender of the Faith, &c. To our trusted and well beloved Greeting. We do by these presents constitute and appoint you to be, during our pleasure, captain of a Company of the Association of the inhabitants of the parish of in the county of associated to serve, without pay, for the protection thereof in case of any emergency, at the requisition of the civil power, but not to take rank in our army nor the said Association to be subject to military discipline or to serve out of the said parish, except of their own accord.
> Given at our Court at St. James' the on the year of our reign.
> By His Majesty's command, Portland.[13]

The encouragement of volunteering was part of the government's wider plan for turning public opinion against France and garnering civil help to guard against invasion.

In the West Riding, a meeting of the Lieutenancy of Yorkshire held in Leeds on 9 April, when the Volunteer Corps that existed in the West Riding at the time, 'resolved to serve beyond their districts in case of invasion', and with a resulting gap in local defence, Earl Fitzwilliam hoped:

> That all persons who are desirous of enrolling themselves in any new Volunteer Corps for the purposes aforesaid, do form themselves into troops and companies and send the names of the persons composing such troops or companies, together with the names of those gentlemen whom they wish to be appointed to command them, to the Lord Lieutenant, for his Lordship's Approbation, or to Mr William Brooke of Wakefield, Clerk of the General Meetings, or to Mr Bolland Attorney in Leeds, to be transmitted to his Lordship previous to the twenty-third instant to which day this meeting is adjourned. William Brooke.[14]

Driven by nationalist fervour Earl Fitzwilliam, as Lord Lieutenant of the West Riding, was inundated with requests to form Armed Associations.[15]

## Civic Rivalry

The formation of Armed Associations was not without its problems. In the West Riding, one of the first requests came from William Rawson, a rich mill owner near Halifax. He asked permission from the Earl to be given the authority to allow him to form his employees into a military force to aid 'the civil powers and to defend their King and Country against all enemies within the Parish of Halifax'. Rawson moreover urged that all manufacturers were to form their own workmen into armed companies to guard against the unemployed and disaffected who 'would probably do the country as much harm as an enemy'.[16] Rawson's calls for private, vigilante, paramilitary forces failed to gain acceptance by Earl Fitzwilliam. The Castleford Potteries made a similar pledge of service in May. The best-known pottery in Castleford was that of David Dunderdale & Co. From 1790, Dunderdale made high-quality products similar to those produced at the Leeds Pottery. The pottery was intended for export, so the company got into difficulties when it could not be exported to the Continent during the Napoleonic Wars. The Castleford Potteries committee, headed by Dunderdale, requested that the government finance the clothing, arms and equipment, and that 'as the members of the Association were members of Sick Clubs and Friendly Societies which precluded military service' requested similar benefits be provided 'to prevent any injury happening to themselves or their families by having entered into this engagement'.[17] To ensure that the force was efficient, well trained and disciplined, the committee ordered that the Castleford Potteries Association members were to drill at least once week for three hours.[18] Despite the enthusiasm of the members, the Association was never formally accepted

Another short-lived formation was the Bingley Armed Association. In May 1798 it mustered fifty men but had disappeared by July 1798.[19] Another unit that never seems to have 'gotten off the ground' was in Pontefract. A meeting was held:

> For the purpose of considering of the propriety of an Armed Association to assist the Civil Magistrates, in preserving the internal tranquillity of the said borough, in case the Volunteers should be called away. Many excellent resolutions were entered into, and a very respectable corps will be immediately formed.[20]

A committee was formed, and it agreed that the Association was raised to defend the Borough of Pontefract and the villages of Tanshelf and Monkhill, the members were not be aged above 60 and were to provide their own arms, uniforms and equipment.[21] The Pontefract Armed

Association never materialised as an independent formation, instead three companies were added to the Pontefract Volunteers.[22] Barnsley Armed Association comprised 40 Independent men (that is, those able to buy their own uniforms and equipment) as Yeomanry and 200 infantry, but again seems to have been a fairly ephemeral corps.[23]

Yet another 'stillborn' Armed Association was proposed in Horbury. Here the vicar of the parish was the chairman of the Horbury Loyalist Association which had declared in 1792 that 'the government of these realms, consisting of a King, Lords and Commons, in whom are combined the advantages of monarchy, aristocracy and democracy, is the most perfect form of all governments'.[24] The vicar of Horbury, Rev. John Taylor MA and the Parish Clerk Rev. William Rayner, were at the forefront of crushing sedition and Jacobinism in their parish and it is little wonder that in 1798 the good reverend led his Loyalist Association to take up arms. He proposed to raise an infantry company of fifty men, clothe and equip it at his expense, ostensibly to keep the peace and serve in the wapentake of Agbrigg. Horbury, lacking a Volunteer corps, was undefended against 'home-grown traitors' as Rayner opined to Earl Fitzwilliam:

> That in so populous manufacturing place as this, (containing near three thousand inhabitants) . . . have some Jacobins amongst the dregs of the people & against those only (for the French can never come here) we are endeavouring to array ourselves.[25]

The good vicar was prepared to resort to acts of violence, if necessary, to keep the peace.[26] No doubt he was thinking of the Wakefield Constitutional Society, two leaders of which had been arrested and gaoled in 1792 for sedition, another had travelled to Paris to experience the revolution first hand, and a fourth had been present at the British Convention held in Edinburgh during November and December 1793, and would go onto emigrate to France, plotting invasion and to assassinate William Pitt and George III. With such men living 'on his doorstep' as it were, and Horbury having at the time witnessed a secession of 'Thom Paine Methodists' from the Wesleyan Chapel in the village, the Vicar's fear of being 'murdered in his bed' by 'home grown terrorists' was perhaps justified. In the nearby townships of Stanley and Wrenthorpe, Thomas Fenton of Hatfield Hall proposed to raise an Armed Association:

> because the lower orders of people who are usually are employed in Wakefield reside in these townships & should any disturbance take

61

place amongst them, this association would be ready to support the civil power without rendering the services of the military . . . the subscribers to the resolutions I take the liberty of adding are in general families & are not likely to enter into any other corps.[27]

The committee resolved that the minimum qualification for enlisting was to own property worth £10 a year, or renting property worth a minimum of £15. Each member had to provide their own uniform. Thomas Fenton headed the committee, other members including Francis Maude, barrister, and Jeremiah Glover, a gentleman. Farmers Joseph Charlesworth, John Nichols, Thomas Lake, William Hampshire, William Rawling, Thomas Gill and James Burrell, as well as William Haigh a stuff maker and William Firth a clothier, were also committee members.[28] Despite much sabre-rattling, the association was never formed. Likewise, a corps of Volunteers had been proposed in Doncaster on 31 May 1794, but again nothing had come of this and one was again proposed on 7 May 1798.[29] For whatever reason, as with the Horbury Armed Association, and that at Stanley and Wrenthorpe, after an initial flurry of activity, nothing more was heard of the Doncaster Armed Association.

In Wakefield, a meeting was held at the Moot Hall on 21 April 1798, chaired by the town Constable, William Whitaker to:

deliberate upon the propriety in the present crisis of forming an Armed Association under certain regulations to assist the magistrates in the civil society, and the defence of the town and neighbourhood, in case the Volunteers should be called out elsewhere.[30]

It was agreed to form an Armed Association, but the members were to come 'only from respectable and positioned households'. Resolutions included:

to provide their own Cloathing, Arms, and Accoutrements, and that the said Arms and Accoutrements so provided, shall, within Six Months after Peace is proclaimed, be sent to Government by the Commanding Officer, as the voluntary Gift of this Association.

That a Committee of Eleven Gentlemen be now appointed to regulate and direct the Cloathing.[31]

Members had to be nominated by two other members and elected by a two-thirds ballot. Members had to be 'Gentlemen'. By 30 April 1798 eighty-six members had been enrolled. The first commissions were granted by the Lord Lieutenant, Earl Fitzwilliam on 21 June 1798. Officers were as follows:[32]

Infantry: Captain Andrew Peterson, Lieutenant Charles Rickaby, William Walker as Ensign.

Cavalry: Captain John Naylor, Lieutenant John Risendale, John Shackleton, Cornet.

The first meeting of the Association was held on 21 June 1798 at the New Assembly Rooms in Crown Court. Thereafter the Association disappears and may never have become 'embodied'; certainly by 1799 it no longer existed, and never submitted any returns to the Earl. Henry Peterson, father of Andrew Peterson elected commanding officer, reported to Fitzwilliam, that considerable number of townsfolk objected to his appointment due to him being Dutch.[33] This tension in the town may well explain the failure of the Armed Association. If we are judge loyalism on the number of men to actually enrol, it seems that the middle class were happy to propose committees and money to form associations, but when it came to active participation, major obstacles were encountered. It was not just in the central belt of the West Riding where difficulties were encountered of transmuting enthusiasm to active participation.

In Otley, William Vavasour was named Major Commandant of two companies. The Association was formed at the request of Walter Ramsden Fawkes, to ensure 'that the town of Otley Shd be well protected'.[34] The reasons for this was because:

the situation of Otley strongly points out the necessity of it being well guarded – for two days in week, it is full of corn & may fairly be called the granary from which all Craven & the northern parts of Lancashire are supplied – it is at a great distance from other towns which are almost all now in a state of defence, while it is itself unprotected. The association will consist of one hundred & Fifty – they will cloath themselves & c but solicit through the recommendation of your Lordship – arms & accoutrements, to be returned when required.[35]

Fawkes was worried that at a time of national famine Otley could be an easy target for food protesters and wanted to ensure that the grain market was protected. Commissions were granted on 6 June 1798, but it had disbanded by 1799 as it submitted no returns in that year. Had it ever been fully formed? Earl Fitzwilliam's papers also record Armed Associations being proposed in Bradford, Dewsbury, Staincross, and

Strafforth and Tickhill, none of which seem to have 'gotten off the drawing board'.[36] Given the number of Armed Associations that lasted no more than weeks, we are not seeing a mass endeavour to form a unit which cost both time and money, but the middle class being committed to a lot of 'sabre-rattling' and 'bonhomie' rather than anything more proactive to defend 'hearth and home'.

## Armed Association Infantry

As we have noted, in many cases, loyalist fervour and desire to enrol only lasted a few months, yet several towns did successful form Armed Associations. We look at case studies from the West Riding once more.

Unlike 1797 which witnessed a single infantry corps being created, six corps of infantry were raised in 1798 embodied as Armed Associations. In Rotherham, the Armed Association mustered 300 men by the end of June.[37] Samuel Tooker, magistrate and landowner in Rotherham, asked Earl Fitzwilliam what allowances were being provided by the government for uniforms, so the committee could begin a subscription list and make a budget for the uniforms. He noted that the men of the Armed Association were dressed the same as the Loyal Sheffield Volunteers, i.e., dark blue faced red. Tooker also informed the Earl of the difficulties had in appointing a Major and Adjutant.[38] The gun founder Joshua Walker was named Lieutenant-Colonel Commandant.[39] Walker provided the corps with a pair of field guns: it is these guns that are now, we presume, in Kelham Island Museum, Sheffield.

In Leeds, after an initial proposal in April 1798 'for the defence of the Borough in case the Volunteers were called off from the town', nothing seems to have actually happened till the end of June, when a meeting was held in the Mixed Cloth Hall which resolved to form a single battalion, without flank companies, formed into two companies, named First and Second. The companies were to drill at Kirkstall. Benjamin Gott, Mayor of Leeds in 1800, loyalist and churchman, was Captain Commandant of the 'Leeds Armed Association.' The other officers were Benjamin Pulleyn commanding 2nd Company, Thomas Shaw was adjutant, William Glover, Frederick William Oates and Thomas Butler were named Lieutenants, and Maurice Logan was appointed surgeon.[40] Glover and Oates were members of Call Lane and Mill Hill Unitarian Chapels, and were both leading members of the Leeds wool merchant community. From the rules of the Association dating from April 1798 we learn that:

each member provide himself with an Uniform consisting of a double breasted dark blue Coat with a black Collar and plain yellow buttons, a white waistcoat [sic] a pair of White Linen Pantaloons or overalls a round Hat looped up on one side and a Feather.[41]

However, this idea was quickly abandoned, as a resolution of 27 June 1798 states:

the uniform should be a scarlet coat with black velvet collar, lapell, facings & cuffs, white buttons with a Fleece & L A in Roman characters. Under – a white waistcoat of any description of cloth & make and white linen pantaloons or overalls, black velvet stock, black cloth gaiters, and a round hat with a black cockade. The hair with or without powder except when a notice for attendance expresses full uniform and then it is understood that each individual must appear in powder and if he wears his hair long to have it plaited and turned up under the hat.[42]

The Association disappears from the *Leeds Intelligencer* during 1800, when we assume the corps disbanded.[43] For an organisation that existed for little over 18 months, it is remarkable that a regimental coat attributed to Lieutenant John Butler was housed in Leeds City Museum. However, as the coat was on loan, its whereabouts in 2023 are totally unknown.

Unlike nearby Halifax which formed a cavalry contingent, which we come to, the townsfolk of Huddersfield raised a mixed force of infantry and cavalry to supplement the Volunteer infantry. To do so, a meeting was held at the George Inn, Huddersfield, on 23 April 1798:

In pursuance of a public advertisement, to take into consideration the propriety of forming an Armed Association for the protection of the town and neighbourhood. April 23,1798.

Sir George Armitage, Bart., in the Chair.

Resolved: -

First -That at the present alarming crisis, when we are threatened with immediate invasion, it is expedient that an Armed Association be formed to assist the magistrates in preserving the peace of this town and neighbourhood, in case the Volunteers who have so nobly offered their services should be ordered away to oppose the landing of the enemy.

Second – The Huddersfield Armed Association do consist of one troop of cavalry and two companies of infantry, to serve without pay and to be armed and clothed at their own expense, who shall not be subject to martial law, nor be liable to march further than ten miles from Huddersfield.

Thirdly – That, if Government should approve of this measure, the following resolutions be adopted for the regulation and good order of the said Association.

Fourthly – That the uniform of the cavalry shall be a plain scarlet hussar jacket, three rows of silver buttons, silver chain to each shoulder, with silver fringe and bullion, helmet cap inscribed, 'Huddersfield Volunteer Cavalry', black bear skin on the crest, white plume with red top, white leather breeches, military boots, blue cloak and military horse-furniture. That the uniform for the infantry shall be a blue coat, with scarlet collar and cuffs, and gold epaulets, white waistcoat, white linen pantaloons and black gaiters, a round hat with a feather and a loop, sword hung to a white shoulder belt, pouch to another to cross. That all reasonable economy shall be observed in everything relating to the said Association, The times for learning the exercise shall be regulate 1 by the Committee, so as to interfere as little as possible with the other engagements of this Association.

Fifthly – That each member on his entering into this Association be required to take the oath of allegiance.

Sixth – That a committee be formed for the purpose of regulating the admission of members into this Association conformably to the directions contained in the Circular Letter of the Secretary of State; that they do appoint officers, and make all other necessary regulations respecting the said Association.

Seventh – That the said Committee do consist of the following gentlemen, who shall meet at the George Inn every Tuesday and Friday evening, at six o'clock, in order to receive the names of such persons as may choose to enter into this Association and to carry into effect the aforesaid resolutions; any five of whom may be competent to act, viz.: -

Names of Joseph Radcliffe, Esq., Rev. Mr Wickham, Committee. Thomas Atkinson, Mr. Wm Horsfall, Mr. Jo. Atkinson, sen., Mr. John Whitacre, Mr. Law Atkinson, Mr. Benjamin Haigh, Mr. Abraham Horsfall, Mr. Thomas Holroyd, Mr. Firth Macauley, Mr. Henry Stables, Mr. Thomas Allen, Mr. Rowland Houghton, Mr. Robert Scott, Mr. John Houghton, Mr. Jonathan Roberts, Mr. Daniel Crosland, Mr. William Roberts, Mr. Shires, Paddock, Mr. R. R. Batty, Mr. Armytage, Highroyd, Mr. John Brook, Flashes, Mr. Walker, Lassels [sic] Hall, Mt. William Armytage, Almondbury, Mr. Harrop, Holmfirth, Mr. John Roberts, Longwood House, Mr. John Dobson, Huddersfield, Mr. Jo. Brook, Huddersfield, Mr. James Dyson, Mr. Godfrey Webster, Mr. Edward Hawxby, Mr. Thomas Nelson, Mr. Sturges, sen., Mr. Jo. Taylor, Mr. Thomas Houghton, Rev. Mr. Coates, Mr. Turner.

Rules and Regulations.

Resolved; That the thanks of the meeting be given to the chairman. (Signed) G. Armytage, Chairman.

That the members of this Association be divided into troops and companies of not less than fifty men each, one captain, one lieutenant, one cornet, two sergeants, one trumpeter, and two corporals to each troop of cavalry; one captain, one lieutenant, one ensign, three sergeants, two corporals, one drummer and one fifer to each company of infantry, and one adjutant to the whole. Such commissioned and non-commissioned officers to be appointed by the committee, and the commissioned officers to be subject to his Majesty's approbation, and to act under his Majesty's commission.

2 – That as regularity and discipline are of the utmost consequence, we agree to obey our officers, and each officer his superior officer, when on duty, and in order to obtain a knowledge in the use of arms, we will attend the drill every Monday and Thursday evening at 5 o'clock precisely during the first two months after we commence exercise.

That as punctuality is essentially necessary in the prosecution of this undertaking, we hereby agree that each officer and non-commissioned officer shall forfeit and pay, on demand, the sum of two shillings, and each private one shilling, to the person appointed to receive the same, in default of their not being present each day of exercise when the roll is called over, unless prevented by illness, or being more than seven miles distant from Huddersfield for the Infantry, and ten miles for the Cavalry; (afterwards it was agreed by the Cavalry to forfeit for absence: the major, seven shillings; captain, six shillings; lieutenant, five shillings; cornet, four shillings; sergeants, three shillings; corporal, two shillings; private, one shilling, each day).

That each member of the Cavalry Corps shall be provided with a sabre and one pistol, the sabre to hang from a white waist-belt.

That each member of the Cavalry Corps shall deposit ten guineas when sworn in, to the person appointed to receive the same, towards furnishing their clothing and arms &c., &c. and to pay for the remainder of their clothing and arms &c. when they are delivered to them.

That each member of the Infantry Corps shall provide himself with clothing, conformable to the 4th resolution, exact in and as near as possible in quality, and exact to the pattern dress proposed by the committee. And we also agree to pay for the arms and accoutrements when delivered to us by the committee.

Major Commandant of the Association of the Parish of Huddersfield – Officers. Joseph Radcliffe, Esq.

Captain of Cavalry-Law Atkinson, Esq. Lieutenant-Firth Macauley, Esq., Clough House. Cornet-Joseph Brook, Huddersfield. Captain of Infantry-Henry Stables, Esq., Huddersfield. Lieutenant-William Hirst, New Street. Ensign-Godfrey Webster, ditto. Captain-John Roberts,

Esq, Longwood House. Lieutenant-Joseph Taylor, Birkby. Ensign-Jos. Hudson, Huddersfield. Adjutant-John Duckworth, Huddersfield.[44]

William Horsfall would come to national prominence when he was assassinated in 1812 by Luddites, having been targeted in 1803 for introducing machinery to his mill at Marsden, and taking a strong stand against trade unionism and workers' rights.[45] The Sheffield Armed Association Infantry, commanded by Captain Samuel Robinson commissioned on 9 July 1798, consisted of about 160 men, and disbanded in spring 1800.[46] We look at this troubled unit later.

Turning to North Yorkshire, things did not run as smoothly as the West Riding. If the French were coming, in order to organise the defence of a county, what was needed was an accurate breakdown of the Volunteer troops already available. In authorising the formation of Armed Associations, it was important that local needs for manpower were met. This relied on efficient Lords Lieutenant. The Lord Lieutenant of the North Riding, the geriatric Lord Fauconberg, was not as capable as the efficient Earl Fitzwilliam in the West Riding. In trying to establish local needs for additional volunteers under the Armed Associations Act, Fauconberg was informed somewhat tentatively that 'there is a corps of Volunteer infantry at Whitby I believe established for the local defence of that place. There are also two troops of Yeomanry cavalry commanded by Lord Morpeth and Mr Ch Duncomb jun.' The Earl's agent added that he thought 'there be a corps of Volunteer infantry at Scarborough. We have directed Mr H Colling . . . to make immediate enquiry if there be any other Volunteers corps.' Basically no one had any idea of the strength of the Volunteer forces in the Riding. The War Office informed the Lord that corps existed at Dickering (180 men), Knaresborough (50 men) Newburgh (60 men), Richmond (60 men), Ripon (50 men), Scarborough (240 men), and Whitby (240 men).[47] Clearly, the Lord Lieutenant's office was far from an effective organisation. In consequence, Armed Associations were formed across the North Riding: Scarborough formed a company of sixty men as well as a troop of cavalry,[48] Armed Associations were also formed in Masham, Northallerton and Catterick.[49] In rural Stillington, the villagers proposed to form an Armed Association for local defence, but their offer of service was declined as the men refused to serve outside the parish.[50] Having had threats made against his life for being a French agent and disloyalty – clearly one could not be opposed to war for the sake of conscience – the Rev. Wyvill, with his neighbour the recusant Catholic Thomas Scroope of Danby, proposed to form a troop of cavalry to 'get the mob off their backs'.[51]

His offer was declined. Despite these issues, by May Lord Dundas had received so many offers that official policy was to accept only offers 'from Respectable Householders' who lived in 'populous towns' with over 1,000 inhabitants.[52] The abortive Irish Rebellion showed to many the danger posed by internal threats to 'hearth and home' – especially when viewed by the propaganda of William Pitt – and as the Crown had hoped, had resulted in a new wave of volunteering: the desire to defend 'hearth and home' outweighed any desire to defend the locality or nation: it was deeply local patriotism. For example, the Marlborough Armed Association were prepared to serve in an area just five miles from the town, and at Hitchin, the Armed Association would only serve in an area of three miles around the town.

Yet, it is undeniable that the Armed Associations were successful in 'filling in the blanks on the map' where Volunteer units had not yet been raised. So far no units had been raised in Shropshire, four years since the first legislation had been passed. We wonder what factors resulted in the county withholding service? A meeting was held in Shrewsbury on 11 May 1798, to form an Armed Association comprising infantry and cavalry. The press noted:

> That the Arms and Cloathing of this Corps shall be as little expensive as possible (each member of this Association being intended to provide his own) at the same time it is expected that they shall be strictly Uniform.
>
> That the Dress of this Corps of Volunteers shall consist of a Scarlet Jacket, with Black Velvet Facing and Yellow Buttons stamped with the Shrewsbury Arms, and the letters (SV) underneath, denoting 'Shrewsbury Volunteers', with Kerseymere Waistcoat and Breeches with Buttons the same as the Coat, Black Cloth Buskins, a Round Hat with a Black Feather, and a Black leather Stock.[53]

A similar corps was formed at Wenlock.[54] Likewise, in Staffordshire no Volunteer units, other than the county Yeomanry, existed and the 'Staffordshire Infantry Volunteers' only came on line during 1799 as an Armed Association. Another of the corps raised in the county was the 'Lichfield Loyal Association' which resolved that:

> That such of the Friendly Societies, where there are members exceeding the Age of Forty, yet very able and effective Men, do form themselves into a Corps or Company, to be called PIONEERS, and to carry such Arms, as Government shall think proper to intrust them with, namely, Pikes and Broad Swords, or Hangers . . .
>
> That another Company do consist of Journeymen, Apprentices and Servants . . .

That these two Bodies of Volunteers shall at the Charge of Government be properly Accoutred, but each to pay Seven Shillings and Sixpence on the delivery of a Drill Frock to him (which then becomes his own Property,) in which he is to learn and perform his Exercise, for the Preservation of his own Wearing Apparel.

That the other Body of Volunteers shall be comprised of able and effective Men . . . to be Accoutred or Armed, at all times by Government, as directed by the late Act of Parliament.

. . . that each Company shall consist of FIFTY MEN (exclusive of Commissioned Officers) namely, Forty five in the Ranks, two Serjeants, two Corporals, and one Drill Serjeant, as also two Boys, the one as Drummer, the other as Fifer: each Serjeant to carry a Halbert, and wear a Sword or Hanger.

. . . Each commissioned and non commissioned Officer to cloath himself in, and wear at his own expence a certain Uniform, or Dress, to be fixed upon by a Committee.[55]

The Armed Association Act undoubtedly helped 'fill in the blanks' on the map of town which had not previously had a volunteer force for local defence.

## Men of the Armed Associations

The Armed Associations have left a very ephemeral paper trail, even amongst the comprehensive papers of Earl Fitzwilliam, who has left students of history one of the most complete archives from any Lord Lieutenant of the epoch. Ultimately, six infantry Armed Associations were formed in the West Riding: Leeds, Rotherham, Halifax, Sheffield, Otley and Huddersfield. However, from the muster lists of those that did not become active units we gain something about their composition. One of the enduring questions about the Armed Associations is to assess if they were formed from the elite of a town or had a broadly similar range of membership to the Volunteers. So far, we have only been able to locate two muster lists: Wakefield, and Stanley. When we look at Wakefield Armed Association's membership list – the names of eighty-six men submitted to Earl Fitzwilliam on 30 April 1798 – and compare it to the county poll book for 1807 (the earliest the author has been able to locate), aligned with pew rent and baptismal registers, we can say something about the trades and political and religious affiliations of the members:[56]

John Soulby: Unitarian, wool-stapler, Whig
John Pullein: Anglican, grocer, Tory
John Goldthorpe: Anglican, grocer, Tory
George Bromhead: Anglican, liquor merchant, Tory

Richard Morville: Anglican, merchant, Tory
George Strafford: Anglican, builder, voted for Wilberforce and Milton
Thomas Armitage: Anglican, bricklayer, Tory
John Couldwell: Anglican, butcher, Tory
Richard Heald: Unitarian, gentleman, Tory
John Ridsdale: Anglican, merchant, Tory
Thomas Hartley: Anglican, grocer, Tory
Robert Wilson: Anglican, innkeeper, Tory
Thomas Yeamans: Anglican, linen draper, Tory
Joseph Tolson: Anglican, wool-stapler, Tory
John Pemberton Heywood: Unitarian, solicitor, Whig
Christopher Sidebottom: Anglican, plumber, Tory
William White: Unitarian, wine merchant, Tory
William Hallilay Hodgson: Anglican, merchant, Tory
William Dawson: Anglican, gentleman, Tory
John Holdsworth: Unitarian, merchant, Whig
John Sunderland: Anglican, maltster, Tory
Richard Scholes: ?, carver and gilder, Whig
Thomas Lee: Anglican, gentleman, Whig
John I'Anson: Anglican, woollen draper, Tory
William Walker: Anglican, breeches maker, Tory
Harper Soulby: Unitarian, wool-stapler, Whig
Thomas Lumb: Unitarian, gentleman, Whig

Of the seventy-three other ranks, not including the committee, it is remarkable that twenty-seven can be identified as voters, and seven identifiable as Whigs from the 1807 election poll. Thus 36 per cent of the Wakefield Armed Association were voters. Of the seventy-three men, 10 per cent were medium artisans such as plumbers, 57 per cent were high artisans, 23 per cent were professionals and 10 per cent gentlemen. The men were all to be respectable householders i.e., property owners.[57] Many of the voters were actually affluent middle-class artisans and merchants as just four were recorded as gentlemen. Of the eighty-six members we find the following who paid pew rent at Westgate Chapel:[58]

Benjamin Heywood, James Milnes, Richard Heald, Thomas Burrell Jnr, Thomas Holdsworth, John Pemberton Heywood, William White, Joseph Clarkson jnr, John Farrar, John Shackleton, Richard Burrell, William Heald, William Burrell, John Holdsworth, Joshua Burrell, Thomas Lumb, John Robson, James Bell, John Soulby, Harper Soulby, William Dawson.

Indeed, these men were all merchants, mill owners, business owners and other professionals, forming the elite of Wakefield society.

They had a vested interest in maintaining the status quo even if it meant backing a government that, ideologically, these men rejected. Participation does not automatically assume a deep-seated sense of patriotism: as men of property and status, they had a lot to lose if the French landed or rioting as in 1795 broke out again caused by a 'cost of living crisis'. These men wanted to protect their property first and foremost, everything else that came with volunteering being very much secondary. The Association was overwhelmingly a mobilisation of the middle-class voters in the town. Just one man, Thomas Scott, is identifiable as a Methodist: he was appointed Trustee of West Parade Wesleyan Chapel in December 1803 and had been a member of the congregation since 1795. He was not eligible to vote. Many of the voters were actually affluent middle-class artisans and merchants as just four were recorded as gentlemen. Compared to the Royal Wakefield Volunteers, these men were the elite of the town, and cut across the political and religious divide at a time of *'la patrie en danger'*. Of the 167 men of the Royal Wakefield Volunteers, just 12 were voters: [59]

> Michael Bentley – Tory, cloth merchant, Anglican
> John Statter – Tory, cloth draper, Anglican
> Samuel Oates – Whig, husbandman, Unitarian
> Thomas Foljambe – Tory, gentleman and notary, Anglican
> Robert Webster – Tory, carpenter, Anglican
> Charles Tunnacliffe – Tory, plasterer, Anglican
> Joseph Penney – Tory, shoemaker, Anglican
> Thomas Glover – Tory, cloth dresser, Anglican
> Joseph Holdsworth – Tory, cloth merchant, Methodist
> Joseph Scott – Tory, cloth dresser, Methodist
> William Holdsworth – Whig, merchant, Unitarian
> William Dawson – Tory, gentleman, Anglican

Just 7 per cent of the Volunteers were voters, 20 per cent less than the Armed Association; the Association appealed to a different stratum of society. Yet the corps was never formed.

Looking at the Stanley Armed Association, we find Thomas Fenton who was the leading coal mine proprietor of the era, Francis Maude, a barrister, and Jeremiah Glover, described as a gentleman. Of the fifty-one men enrolled, 50 per cent were farmers and 40 per cent were involved in the woollen trade, leaving the remaining men as respectable business owners: one man was a publican, one a carpenter, and one a gardener.[60]

Therefore it seems undeniable, based on these examples from the West Riding, that the government's desire to mobilise the 'possessing class' into the Armed Associations was effective. Perhaps the Crown felt that those who had a lot to lose from invasion and riot at home would rally to the colours. In this respect, the Act did encourage more of the 'possessing class' to join up, but for practical reasons of safeguarding property rather than patriotic or nationalistic sentiment, although this probably did exist in many who did join.

Chapter 7

# ASSOCIATION CAVALRY

At the same time as infantry Armed Associations were formed, the more affluent bourgeois formed Association cavalry troops. In the four months between April and July 1798, the number of Volunteers increased from 54,000 to 116,000. The sheer numbers caused fears in government that an armed populace might be dangerous. However, Lord Dundas held a contrary view and felt the Volunteers would serve to unite the country, remarking:

> You will recollect, many parts of this country which were most disaffected, but were insensibly cured of it by being enrolled under arms along with others of a different description. If, on the other hand, they are not so associated, they become prey to the intrigues of traitors and enemies, being debarred the privilege of bearing arms on the right side.[1]

About this, my friend Dr Peter Hicks remarks:

> Pitt's (and Dundas's) opinion was also that military service reduced social tensions. They believed that all parts of society (even Catholic Ireland) could be mobilised to resist the French threat, and that that experience would have a powerfully unifying effect on the nation. All classes (they thought) would discover the power of the national bond under the threat of foreign conquest; radicalism would be marginalised by military participation as the lower orders were brought into closer contact with and acquired greater confidence in their superiors.[2]

Nationalism and anti-French sentiment were in essence weaponised to rally the country behind the Crown, in the hope of ending dissent and nullifying the threat of home-grown insurrection. In this regard, the Crown was hopelessly wrong. Sir William Milner, MP for the City of York, William Wrightson of Cusworth Hall and forty-five other men of consequence felt otherwise: peace was the answer, not the continuation of an unpopular and costly war, and sought a county meeting to petition for peace and a general election to remove Pitt. Yet such voices were an increasingly small minority as the nation was increasingly radicalised against democratic ideals.

So successful was Pitt's propaganda war in mobilising public spirit, that at the end of 1798, 229 infantry Armed Associations had been formed, and 63 cavalry. Many of the proposed Association cavalry corps became Yeomanry troops: 106 troops of Yeomanry existed at the close of 1797, and this almost doubled to 203 troops by the end of 1798, increasing to 210 by 1800. Clearly the appeal of Association cavalry was very marginal indeed.[3] Perhaps this was due to instructions issued by Henry Dundas in May 1798 to the Lieutenancies to refuse new offers when it was felt that Volunteer forces were already adequate. Dundas made it clear, that proposals for Associations from inland towns of fewer than 2,000 inhabitants, or made on limited conditions, were to be immediately rejected.[4] Another deterrent to forming a troop of cavalry under the Armed Association Act was money: members had to provide their own mount, uniform, saddlery and equipment and received no pay if mobilised. This made the force socially exclusive, to men of wealth and property, and made the conversion of an Armed Association cavalry troop to Yeomanry highly expedient. The first Armed Association cavalry troops were formed in 1797: the Loyal Birmingham Associated Cavalry or 'True Blues' was formed when a meeting was held at the Shakespeare Tavern on 9 September 1797, chaired by the Bailiff James Reynolds 'for the protection of the Town and Parish'. A second troop, known as the Loyal Birmingham Light Horse Volunteers, was formed on 7 October.[5]

After these troops had been formed, a further sixty-three would be created during 1798. One of these, was in Shropshire, which witnessed the raising of the 'Brimstree Loyal Legion' in April 1798, with cavalry troops at Shifnal and Apley. About uniforms, it was resolved that:

EVERY Volunteer serving in the cavalry, is to provide himself with a horse, to be approved by the commanding officer; also, with a scarlet jacket with blue collar and cuffs, white buttons bearing the cypher B.L.L. with a crown at the top, white waistcoat, white leather breeches, long black top't regimental boots, plated spurs, black stock or handkerchief and helmet.

THE officers to be distinguished by red and white feathers.

ARMS & ACCOUTREMENTS.

... They will consist for the cavalry, of a goatskin and regimental bridle, sword, sword belt and knot, horse collar, pistol, holster on one side and cartouches on the other.[6]

In Wolverhampton, a cavalry troop was formed alongside an infantry company, and likewise in Dudley a meeting was held on 13 April 1798, with a view to form a 'Corps of Cavalry and Infantry'.[7] A mixed force was raised in Deptford, the dress of the cavalry being agreed on 28 April 1798 to be:

A dark blue jacket, red cuffs and collar, ornamented with lace as per pattern, white kerseymere waistcoat, single breasted; white leather breeches without any buttons at the knee; helmets as per pattern with a device on one side of a crown and letters GR in a circle, and the word 'defence' under them, military boots and spurs as per pattern.

Every Volunteer for the cavalry had to subscribe 10 guineas, and for the infantry 5 guineas.[8] This subscription prevented working-class and lower middle-class participation. 'The Kidderminster Armed Association' advertised its enrolment in the local press in May 1798.[9] In Lancashire, 'The Bolton-Le-Moor Cavalry Association' mustered sixty-five men in a single troop when its standard was presented in June 1799.[10]

In Dewsbury both an Armed Association and Light Horse Volunteers were to be raised in April 1798: the infantry never seem to have materialised, but the Light Horse Volunteers seem to have existed albeit unofficially till 1801 or perhaps 1802.[11] A similarly ephemeral unit was 'The Wakefield Independent Cavalry'. The unit was raised in July 1798, 'from householders with property worth 50l' and to muster a troop of fifty men. Unitarian merchant prince James Milnes of Thornes House was gazetted Captain, John Lee as Lieutenant and fellow co-religionist Benjamin Heywood as Cornet.[12] Milnes provided £1,000 to clothe and equip his troop from his own funds. On 8 July 1799 the corps mustered thirty-one all ranks, the same number being under arms on 1 August 1800.[13] The troop appears to have been wound up at the end of 1801.

In York, the Armed Association was formed to 'serve without pay for the Internal Defence of the country, in case the present force of Volunteers, already trained, should be called into actual service'.[14] The York Armed Association committee agreed the unit was to comprise a troop of cavalry, 80 men strong, and 150 infantry. The Association was to be called out for 'the suppression of Riots, the defence of property and the maintenance of good order, under the authority and direction of the Magistrates of the City'.[15] The Armed Association Infantry seems to have been 'stillborn', and we hear nothing more of it. The cavalry element was formed, as the 'City of York Gentlemen Cavalry', an independent troop of Yeomanry. It was accepted by Earl Fitzwilliam in May 1798 with the first commission granted on 20 June 1798 to William Duffin. An 'elegant standard', the gift of Captain Duffin, was presented on 28 October 1799.[16] In Rotherham, a similar story emerges as with infantry units proposed in Wakefield and elsewhere: a cavalry troop was proposed in April, yet the returns sent to the War Office in 1799 lists no troop of cavalry here.

In Halifax, rather than form an infantry force to supplement the Volunteer infantry, a cavalry force was raised. The Armed Association Cavalry was dominated by the slave-trading Ingram family: William Ingram (1768–1824) was Captain Commandant, and his son Richard was Cornet.[17] According to the Trans-Atlantic Slave Voyage Database, William, in partnership with his brother Francis and James Rigby of Liverpool, conducted twenty-six slaving voyages. He transported 7,010 slaves, 6,100 going to the West Indies, some two-thirds being delivered to Jamaica. His voyages went to West Central Africa and the Congo Basin, thence to the West Indies and brought back rum, tobacco, dyestuffs, spices and sugar. From the Association's regulations of 1798 we learn that:

Rule 5. That every Member at his own Expence shall furnish himself with the following Cloathing – Arms and Accoutrements, all made to pattern, a regimental Bridle and Saddle, with Cloak-Pad and Straps – a Cartouch Box, containing twelve Rounds, fixed in the right Holster, a Sabre, – a whited Leather Sword Knot, a whited leather Shoulder belt, a Pistol, a regimental Blue Coat Cloak, with Scarlet Collar and Lining, a Dress Uniform agreeable to Rule 6, and an Undress Uniform agreeable to Rule 7; and each commissioned Officer to procure a crimson Silk Sash.

Rule 6. That the Dress Uniform shall be a Scarlet Hussar Jacket with Silver Lace, Black Velvet Collar and Cuffs, White Leather Breeches, long black topp'd boots, plated Spurs with horizontal Rowels, Black Velvet Stock, with a narrow white Turn Over, frilled Shirt, Hair well powdered, Short Sides, Queue tied rather close to the Head, Silk Rosette, white wash Leather Gloves, and Helmet with white long feather.

Rule 7. That the Undress shall be a plain Blue Jacket – Pantaloons of Blue Cloth, with the Insides of Black leather – Half Boots – and other particulars as in Rule 6.[18]

The regulations stated that the jackets of all ranks were to be scarlet with silver braid and lace, and no indication of rank is suggested other than officers' sashes. The reference to 'Insides of Black leather' must indicate strapping on the pantaloons, which may therefore have been cut looser, as overalls. The helmet turban colour is not indicated. William Ingram's daughter presented a standard on 4 June 1799.[19] Richard Ingram was a man with little or no morals when it concerned personal gain: he was caught embezzling the men's pay and marching guinea when called out to act against food riots in 1799 and 1800 when they had marched to Saddleworth with the Huddersfield Fusiliers, and again in 1805.

Halifax was not alone in forming ostentatious cavalry troops. In Sheffield, Rev. James Wilkinson informed Earl Fitzwilliam that:

> some gentlemen of Sheffield have proposed to enter into a fresh military association for the defence of the town and neighbourhood against riots, insurrection, seditious assemblies and public disturbances in the breach of the peace, for the protection of the magistrates in the execution of the Laws & the duty of their offices. They propose to unite in raising a body of cavalry about a hundred in number to consist of the gentlemen, subscribers to bear the expence, in person or their substitutes who are to be person well known & of good character.[20]

Despite the optimism shown in April, the Sheffield Cavalry came to a juddering halt in summer 1798, and new exertions were made to form the unit, as despite forty men enrolling, nothing actually happened in organising uniforms, training, appointing officers and NCOs etc, to the great chagrin of the local magistrates. Charles Hawksley Webb organised a meeting at the Angel Inn, Sheffield on 20 May to appoint officers and a new committee.[21] The earliest commissions are dated 5 July 1798. The corps comprised two troops and were commanded by Captain Commandant Charles Hawksley Webb and Captain George Browne. A standard was presented by Lady Fitzwilliam on 1 November 1798.[22] Each troop had one trumpeter, and two trumpets were presented on 6 December 1798.[23] About the dress of the two troops, the committee agreed:

> the uniform jacket dress noted by the majority of the principles is scarlet, turned up with black velvet, trim'd with gold lace after the manner of the Sommersetshire [sic] Officers Dress, which suppose [sic] to be somewhat the style of the Hessian dress, generally adopted.
>
> The Helmets, swords, pistols, bridles &c already ordered according to approved patterns.[24]

At the time the above was written, the Somersetshire Fencible Cavalry were currently in barracks at Sheffield. It is not clear whether gold lace was proposed for officers alone or for all ranks. 'Hessian' here seems confused with 'Hussar'.

The increase in the cavalry force was no doubt most welcome, as the Yeomanry had proven so far to be the most effective body of volunteers for local defence. With a preliminary peace treaty being signed with France in October 1801, the majority of these various cavalry troops were stood down, along with the Armed Associations and Volunteers.

Chapter 8

# 1803: NEW FORMATIONS

The Armed Associations, Yeomanry and Volunteers were stood down in summer 1802 on the coming of peace with the Treaty of Amiens. When war broke out again in May 1803, Charles James Fox blamed the Prime Minister Henry Addington for not standing up to the King. The British government had not left Napoleon 'any alternative but War or the most abject humiliation' and that the war 'is entirely the fault of our Ministers and not of Bonaparte'.[1] For those who supported war, the Rev. Munkhouse in Wakefield was typical:

> who would not, at this awful crisis, come forward and say – Before God and my Country, I swear to defend her rights and independence with the last drop of my blood? If there be any such among us, in God's name transport them to the soil of France, so rank and foul with traitors, and let them come in the ranks of the tyrant's army to meet, on their native shores, the just vengeance of their countrymen.[2]

Despite the Volunteers having of been little practical value compared to the regulars, as a potent means of rallying the nation behind the Crown they had exceeded all expectations. The revival of the movement was on a larger scale than ever before: rather than waiting for government prompting, Volunteers willingly returned to the colours. In Aylesbury, one notably civic dignitary declared that the 'Wolves of France are howling at the Doors of the English family' and placed at danger all 'homes of Englishmen' from 'a Palace, a House, a Cottage, or a Chest' adding that 'petty motives' should be put aside at a time of national peril.[3] One who bought into the Crown's fears was stalwart anti-war liberal Samuel Shore of Sheffield, and another was Samuel Hamer Oates of Leeds. Shore wrote to his mentor and friend Rev Wyvill from Meersbrook Hall, near Sheffield:

You would probably smile to see your old friend strutting about in a red jacket with a hat of some elevation and feather plucked from the neck of the bird of the gallic name to raise it a foot higher so that he could not even enter your lofty door without lowering this part . . . I must now inform you that we have a company of volunteer infantry in the Parish of which they chose me Captain, my son is a lieutenant . . . we are eighty three in number, and I must do the men justice to say, except perhaps, with a very few that they had no other motive for stepping forward at this crisis than a desire unite with [illegible] an invading enemy. The spirit of the country has been highly laudable and patriotic.[4]

If Shore and Oates abandoned the cause of peace, many still supported it. The Rev. T. Lindsey opined 'it is only by active & [illegible] measures, that we can hope to extricate ourselves out of this preposterous & unnecessary war'.[5] Similar sentiments were held by the veteran radicals Thomas Walker of Manchester and Gamaliel Lloyd of Bury St Edmunds.

Yet were the French actually coming? As our companion Frontline volume, *French Invasions of Britain and Ireland 1792-1815*, explores, any invasion of England in 1803 was not being planned in Paris.[6] Ireland was the focus of French planning throughout 1803, 1804 and 1805. Lord William Cavendish Bentinck at the end of August 1803 reported that:

They (the Irish) have begun according to their ancient custom. If this country be not attended to, it will be lost. These rascals are as ripe for rebellion as ever. The Government at present is very active. It has seized a great number of rebels and some of their chiefs. A great many Frenchmen, and Irishmen in the service of France, are said to be concealed in Ireland. Parliament has taken the precautions which circumstances required, by authorising the trial of all the rebels by Martial Law, and by suspending the Habeas Corpus. It will be necessary to put in execution the penal laws against the Catholics. If an opinion on the subject were necessary, mine is, that the grand attack will be made upon Ireland, where they (the French) will certainly be joined by a considerable number.[7]

In London, Irish and English radicals were plotting to assassinate the King and establish a republic.[8] The country was more divided than ever. The famine of 1799 had scarcely abated by the time war broke out again. Addington, learning the lessons from the 1790s, declared a national crisis, on very flimsy evidence that the French were going to invade, using 'fake news' to rally a divided nation to the Crown. To do so the Volunteers figured large in a largely propaganda war. The *Leeds Intelligencer* reported:

the Bill for the Defence of the Country provides that returns be made of all persons from the age of fifteen to sixty, distinguishing such of them as are capable of active service and as are engaged in any Volunteers Corps &c. and which of them are willing to engage themselves to be armed, attired, trained and exercised for the defence of the United Kingdom; and upon what terms they are willing to engage in case of emergency, either gratuitously or for hire as boatmen or bargemen, or as drivers of carriages or horses, or drivers of waggons, carts, cars, or cattle or as pioneers of labourers . . . Proper officers are to be appointed, and to be ready for arraying, training, exercising and commanding such men as shall be willing to engage themselves to be armed, trained and exercised, and also proper persons to be in the like manner, ready, in case of need, for superintending the execution of several other duties which may be necessary to be done. Person who may enrol themselves in any Volunteer Corps, subsequent to the date of this act, shall not be liable to be placed under the command of any General Officer commanding within the district in which they may be formed, except in conformity to the terms of their offers of service. Any officers of Volunteers making false returns of their several Corps to forfeit £200 each.[9]

The Defence Act of 11 June required Lords Lieutenant to return the number of men aged 16 to 60, listing those serving in existing units, those willing to serve, and those unwilling or unable to serve. Records of the number of horses and wagons in each parish were to be made.

Under the Act, it was reported that in the West Riding and York 1,989 men were eligible for service, 577 in the North Riding and in Kingston upon Hull and the East Riding 452 men, making a total of 3,018 men in the Militia or Volunteers.[10] A county meeting was held at York on 28 July called by Earl Fitzwilliam, Bacon Frank, magistrate of the West Riding, John Blaydes, magistrate of the West Riding, Godfrey Wentworth, William Cookson merchant manufacturer of Leeds, Richard Slater Milnes who had sat as Whig MP for York 1784–1802, John Lee of Wakefield, Benjamin Gott the Leeds industrialist, William Smithson, Walter Fawkes, William Wrightson, James Milnes of Thornes House, John Naylor of Wakefield, Benjamin Heywood of Stanley Hall, and James Torre of Snydale Hall amongst others.[11] At the meeting Walter Fawkes declared that every able bodied citizens was to 'prepare then to receive these invaders, apply yourselves to the use of arms . . . sink not into apathy from the opinion that the danger is distant' and were to 'form themselves once more into Volunteer corps'.[12] The vicar of Ackworth, William Robert Hay, the Jacobin-hunting Justice of the Peace, was amongst the first to form a Volunteer corps, as he informed his friend Isaac Hawkins Browne MP:

I have made a point of attending all public meetings when I was invited and endeavoured to make myself useful. Feeling that the times were pressing, I stood occasion to prepare a sermon which I preached & instantly called my parish together, who came forward with their services in a way did them honor, and know am principally engaged in promoting the arrangement of the Pontefract Volunteers, of whom my squad are to form part. I think you will not disapprove of our loyalty when I tell you we have sixty infantry, all stout men and have 7 men & horses to the cavalry.[13]

Despite initial enthusiasm and a flourish of activity, by mid-July it was apparent that the Act was not going to generate sufficient men. Almost immediately the Act was replaced by the General Defence Act of 27 July 1803. Called a 'Levy *en Masse*' it was an almost exact copy of the French Army's conscription system! The Act required all men aged between 17 and 55 were to be placed into four classes, those of the first class to enrolled in the Militia or Volunteer corps.[14] News of the passing of Act took time to be disseminated to Lords Lieutenant and thence to parish level.

The new Act was not greeted with enthusiasm. In an anonymous letter, William Robert Hay confided to Isaac Hawkins Browne MP what occurred in Leeds on the Act being made public:

the whole meeting was in confusion as almost all offers in addition for monies gentlemen patriots had held out as inducement to persons to Volunteer, they were as eligible as their neighbours & unable to exempt themselves from the operation of the act – they would not be got over – the fear was that large numbers would retract their offers & the spirit of the county be completely broken. If a general rule of taking 6 times the Old Militia were enacted that would put aside the genuine principle of Volunteering – I never witnessed a more anxious and embarrassing scene – the offers of service then taken Ld Fitzwilliam & [illegible] transmitted to Govt were very numerous & continued to be presented. We were in my [illegible] discussion for 4 hours when I was fortunate enough to frame a motion which seemed to meet with the approbation of all parties to this effect – That the meeting Sh'd be adjourned for a fortnight for the purpose of making for accurate returns of the number of Volunteers [illegible] and that in the meantime, Gentlemen be requested in their respective neighbourhoods to exert themselves strenuously in promoting Volunteer service in order that his Mag might be the better [illegible] to make that selection from them as he in his wisdom might think most convenient for the public service – I hope this will have some effect in [illegible] dissatisfaction in the country – but the truth is that Government has been so [illegible] & have [illegible] new arrangements respecting the service have [page torn] have been repeatedly impeded.[15]

In York, the press reported:

> one part of the new plan for the better arrangement of the Volunteers Corps, we understand to be, that such Volunteers as may hereafter be accepted are not to claim any exemption from being drawn for the Militia &c. Another arrangement will be, that Volunteers in future will be expected to find their own arms; and that they are also to be formed into regiments or brigades, and to be occasionally reviewed and inspected by experienced officers, who will be appointed to provide over certain districts. In short, the plan, it is stated, should the exigencies of the state require it, to render them in all respects competent to the defence of the country.[16]

Mass participation of all able-bodied men not already members of a military corps was enforced through fiscal forfeits. Once sworn in, Volunteers no longer had the power to leave the corps as and when they wanted. Non-attendance at compulsory training sessions and not completing the service period were to be treated as desertion. If a man left the corps, they became eligible for the Militia ballot.[17]

The Militia ballot was perhaps a major spur for men to volunteer. If balloted to serve the Militia whilst a member of a Volunteer corps, he became liable to serve or provide a substitute upon leaving the corps. Militia service entailed full-time military service away from home, under the same conditions as the regulars for three years: avoiding the Militia was no doubt a driving force for many to enlist as Volunteers. Volunteering provided an opportunity to take part in military service, avoid the Militia and take no part in fighting, and were unlikely to be induced to join the regulars as many Militiamen were. Indeed, one critique commented that the men enrolling in the Volunteers 'put on a soldier's habit to avoid a soldier's duty'.[18]

The status of Volunteers as part-time soldiers led to legal challenges, especially over the freedom to resign. Radical and noted lawyer Thomas Erskine emphatically affirmed the legal right of the Volunteers to resign as they were civilians and not soldiers. Erskine's declaration of January 1804 was read 'with great avidity' by the working class of the West Riding and indeed had tendency to 'un-hinge' the minds of the Volunteers who apparently had no awareness that they had legal rights and could resign, just as if leaving employment.[19] Volunteers were required to provide good reasons for resignation, usually ill-health or long-term absence from the locality due to work. In order to keep men in the ranks, attractions could be offered against large-scale resignations. For example, the officers of the Belper Volunteers in Derbyshire paid a total of eight guineas in March 1804 'for drink on the Inspection Day, on being told they had the power to withdraw, but not one man would resign'.[20]

Be that as it may, the levy was used to encourage volunteering in underrepresented rural areas. Volunteers had to engage to serve 85 days paid exercise a year, reducing to 20 days from August 1803. The first two classes of men were those aged 17–30 that were unmarried and 30–50 that were again unmarried. The third class was for married men aged 17–30 with two children aged under 10. Men in these three classes were to be exercised for two hours a week and given military training. Journeymen and labourers were paid to attend. All other men were assigned to the fourth class from which 'Special Constables' were to be drawn. Service under the levy did not provide exemption from the ballot for the Militia or Army Reserve.[21] In August, for corps enrolled under the June Acts, a clothing allowance of £1 for every three years' service was provided, as long as the corps was willing to serve anywhere in the country, and 1s a day for 20 days' training. It was hoped the allowances would provide an incentive to serve.

To defend the vulnerable south coast, William Pitt wrote in his capacity as Lord Warden of the Cinque Ports to Lord Hobart, the Secretary of State for War, on 27 July 1803:

> I have the honour of transmitting enclosed a Memorandum of the proposal which I laid before your Lordship this morning for raising a Regiment of Volunteers within the Cinque Ports, to serve in case of invasion in any part of England, and to consist of three Battalions: and I have to request that your Lordship will submit the same to His Majesty's consideration.

In July 1804 Kent was divided into three Volunteer Brigades, and the 3,000-strong Cinque Ports Volunteers were incorporated into the Cinque Ports Infantry Brigade along with the Deal Infantry and the Ramsgate and Margate Marksmen under the overall command of Brigadier General Charles Hope. These men would form an immediate line of defence if the French landed.

## Earl Fitzwilliam and the Volunteers
In the north of England, the first Volunteer corps to re-appear in the West Riding was the Royal Wakefield Volunteers. A meeting was called in Wakefield on 23 July to consider the propriety of addressing

the King, and to make steps to organise a defence of the county.[22] In response, the Tammy Hall, the largest public meeting place in the town, was let by its trustees to be the venue for a meeting on 1 August 1803. The meeting, chaired by Jeremiah Naylor,

> Resolved, that we whose names are undersigned, will immediately enter into an Association and form a Corps of Infantry to serve in any part of Great Britain, in case of actual invasion or the Appearance of the Enemy in Force upon the coast, and for the suppression of any Rebellion or Insurrection.
> Resolved,
> That we will serve without pay, unless called out on actual service, but that the government be solicited to furnish Arms and Accoutrements.
> Resolved,
> That the Chairman be requested to wait upon the Constable to desire that a Meeting of the Inhabitants of Wakefield may be held on Saturday Next at Twelve o'clock at the Moot Hall for the purpose of laying before them these resolutions and for obtaining the co-operation of the inhabitants in such manners as may be thought best adapted for carrying the same into Effect.
> Resolved,
> That the thanks of this Meeting be given to the Chairman, Jeremiah Naylor.[23]

Five days later, a meeting was held in the ancient Moot Hall, Wakefield on 6 August, chaired by John Smyth MP for Pontefract, which agreed:

> that the whole Parish of Wakefield, as well as the Townships of Altofts, Acton, Crofton, Normanton, Sharlston, Sandal, Snydale, Warmfield, Walton and Whitwood shall be invited to join in the Association of Volunteers . . . That a subscription be opened to raise a sum of Money for defraying the Expenses of the Corps, until they be called for actual service, such money to be lodged in the bank of Messrs Ingram and Co . . . that a Committee be appointed, and that same do consist of subscribers of Twenty Pounds and upwards, and that any five of the said Committee be empowered to act . . . That Mr Tolson, the constable; Mr Kennet, Mr Andrew Peterson, Mr Daniel Smallpage, Mr Jeremiah Naylor, Mr Joseph Scott and Mr Whitaker be desired to solicit subscriptions in the Town and neighbourhood, and that the different townships admitted to this association be desired to do the same, and lodge with money when called for, as directed by the said committee.[24]

A return of 12 August 1803 sent to Earl Fitzwilliam by Daniel Smallpage, church warden, chandler and soap boiler, stated that 350 men had returned to the colours. He further made a request to the Home Office that 'the corps should be allowed to take back its blue regimentals and assume the title of Royal hitherto granted in the last war'. The Home Office replied that they had never heard of such a request before. Royal intervention allowed the corps to retain blue facings and become again 'The Royal Wakefield Volunteers'.[25] By 5 September a further fifty men had been enrolled and taken the oath of allegiance.[26] William Rookes Leeds Serjeantson was Lieutenant-Colonel, assisted by Major Jeremiah Todd Naylor. The officer's appointments were published on 10 October:[27]

Lieutenant-Colonel Commandant: William Rookes Leeds Serjeantson
Lieutenant-Colonel: John Tottenham
Major: Jeremiah Todd Naylor
Captains: Benjamin Kennet, George Oxley, William Whittaker, Andrew Peterson, Robert Allot, Joseph Scott, Edmund Steer, John Jackson
Lieutenants: John Maude, John Hurst, George Allot, Peter Richardson, William Shackleton, James Craven, George Addey, Michael Bentley, William Dawson, Thomas Foljambe
Ensigns: John Lee jnr, Richard Burrell, Thomas Lee, W T Batten, John Hill, Charles Topliss

The corps mustered at Heath Common with the Wakefield Troop of Yeomanry Cavalry under the orders of Captain Sir Edward Sylvester Smith, Lieutenant Daniel Gaskell and Ensign William Naylor on 1 January 1804, the men 'wearing new regimentals'.[28] The field day was followed by a dinner at the White Hart Inn for the officers and NCOs, the other ranks being hosted at other inns across the town.[29] The colours were represented on Heath Common on 24 February 1804.[30] The 'Loyalist and St George Club' presented the corps on 6 December 1805 with a ceremonial baton for 'loyal and devoted service to the country and monarchy'.

Close behind Wakefield in declaring its loyalty came Huddersfield when a meeting chaired by Joseph Radcliffe JP was held at the George Hotel on 29 July. The meeting resolved to summon 'the gentlemen, clergy, merchants, inhabitants of the several Parishes of Huddersfield, Almondbury, Kirkheaton, Kirkburton and the township of Quick in the Upper Division of Agbrigg'. The second meeting was held on 1 August, with the resolutions of the meeting being that a 'corps of Volunteer infantry be raised in the district on a large scale a scale as possible, so as to be respectable and a corps of Volunteer cavalry'. Sir George Armitage Bart was named commander of the infantry and Sir John Lister Kaye of the cavalry. Law Atkinson was named clerk to the committee and held the subscription list and enrolment ledgers. On 29 August the committee ordered that:

> each township within this division is required to enrol as Volunteers Resolutions six times the number of men as are balloted to serve in the old militia, thereat. and it is recommended to the several townships to select such men as are unmarried, and have the fewest incumbrances.
>
> That John Lister Kaye, Esquire, be requested to attend at Huddersfield to enrol the men, and to administer the oath to the corps of Cavalry.
>
> That Sir George Armytage, Bart., be requested to attend to enrol the men, and to administer the oath to the corps of Infantry in the following townships, viz: – Huddersfield, Kirkheaton, Dalton, Whitley, Lepton, Almondbury, Lockwood, Marsden, Quick, Mirfield and Hartishead-cum-Clifton.
>
> That Josh. Radcliffe, Esquire, be requested to attend to enrol the men, and to administer the oath to the corps of Infantry in the following townships, viz.: – Longwood, Lindley-cum-Quarmby, Linthwaite, Golcar, Scammonden, Slaithwaite and Lingarths.
>
> That George Armitage, Esquire, of Highroyd, be requested to attend to enrol the men and to administer the oath to the corps of Infantry in the following townships, viz: – Honley, Meltham, Netherthong, South Crosland, Farnley Tyas, Kirkburton, Thurstonland, Shelley, Shepley, Wooldale, Foulstone, Cartworth, Holme, Hepworth, Austonley and Upperthong. That each of the above-mentioned townships be required to complete their lists with the least possible delay, and that Sir George Armytage, Baronet, Josh. Radcliffe and George Armitage, Esquires, be requested to inform the gentlemen of the respective townships when it will be convenient for them to attend to enrol and to administer the oath.[31]

The meeting further resolved that:

> John Lister Kaye, Esquire, be requested to apply to Government for the allowance for contingencies, and to order the clothing and accoutrements for the corps of Cavalry. That Sir George Armytage, Baronet, be requested to apply to Government for arms and other allowances, and to order the clothing and accoutrements for the corps of Infantry and that the expense of clothing each man do not exceed the sum of £2 12s. 6d. That the gentlemen in each Township are requested to collect the whole of the subscriptions of Five Guineas and under, and to pay the same into the Bank of Messrs. Perfect, Seaton, Brook and Company on or before Friday, the 9th September. That all subscribers of above Five Guineas are requested to pay 25 per cent. on their respective subscriptions into the hands of Messrs. Perfect, Seaton, Brook and Company, on or before

Friday, the 9th September. That a list of the subscribers to the corps of Volunteer Cavalry and Infantry in the Upper Division of Agbrigg be inserted as soon as completed in both the Leeds papers.[32]

A day later in Halifax the Rev. Dr Coulthurst chaired a meeting on 30 July for the 'propriety of making an offer to government to raise a Volunteer Corps in the Town and Parish'.[33]

On 15 August a meeting was held in York to re-form the York Volunteers, which were to act in the city and immediate suburbs and not serve 10 miles beyond the city. All subscribers who gave over £20 were considered committee members. It was envisioned that a mixed force of infantry and cavalry was to be raised and a subscription was opened to fund the corps. The City Corporation gave £500 and the Mayor, Thomas Hartley, gave £50, William Mordaunt Milner, the city's MP, gave £300 and Lord Dundas £200. The Archbishop of York gave £150 and the Deanery of York £300. At a subsequent meeting held in the Guildhall, the committee agreed to give £7 to any man joining the cavalry force to cover the cost of his uniform and equipment.[34] William Mordaunt Miner was named Colonel Commandant, the corps mustering 570 men by the start of September.[35] Colours were presented to the original regiment on 20 December 1803 by the Mayoress.

For the Ainsty of York, Hall Plumer, the Lieutenant of the Division, called a meeting at the Rose and Crown Inn, Tadcaster on 18 August to raise a Volunteer force. It was in theory also a mixed force of infantry and cavalry.[36] Colours were presented on 18 January 1804 by Mrs Plumer.[37] By 5 September 400 men had been enrolled and taken the oath of allegiance.[38]

As well as infantry, the Yeomanry was reformed. Earl Fitzwilliam called a county meeting on 11 July in Doncaster to re-establish the Southern Regiment of Yeomanry Cavalry.[39] The meeting of the Lieutenancies and Magistrates resolved:

> On Monday last at a Meeting of the Lieutenancy of this Riding, was held at Doncaster, in order to consider the best means of augmenting the defensive force of the country; when it was unanimously resolved to make a corps of Volunteers Yeomanry Cavalry in the Wapentakes of Strafforth and Tickhill, Staincross, Osgoldcross, Agbrigg and Morley.
>
> The Meeting of the Lieutenancy of the West Riding held at the Hotel in this town on Thursday last, was very numerously attended; when it was unanimously resolved that a requisition should be made to the County Sherriff to call a County Meeting.[40]

Subscriptions for the regiment included £500 from Francis Ferrand Foljambe, £100 from Thomas Fenton, £200 from Bryan Cooke, officer commanding Doncaster Troop, and £150 from J.W. Childers.[41] The officer's appointments were published on 3 October 1803.[42] By the end of the year, the Southern Regiment comprised 612 men in 12 troops based in Barnsley, Tickhill, Doncaster where the headquarters was established, Hatfield, Rotherham, Kiverton, Pontefract, and Wakefield two troops at Wath, and two in Sheffield. The Northern Regiment mustered eight troops and 384 men. Other independent troops came under the designation of the 2nd Regiment. The Craven Legion Yeomanry were raised in 1803 under the orders of Lieutenant-Colonel Richard Wainmann, and mustered five troops of 200 men in total in spring 1804, and was associated with an Independent Association of Infantry which was taken into the local Militia in 1808. The total cost of clothing and equipment was estimated at 'not much less than £10,000' (the infantry included) and described in 1804 as 'uniformly handsome and good, but by no means tawdry or extravagant'.[43] The colours of the Craven Legion were blessed by the Rev. Josiah Dawson on 17 February 1804 and presented by Lady Ribblesdale.[44] Other Independent Yeomanry troops included the Harewood Cavalry commanded by the Hon. Henry Lascelles, one troop of seventy-two men, and the Knaresborough Cavalry, comprising a single troop of forty-eight men headed by Captain Thomas Slingsby and a West Riding Corps of Volunteer Cavalry commanded by Captain the Hon. William Gordon of Stockeld Park, a single troop of some forty-five men. On 18 January 1804 the troop received its 'colours' from the Countess of Aberdeen.[45]

Be that as it may, the formation of Volunteer corps proceeded across the West Riding and the Country as a whole. In order to organise the West Riding's response, Earl Fitzwilliam called a county meeting on 4 August which resolved:

> unanimously and strongly recommend the forming of such Volunteer Corps in every place where it is possible to be done . . . for the purpose of encouraging Volunteers under this act, it is strongly recommended that a subscription be entered into in the respective Parishes or such other districts.[46]

We find from the list of subscriptions that Lord Harewood gave £2,000, John Smyth of Heath offered £400 as did Walter Spencer Stanhope of Cannon Hall, Barnsley, Godfrey Wentworth of Woolley gave £550, Walter Ramsden Fawkes £500, and so too Edwin Lascelles and his brother Henry. William Sotherton gave £100 to the general-purpose committee, £50 to the Yeomanry Cavalry and £26 5s to the Pontefract Volunteer Committee. Charles Wilson gave £100 to the Leeds Volunteer Committee, £50 to the Yeomanry cavalry and £26 5s to the Pontefract Volunteer Committee. From Wakefield Benjamin Heywood, as well as John Naylor and Thomas Lumb each gave £100. We also note that James Milnes of Thornes House gave £1,000, and the Archbishop of York gave £2,000, £300 of which was specifically for York Volunteers.[47] By 27 August, a staggering £18,729 10s had been raised: Francis Foljambe gave £500, so too the Duke of Leeds and Lord Viscount Downe, and Earl Fitzwilliam had given £2,000.[48] The invasion scare and formation of new Volunteer corps gave the leading merchants, manufacturers and other members of the increasingly wealthy middle classes across the West Riding the opportunity to display their largesse. It also allowed for middle-class involvement in the running of civic institutions which helped raised the profile of the urban bourgeoisie, making them firmly part of the loyalist establishment. The defence of wealth inequality and property was a key factor in attracting broad cross-party support for Reeve's ideals in 1792 and also to the Volunteer system: both Whig and Tory understood that broad ideas of liberty and equality were explosively incompatible with wealth accumulation. The rich 'bourgeois' had as much to lose from Jacobinism and reform as the aristocracy.[49]

By the end of August, the Leeds Volunteers were 1,000 strong, at Huddersfield 500 had enrolled, and Walter Ramsden Fawkes had formed the Wharfdale Volunteers.[50] Sheffield by mid-August had raised 700 men, 1,000 men had enrolled in the York Volunteers, and Huddersfield reported 3,000 had joined the colours![51]

When the Volunteer corps had been reformed, the Crown accepted all offers of corps' formation via the Lords Lieutenant, but in August 1803 a new limit was set per county as six times the Militia quota: a number of corps were merged with neighbouring formations or disappeared entirely. In order to limit participation, the corps selected for continuation were based on the respectability of the men in the corps, location, composition, and the likelihood of the men to join the Militia. Despite such restrictions, by the end of the year 380,000 men were Volunteers, serving under the same set of regulations. Lord Dundas argued the force was too large and badly trained, and would have preferred a well-trained reserve of give-or-take 200,000 men.[52]

Unlike 1794, when the Duke of Norfolk in his capacity as Lord Lieutenant had accepted virtually every offer of service to form a Volunteer corps, his successor Earl Fitzwilliam took a more selective approach. He was not convinced of the need for forming Volunteer units: thanks to the events in Sheffield where the Sheffield Armed

Association had threatened to open fire on the magistrates and other corps had mutinied as we discuss in a later chapter, Fitzwilliam was a worried man. Writing to Hobart, the Secretary of State for War, he noted that he was in favour of limiting the number of Volunteer corps and cautioned that 'the indiscriminate arming of the people' could be 'attended with great danger'.[53] He explained his motives in a letter to Lord Pelham:

> I had previously as far as I could, endeavoured to prepare the country for that arrangement in the Volunteering system which the present state of things now renders necessary for the tranquillity and safety of the country. We must avoid as far as the case will admit having small detach'd corps, at least withing the manufacturing district: we must try to get some distinguished persons to be at their head & I cannot help thinking, that it would tend much to security, if adjutants and some Non-Comm'd officers were allow'd: it would be keeping instruction, consequently authority, in the hands of persons accustom'd themselves to look up to their commanding officers with respect & deference & direct therefore the minds of those under their instruments to the same points: it would still have a more beneficial effect in preventing the busy, active spirits (description of person one must suspect) of taking a lead amongst the ignorant hands, which they will, if that lead is previously in other hands.[54]

Fitzwilliam had legitimate concerns that 'undesirable elements' were joining up to learn the use of arms to turn them against the state, which Magistrate Busfield feared was already happening in Bradford. The 'evil spirit of sedition is by no means laid in this neighbourhood', reported Busfield to Earl Fitzwilliam, noting that the opportunity to be issued a musket and receive military training without any oversight was received 'avidly by many who are suspected of being disaffected'.[55]

Fitzwilliam was far from happy with the Act. True to his Whig principles and opposition to a standing army, the Earl claimed to express the sentiments of 'every considerate man' in the West Riding, in expressing his fears that the Levy *en Masse* would create an army under no control. He added that if the government was adamant volunteering was to be massively expanded, he warned command of the various units would devolve on inferior men – therefore of dubious loyalty to the state – because 'no men of consequence, rank and respectability would submit to take commissions'. Furthermore, Fitzwilliam was concerned that if smaller, unsupervised corps were formed in the same ad-hoc fashion as in 1794, he felt that for many, the Volunteer system would become 'play time, and arms play things'.[56]

Despite his objections to the enlarged nature of volunteering, Earl Fitzwilliam in his capacity as Lord Lieutenant had to support the government's mandate. However, he had ultimate power to decided which offers of Volunteer corps' formation to proceed with by forwarding them onto the War Office: in doing so he was able to revise the nature and scope of the Volunteer units in the Riding. We know from his own correspondence, that Fitzwilliam had received offers to form twenty Volunteer corps by August, but chose to accept just nine troops of Yeomanry.[57] This still left 165 infantry companies and 24 troops of cavalry which had applied for acceptance to be approved.[58]

## Fitzwilliam's Reforms

Whether what happened next was a reflection of national policy or not, Earl Fitzwilliam as Lord Lieutenant of the West Riding sought to bring some sort of order to the chaotic nature of volunteering. Rather than accepting a multiplicity of corps in a wapentake or parish, Fitzwilliam strove to amalgamate smaller units into larger, more cohesive more and militarily useful formations, with a greater degree of supervision, to try and fend of the spectre of the mutinies of 1800 from recuring.[59]

John Shillito, Major of the 'Barkston Ash Volunteers', approached the Earl about the minimum size of a corps and the strength of a company. In a terse reply, the Earl deemed the minimum number of men in an infantry unit to be 120, noting:

> In the meantime, I think it candid to explain that no Volunteer establishments that does not consist of three companies is considered as a corps: if not that establishment, it is not a Corps, is held exempt from being liable to be placed any regiment His Majesty may have pleasure to attach it to, when called into active service.

He closed the letter noting that if Shillito was indifferent to him and his men being placed in an existing corps then he would forthwith agree to the formation of the unit, or if being placed in an existing Corps was an issue, then Shillito would be told to recruit the proposed unit up to three companies.[60] Shillito's Barkston Ash unit, despite mustering 120 men was not accepted. Shillito, commanding just 120 men and facing demotion to Captain, readily agreed to the Earl's plan and the 'Barkston Ash Volunteers' became the nucleus of a much larger wapentake unit, affording Shillito the rank of Major. Did title and therefore status drive Shillito, or a desire to defend the nation? Perhaps a mix of the two. In March 1805 the Sherburn and Tadcaster companies of the corps demonstrated the 'light infantry movements' on a field day. Ultimately, Shillito was Major of a six-company-strong battalion headed by Colonel Mervin Vavasour.

As we have noted in the case of Shillito the Earl wielded considerable influence in accepting or declining the offer of service and became directly involved in how units were recruited. In order to bring a 'commonsense' approach to the re-formed Volunteers, rather than allowing the ad hoc system of 1794, of small independent companies, Earl Fitzwilliam favoured larger corps over smaller, township-based units. Desiring to form largely wapentake based corps, Fitzwilliam was able in his own way to temper government policy. This did not go always go smoothly or well. It was on his recommendations that the 'Staincross Volunteer Infantry' would become wholly recruited from a single wapentake, and that smaller units were not accepted or forced to amalgamate with units raised nearby. In this, the Earl was partially successful.

A good example of Fitzwilliam's endeavours being thwarted by local rivalries concerned the towns of Dewsbury, Ossett and Soothill. In Dewsbury, John Halliley, a wealthy merchant of 'Halliley, Brooke & Halliley' who owned Aldams Mill on Westgate in the town, in August proposed to the Earl to form a unit of Volunteers.[61] By October, he had appointed his officers: Abraham Greenwood was named Major, his son John Halliley jnr as Captain commanding the grenadier company, the others being Captains Thomas Rylah and Edward Hipposon, Lieutenants John Heald Jr, Thomas Bramley and Edward Lancaster, and Ensigns Timothy Parker, George Bromley and John Chaster.[62] The company was inspected on 24 October when the corps had three companies of 60 men, totalling 180 other ranks, nine sergeants, nine corporals and three drummers. They had no arms, but had been allocated funds for clothing.[63]

Less than five miles from Dewsbury, the townsfolk of Ossett had raised their own Volunteer corps. The vicar of Ossett, Rev. Edward Kilvington, informed Earl Fitzwilliam that, independent of what Halliley was organising, he had raised a company of seventy-three men and reported that they had been enrolled under the same terms as the men in Dewsbury. Furthermore, he informed the Earl that he had opened a subscription to fund the men's clothing.[64] The Ossett enrolment list was headed by William Ingram Jnr. Of the seventy-three men on the roll, twenty-six were illiterate and signed the list with a 'X' next to where they were told their name was written.[65]

Hard by Dewsbury is the small town of Soothill, where yet another small Volunteer unit was raised. The Earl sought that the three small and ineffective units were to be amalgamated. Thus, Dewsbury which mustered 135 men was amalgamated with Soothill's some 96 men, and

Ossett's 75 men, forming the 'Dewsbury, Ossett & Soothill Volunteers'.[66] Perhaps inevitably local rivalries broke out: the townsfolk of Ossett refused to serve in a Dewsbury-based Volunteer unit, despite the town of Ossett being in the Parish of Dewsbury. Matters were made worse when civic rivalry about where the force was to be based, the name of the force and a lack of a suitable commanding officer to take command, with the resignation of John Halliley in disgust at the forceful amalgamation of his unit, meant that Fitzwilliam had no option but to disband all three![67] Clearly the zeal of the officers was tempered by the lack of recruits and the desire not serve as part of another corps. Local pride and civic or even parish rivalries would to an extent hamstring the formation of Volunteer units as we shall see. Clearly the hatred of the French and the desire to protect hearth and home did not outweigh dislike of men from the neighbouring town or village.

A similar problem arose with the long-standing rivalries between Wakefield and the small town of Horbury, part-way between Wakefield and Ossett. Here the 'Horbury Volunteer Infantry' was headed by the Rev. John Taylor. In theory vicars could not command Volunteer formations, but such requirements do not seem to have bothered the good reverend. His second-in-command was Richard Carr, the Parish Clerk. The Earl refused to accept Horbury as an independent Volunteer corps, who were told, that they were to merge with the 'Royal Wakefield Volunteers'. The disgusted Richard Carr informed Earl Fitzwilliam that 'we sh'd be considered as attached to Wakefield and under the direction of the commanding officer there and our drill the like command' but he added 'only when the French landed or the corps was called upon in riot suppression'. Carr furthermore hoped that the Horbury corps would remain independent of Wakefield and:

> would not join them in their exercise but at hours convenient to the Horbury Corps. There are those in our Township who have served in the Militia and will naturally assist us in our duties . . . the Corps to consist of 60 men exclusive of officers, serjeants, corporals and drums and to be cloathed (provided) at our expense. [68]

A month later Carr informed the Earl that he hoped that the company would not be united with the 'Royal Wakefield Volunteers'.[69] Fitzwilliam refused to accept the corps despite Carr's pleading – it mustered under the 120 men minimum – and the corps was amalgamated with the 'Royal Wakefield Volunteers'. A similar story was repeated when the Earl endeavoured create a single corps of Volunteers for Liversidge, Bingley, Birstall and Batley, which again because of regional rivalry came to nought. Out of this came the 'Bingley Volunteer Infantry' headed by Currer Fothergill Busfield, son of the magistrate J.A. Busfield as Colonel, and the 'Loyal Birstall and Batley Volunteers' headed by Colonel Samuel Sykes.[70] We note that the wapentake of Agbrigg and Morley had no wapentake formation: Wakefield seems to have represented at least some of the Agbrigg Division. The Morley Division included Birstall, Bradford, Calverley and parts of Batley, Huddersfield – parts in Agbrigg along with Almondbury – and Dewsbury. Perhaps the size of the wapentake and the major industrial towns precluded a single corps being formed. The Loyal Leeds Volunteers was largely recruited from the Borough of Leeds, which included Armley, Beeston, Bramley, Farnley, Holbeck, Hunslet and Wortley.

Despite desiring wapentake-focused formations, in the southern part of the Riding, besides reforming the pre-1801 units in Sheffield and Rotherham, the Wath Wood corps was formed out of Volunteer offers from the area between Doncaster, Rotherham and Sheffield, and it was joined by units at Ecclesfield, Bawtry and Thorne, the latter two at the extremities of the division. In the wapentake of Tickhill, Doncaster supplied 200 men and a further 300 were raised in 27 villages surrounding Doncaster. William Wrightson of Cusworth was in overall charge as Lieutenant-Colonel Commandant while Captain Elwin commanded Volunteers from Tickhill, Conisbrough, Braithwell, Wadworth, Warmsworth, Edlington and Clifton.[71] In seeking to create larger units, two largely rural parish-based units of Sowerby and Soyland were brought together on 30 September 1804 as the West Halifax Volunteers, headed by James Moore, and mustered 400 men. Yet the parish-based Ecclesfield Volunteer Infantry remained an independent unit headed by Thomas Robson, and again the largely parish-based Roundell Volunteer Infantry headed by William Roundell, which was recruited around Skipton and therefore should have formed part of the Craven Legion, remained independent.[72] Indeed, colours were presented to the Ecclesfield Volunteers on 23 April 1804, the gift of Mr and Mrs Greaves, bearing the motto 'Nothing is Difficult to the Brave & Faithful'. These were later deposited in St Mary's, Ecclesfield, along with six swords and three bugles.[73]

As well as infantry formations, small units of independent Yeomanry cavalry existed at Knaresborough mustering forty-two men commanded by Thomas Slingsby, at Harewood some seventy-two men commanded by Hon Henry Lascelles, Stockeld Park Yeomanry, mustering forty-two men and commanded by Hon William Gordon, and the Leeds Cavalry which mustered seventy-eight men.[74]

One oddity was the formation of an Armed Association in York. The first meeting was advertised in the newspapers on 15 October to serve within the limits of the city and surrounding area in the event of the services of the Volunteers being 'requisite elsewhere', especially in case of invasion.[75] In December it was proposed to dress the company of 120 in a blue coat faced red, the men to provide their own arms.[76] We hear no more of this corps after 20 December 1803. In fact, we know very little about the majority of the corps raised in 1803 beyond the name of their commanding officer.

The last Volunteer unit raised in the West Riding was the 'Addingham Volunteers', incorporated on 12 August 1804 and mustering sixty men. Proposed in 1803, the corps was accepted on 19 November 1803 – despite not meeting the 120-man minimum – under the command of Captain Thomas Langton, Willian Cunliffe and Beckwith Spencer as lieutenants. All three officers resigned on 7 January 1804. The unit took part in the review of Volunteers on Brinsworth Common on 8 October 1804 under the command of Walter Ramsden Fawkes and was amalgamated with the Wharfedale Volunteers. Ultimately, William Cunliffe was appointed Captain on 7 March 1805 and Spencer was named again as Lieutenant the same day.[77]

Schools also seem to have formed their own corps. The *Leeds Intelligencer* reported the Rev. R Hartley, Vicar of Bingley since 1797 and headmaster of Bingley Grammar School, had formed his young charges into a body of Volunteer infantry.[78] A similar unit seems to have been formed at Leeds Grammar School of 'dismounted cavalry, composed of genteel-looking boys'.[79] Leeds also boasted a company of pioneers dressed in blue commanded by former Leeds Mayor Wade Brown. As well as raising Volunteer soldiers, special constables were to be raised across the country. Via the magistrates of the Riding, Earl Fitzwilliam ordered on 11 November 1803 that able-bodied men classed as 'house keepers' not enrolled under the first and second class, were to engage as special constables.[80] In response, on 24 November 1803 in Leeds over 300 men were sworn in as special constables, to aid the civil authorities in the case of invasion. Such measures were not uncommon elsewhere, but here the force seems to have had a paramilitary nature – 'they are to be armed with pikes, and such as are acquainted with the military exercise are to be provided with firelocks'. They were to be classed as staff officers when serving alongside the Volunteers.[81] We are not sure as to their duties.

Chapter 9

# MEN, UNIFORMS AND EQUIPMENT

The re-formation of the Volunteers on a more professional and homogenous footing in 1803 required a similar degree of consolidation of what was worn; the newly raised corps were restricted to the red of the regulars and Militia (or green for rifles), and were strongly encouraged to follow the patterns of the county Militias. As could be expected, in the West Riding Earl Fitzwilliam insisted upon a greater degree of standardisation of dress. Out of this came a cohesive plan for dressing all regiments ostensibly the same across the Riding. The *Leeds Intelligencer* reported:

> the Uniform of the Volunteer Infantry Corps, throughout the Whole of the West-Riding of Yorkshire . . . should be the same in every Respect; and should be similar in Materials and Make to, and not exceed the regulated Prices allowed for the Army; and it is recommended that the Officers of the above Corps be clothed in Serjeants' Cloth.[1]

It was further noted that henceforth all regimental facings would be yellow, with silvered or white metal buttons, silver lace for officers and buttons in pairs. The 'grand ideas' of the Lords Lieutenant counted for literally nothing in desiring to standardise uniforms, if we are to compare the theory to practice from extant garments. Judging from surviving coats and portraits, we note the Wharfdale Volunteers had gilt or brass buttons in threes and buff facings;[2] brass or gilt buttons in pairs with yellow facings were worn by Barkston Ash,[3] York,[4] Leeds,[5] Upper Agbrigg and Pontefract; buttons in pairs and green facings were worn by Sheffield,[6] Halifax,[7] Birstall and Batley,[8] and Bradford,[9] and the 'Royal Wakefield Volunteers' had buttons in singles with blue facings.[10]

Clothing was made by public tender. The clothing of the other ranks is particularly well documented thanks to the regimental committee of the York Volunteers' practice of tendering for materials and tailors by advertising in the local press:

> Any person or persons in this City willing to contract for the delivery of the under-mentioned Articles, or any of them, are requested to send Proposals in writing to the Committee, sealed up, with Patterns inclosed, or to the Secretary . . .
>     740 yards of serjeants broad scarlet cloth from 15s to 16s a yard
>     1800 yards of yard-wide white cloth at 6s per yard
>     300 yards of Black broadcloth (six-fourth) cloth at 7s 6d per yard
>     125 Gross of Gilt Buttons, similar to those of the late Corps
>     600 Caps with regulation feathers, not exceeding 15s agreeable to pattern to be seen at the Guildhall.
>     600 Black stocks.[11]

A week later contracts were made for:

> 25 regulation swords for Sergeants
>     580 belt plates for the privates
>     25 gilt belt plates for the Sergeants
>     A pattern of each of the Plates determined upon are left at the guildhall, and may also be seen this day from Eleven to Two O'clock.
>     Also, proposals for providing 600 caps with devices and regulation feathers, of equal goodness, and the exact pattern of one left at the Guildhall, and may also be seen this day from Eleven to Two o'clock, at a price not exceeding 15s each.[12]

Jacket ('coat'-size) buttons, apparently on an allowance of thirty per jacket, were gilt, 'similar to those of the late York Volunteer Corps'. Contracts were also made for smaller buttons for waistcoats and breeches, and for gaiter buttons, the latter being made from the black broadcloth. The caps bore 'devices', later described as 'a yellow plate with the motto "pro aris et focis" – for our homes and altars, which we have no doubt they will well defend when called on', and 'regulation feathers' – presumably tufts.[13] The first batch of 600 caps with 'Regulation Feathers' was supplied, at the lowest estimate (10s each), by Messrs Haden and Moody of York. The scarlet, white and black broadcloths purchased by the committee were supplied, along with buttons, to the tailors, who were expected to furnish:

a coat, waistcoat, breeches and gaiters, according to the patterns to be seen in the Guildhall. The scarlet, white and black and buttons are provided by and are to be taken from the Committee at their prime cost; all other Articles, Facings and Trimmings are to be furnished by the persons contracting to make up the clothes. [14]

Contracts for the clothing seem to have been made in two batches, of 556[15] and 417[16] respectively. The prospective contractor had to make a minimum of one company's worth of clothing. Each man was to be measured and the 'suit of clothing fitted to the man' i.e., their uniforms were tailor-made, or at least tailored to fit. The patterns and cloth samples had been agreed with the Corps Committee and Earl Fitzwilliam. For the second batch of uniforms the committee were to:

provide scarlet broad cloth as 14s 6d per yard; white broad cloth at 9s per yard; black cloth for gaiters at 4s 5d per yard; coat buttons at 14s 6d per gross; waistcoat and breeches at 9s per gross; gaiter buttons at 2s per gross . . . the contractors must also find all other articles which are to be of equal goodness and quality with those made use of in the pattern produced: the yellow cloth for the facings to be equal in goodness to the white.[17]

The uniform was first worn on 1 December, and reported as 'extremely good and handsome; being a scarlet jacket with yellow facings, white cloth waistcoat and breeches, black gaiters and a black cap'.[18] Greatcoats and knapsacks were also bought in late 1803, and tenders for greatcoat straps were invited in December.[19]

About the clothing of the Volunteers, General Instructions recommended:

The nature of the service will require every individual being in the lightest state of equipment. Besides his arms and ammunition, each Volunteer will only carry one shirt, one pair of shoes and stockings, and combs and brushes. It will be essential, if possible, each man shall start with three days bread, 4 1/25lb. – In the Infantry, one horse for each effective officer will be allowed, including staff, and one extra for each field officer, one per company for officers' portmanteaus; one light two wheeled cart will be allowed for each company; in the light cart, tin kettles sufficient for the company must be carried. It would be eligible that each Volunteer should bring a light blanket or greatcoat; each company should also have a proportion of bill hooks, one for every five men; a canteen for water is also essential, or in its place a strong bottle slung over the shoulder, and a linen haversack for the necessaries and bread; a small portmanteau will contain the baggage of each officer. It is evidence that the necessity of the service requires this light state of equipment, to which every individual will with cheerfulness accede.[20]

One unique aspect of the Volunteers was the use of Prussian muskets and another was the use of black leather cross belts. On 3 November 1803 480 stand of arms were delivered to the 'Royal Wakefield Volunteers', the muskets of Prussian manufacture 'and uncommonly strong'. Doncaster Volunteers received 300 muskets, Rotherham 480 and Sheffield 500, again all Prussian in origin.[21] The Leeds Volunteers likewise had 1,400 Prussian muskets and Bradford 560.[22] Black cross belts were in use in Sheffield in November 1807 as Colonel Fenton wrote to Earl Fitzwilliam, the Lord Lieutenant, asking to exchange the black belts and musket slings for white, and repeated this request in January 1808.[23] Whether this was actually done before the disbandment of the corps and the organisation of the Local Militia later that year is not clear. We note that in November 1807, Colonel Fenton had stated that the black cross belts were 'not so neat and they dirty the cloathes' which was no doubt a comment on the black ball polish leaving marks on the uniform coat. He added that when the regiment was raised, he had requested white belts and slings, and blackened cowhide items were used as no buff was to be had. Fenton also requested his 'heavy Prussian Arms' to be replaced.[24] Leeds replaced its black cross belts with whitened buff in summer 1807, which was reported to have 'given them more the appearance of regular soldiers'.[25] We assume the practice was widespread in the county.

## Training

Volunteers of 1803, like their predecessors, had to attend twice-weekly drill sessions, as well as be 'mobilised' for two weeks for training alongside other corps. The diary of Lieutenant Thomas Asline Ward of Sheffield, housed in Sheffield City Library, provides an insight into the life and times of a Volunteer officer. He had been entreated to join following a sermon by his minister, Rev. Benjamin Naylor of Upper Chapel, Sheffield. Naylor, a Unitarian, had supported the radical reformist ideals of congregation member Henry Redhead Yorke, and bankrolled the *Sheffield Iris* newspaper of James Montgomery. By 1803, the fear of invasion led him to entreat his congregation to join the colours and participate in a war for the defence of their homeland. Ward from his diary tells us he left for Doncaster with his company, 2 April 1804 for 15 days. They arrived 'soon after 4 o'clock our fixed time for dinner at the mess, the officers repaired to the Angel Inn, which for the week is fixed for our headquarters. It is calculated that if each officer contribute ten day's pay it will defray the expenses of his dinners at mess including ale and a pint of port for the whole fifteen days.' Following his evening meal Ward tells us 'we had an evening parade at half-past six o'clock . . . the men appeared with side arms only, being brought up to the Grande Parade by the junior officer of each company from their Private Parade'. He continues, 'at the appointed time, and when the line was formed, the whole of the officers took their posts, ranks were opened, the captains gave their reports to the Adjutant, the band performed several airs marches &c'. One of Ward's 'pet hates' was being billeted in a barrack room: 'I would or could not gain a moments rest', he complained to himself about trying to get a night's sleep because of 'the loud snoring's of the unconscious sleepers, who, stretched out in their warm watchcoats upon the floor, tables and forms, present a very uncommon and novel spectacle to me'. In order to promote a sense of equality amongst the officers Ward tells us 'I should not omit to mention two rules made for the government of our mess room – one prohibiting swearing and indecent language; the other, preventing any allusions to the shop or to the profession of himself.'

The Sheffield Volunteers returned to Doncaster in August 1805. Ward tells us 'August 26, rose at 3, breakfasted on chocolate, attended the parade of the Volunteers before 4, and marched at 4. Arrived by 10 at Conisboro', where we were refreshed with bread and ale; reached Doncaster by 1.' About the training routine he noted 'August 27 – Paraded at 9 and exercised till 2' which set the pattern for the 15 days. About insubordination he tells us

the men of our company having been very talkative on the field this morning, I marched them from the grande parade in the evening to the corn market, where I told them would march till silence was enforced. They went around the corn market 8 or 10 times, when I dismissed some of the most silent. In another round or two, Armstrong and Powell quitted the ranks without leave.

About the return to Sheffield:

September 9 – I rose at half past four, breakfasted on coffee, attended parade at five. We marched from Doncaster before six, halted a short time at Dalton for refreshment given by the Countess of Effingham, and arrived at Sheffield by half-past 12, where Dr Browne presented the men with a purse of 30 guineas. They were also treated by their officers to a dinner with beef, mutton, veal, ham, pudding, pye and cheese before them, everything of a good sort and well cooked.

Clearly being a Volunteer had some perks! About training in Sheffield Ward remarks:

> April 11 1808 – the Volunteers paraded at half-past one near Norwood; May 9 The Volunteers paraded at 2 o'clock and went to Owlerton; May 23 the Volunteers paraded at 4 o'clock and went to a field near Broomhall. Corporal Law of the Light Company, for insolence to his Captain Wade, was drummed out of the regiment; July 11 the volunteers parade at 2 o'clock and went to a field of Beardall's in the Park; July 20 The Volunteers paraded at 4 o'clock and went to Beardall's field.

Clearly only weekly musters were taking place.

## The Men of the Volunteers

Our earlier chapter showed that the possessing classes in most cases, not the urban poor, made up the Volunteers in the 1790s. How did this change with the formations of 1803? In understanding the demographics of the men who were Volunteers, we are reliant on what archive papers exists. For the units created after 1803, the West Riding is particularly well supplied with archive records thanks to the good offices of Earl Fitzwilliam.

The Bradford Volunteers were probably typical of a large industrial town's units in 1803. Approximately a quarter of the men, 26.4 per cent of the total, can be described as labourers or workers connected with the cloth industry. We note 21.6 per cent can be classified as low artisans and 21.2 per cent as medium artisans such as basket makers, publicans, and tin plate braziers: these men belonged to the developing working class that E.P. Thompson identified, who are usually portrayed as, at best, anti-government, and at worst outright radical. The remaining 17 per cent of the men were shopkeepers, tailors and drapers and can be considered as middle class or at least property-owning taxpayers. Nor were these men confined to the ranks: artisans and labourers also formed around half the corporals, and 40 per cent of the sergeants.[26] Although these classifications are crude, they help illustrate the rough occupational make-up of the Volunteer units.

For the 'Barkston Ash Volunteers', we are fortunate that the names of the men in corps enrolled in 1803 have survived as well as their occupations and ages.[27] Of the 120 men, who were formed into three companies of 60 men each, the youngest man was 17, the oldest 55, with the average age being 29. We note three men were high artisans, four men of gentlemanly occupation, and twenty-eight were medium artisans, such as butchers, carpenters and tailors. Of the remaining men, fifty were servants, twenty-one described themselves as farmers and seventeen as labourers. Overall, 3.3 per cent were gentlemen, 2.5 per cent were high artisans, 23 per cent of the men were medium artisans, thus 71 per cent were labourers, farmers or servants.

Again, we are fortunate in having a complete muster list for the Rotherham corps in 1805. From this list of names, we find eight men or 1.8 per cent were involved in the building trade, twenty-one men or 4.7 per cent were shopkeepers or allied businesses, twelve or 2.7 per cent were involved in manufacturing, and five were publicans. The supposition is the bulk of the men, 86 per cent, were labourers or in employment in the various foundries in the town.[28] This would make perfect sense, as the Walkers' company was one of the largest ironworks in the world at the time, and the family dominated the local economy and the Volunteers. This is markedly different to Bradford, but seemingly analogous to Halifax, in that labouring men rather than the middle class were the mainstay of support for the corps.

Despite the paucity of available material, we can say something about the demographics of the men when compared to the work of Austin Gee (see table overleaf):[29]

The make-up of the different corps represents that of the areas from which they were recruited. Barkston, Ash being rural, relied on agricultural labourers, like Dinton. Bradford, then industrialising and lacking a large middle class, resulted in a largely working-class corps, the same with Rotherham. Hexham witnessed a mobilisation of property owners, forming a solidly middle-class, and we suppose Anglican, corps. It is interesting to note that the Sheffield Volunteer Infantry, when re-formed in 1803, had a much higher number of artisans than previously when the corps was almost exclusively formed from labourers. The predominant trades were silver platers, cutlers, file smiths, and saw makers. The unit also had a marked number of opticians and hairdressers in the ranks.

We see a broad spectrum of society volunteering to join the colours, from both Nonconformist and Anglican backgrounds in defence of hearth and home or of the nation at large, superficially seems to have cut across political and religious divides: yet as we shall see this generalisation of the data masks other significant conclusions we can draw from the available data. This phenomenon has been termed 'National Defence Patriotism' by John E Cookson[30] and understood by Linda Colley as intrinsic with the creation of the idea of Britishness.[31] A later chapter explores these ideas.

| Unit | % Labourer | % Low Artisan | % Medium Artisan | % High Artisan | % Professional | % Gentlemen | No recorded trade |
|---|---|---|---|---|---|---|---|
| Barkston Ash Volunteer Infantry | 71 | | 23 | 2.5 | | 3.3 | |
| Bradford Volunteer Infantry | 46.4 | 41.6 | 17 | | | | |
| Corbridge Volunteer Infantry | 30 | | 1.4 | 58.6 | | 4.3 | |
| Dinton Volunteers | 43.3 | | 13.3 | 13.3 | | | 13.3 |
| Hexham Volunteer Infantry | 6.9 | | 2.6 | 87.1 | 1.8 | 1.7 | |
| Oxford Loyal Volunteers | 21.9 | | 16.6 | 41.4 | 3.0 | 2.7 | 5.8 |
| Rotherham Volunteer Infantry | 86 | 2.7 | 4.7 | 1.8 | | | |
| Sheffield Volunteer Infantry | 8.6 | 40 | 12 | 38 | 1.4 | | |
| Walls End Volunteers | 58.3 | | 0.6 | 34.6 | 4.8 | 1.9 | |

## Men of the Yeomanry

Re-formed alongside the infantry, the Yeomanry in theory were still drawn from the rural elites. We have been unable to locate any archive records for the West Riding Yeomanry for this period, so we have to rely on studies already in print. The Devizes Troop of the Yeomanry cavalry was overwhelmingly, 59 per cent, recruited from farmers, 22 per cent were shopkeepers, gentlemen made up 7.4 per cent and professionals 3.7 per cent.[32] Of the 138 men serving in the Aylesbury Troop of the Buckinghamshire Yeomanry, 47.8 per cent were farmers, 10 per cent were professionals, 23.9 per cent were tradesmen (ten men were landlords), 11.5 per cent were artisans, and 1.4 per cent were servants. Significantly, seventy-eight men provided their own mounts in the troop.[33] In Suffolk, of forty-seven men in the troop of Captain Collet, we find thirty-three were farmers, one was a banker, one a butcher, one a maltster, two millers, one corn merchant, two general merchants, one brick maker, one publican, and one liquor merchant. These were all well-to-do middle-class 'gentlemen' as many no doubt understood themselves to be. Every man was able to provide his own mount.[34] In table form the data is as follows:

| Unit | % Farmers | % Low Artisan | % Medium Artisan | % High Artisan | % Professional | % Gentlemen | No recorded trade |
|---|---|---|---|---|---|---|---|
| Aylesbury | 47.8 | 1.4 | 11.5 | 23.9 | 10 | | |
| Devizes | 59.3 | | 7.4 | 22.2 | 14 | 7.4 | |
| 1st Suffolk Troop | 82.8 | | | 15.3 | 1.9 | | |
| 2nd Suffolk Troop | 70.2 | | | 4.7 | 2.1 | | |
| 3rd Suffolk Troop | 75.8 | | | 22 | | 2.2 | |

With troops centred on urban centres we find a high level of middle-class shopkeepers and artisans in the ranks, while in rural areas, as might be expected, we find farmers and tenant farmers predominate.

Chapter 10

# OFFICERS AND GENTLEMEN

So who were the men who led the Volunteers and Yeomanry upon their re-formation? As in 1794, commissions for officers were in the hands of the Lords Lieutenant and the Home Office. The commission for Northend Nichols to be Lieutenant-Colonel of the Upper Agbrigg Volunteers in useful in defining their terms:

> To Northend Nichols, Esquire. By Virtue of the Power and Authority to me given by a Warrant from His Majesty, under his Royal Signet and Sign Manual, bearing date the 22nd day of May, 1804, I, the said Earl Fitzwilliam, Do, in His Majesty's Name, by these Presents, constitute, appoint, and commission you the said Northend Nichols to be Lieutenant-Colonel of the Upper Agbrigg Corps of Volunteer Infantry, but not to take rank in the Army except during the time of the said Corps being called out into actual service; You are therefore to take the said corps into your care and charge, and duly to exercise, as well the officers as soldiers thereof, in Arms, and to use your best endeavours to keep them in good order and discipline, who are hereby commanded in His Majesty's Name, to obey you as their Lieutenant-Colonel: And you are to observe and follow such orders and directions, from time to time, as you shall receive from His Majesty, your Lieutenant-Colonel Commandant, or any other your superior officer, according to the Rules and Discipline of War, in pursuance of the Trust hereby reposed in you.
>
> Given under my hand and seal the 15th day of August, in the 43rd year of the reign of our Sovereign Lord, George the Third, by the Grace of God of the United Kingdom of Great Britain and Ireland, King, Defender of the Faith, and in the Year of our Lord One thousand Eight hundred and Three.[1]

Officers had to be persons of note, as Teesdale Cockell argued to Earl Fitzwilliam about his own unit of Volunteers. He opined to the Earl that the corps lacked any real status in the town and neighbourhood '. . . from not having any person of weight and rank to give it a countenance. Young Sir Rowland Winn is very anxious for its success.'[2] Earl Fitzwilliam was concerned that with the expansion of volunteering in 1803, command of units would devolve on men of inferior character, because, as he argued, no-one of respectable rank and position would be willing to come forward and command a unit not formed from middle-class gentlemen as in previous years.[3] Being drawn from the middle class or from 'merchant princes' and self-made men did not always mean respectability. The officers of the Loyal Sheffield Volunteers were 'studiously ignored' at a civic reception at Doncaster Mansion House by the local gentry, much to their chagrin. As one commentator noted from the period, Volunteer officers were 'riff raff' and not gentlemen, often speaking 'rough dialect'. Officers who did not possess a fortune and property, it was felt, could not command the adherence of their junior officers and men: rank relied on the moral economy and wealth inequality rather than professionalism. Furthermore, officers who were not drawn from the local elites could not liaise with the 'county set' on equal terms: social rank was far more important than competence and ability.[4] The writer of this comment, Thomas Asline Ward, was a Unitarian and trustee of Upper Chapel Sheffield and also the Unitarian Chapel at Underbank near Stannington. His perceived lack of social grace and also his heretical religion marked him out as 'not a gentleman'.

In an ideal world officers were to be drawn from men of consequence in a town, or parochial area to give an air of respectability and also to give them 'moral authority' over their social inferiors. Therefore, they had to be men of property and influence: it comes as no surprise therefore to find that commanding officers were drawn from the leaders of local society. These men were either rich merchants, major landowners, aristocrats, former regular army officers or MPs. In Newcastle for example, the roughly-spoken coal hewer Charles Brandling was named Colonel of the Newcastle and Gateshead Volunteers. Brandling, a man of coarse words and great wealth, was MP for Newcastle 1798–1812, and a prominent local supporter of Pitt. Yet because of his non-aristocratic or even middle-class background, he too fell foul of a lack of the credentials of a gentleman.[5] The Wallsend Volunteer infantry were commanded by John Buddle, a prominent self-made man.[6]

## Volunteer Officers and the Moral Economy

Enrolment in the Volunteers was a political act: it said publicly 'I support Pitt, I support the end of freedom of speech, I support suspension of Habeus Corpus and no freedom of religion'. It said 'I am a Tory' in the majority of cases. Volunteer officers, as civic leaders, had power and prestige in their community. In the northern, largely urban-based Volunteer corps, the officers and men were tinged with counter-revolutionary fervour, and it was these corps that made the most considerable contribution to public order in 1795. Undoubtedly, the staunchly loyalist principles of the units' commanders in places such as Wakefield, Leeds and Sheffield ensured that these corps were particularly zealous in coming forward to assist in suppressing the food riots. However, counter-revolutionary sentiment was just one aspect of the Volunteering system.

As we touched on earlier, officers were drawn from men of consequence in a town or parochial area. They had to be men of property and influence. The public meetings and subscriptions which witnessed the creation of corps superficially appeared to be communal bodies: yet the reality was that they were dominated by rich urban elites, who already controlled town governance and other civic institutions. Formal management fell on the wealthier subscribers: this was no doubt intended to restrict committees to the 'right sort'. These committees were formed by town elites and leaders, and in essence controlled the Volunteers. The Volunteers by and large reflected the aspirations, politics and influence of the committee.

Urban infantry units tended to be commanded by 'merchant princes'. Bucking this trend, we note that the Skyrac Volunteers were commanded by Michael Angelo Taylor, who sat as MP for Aldborough 1796–1800, Durham City 1800–02, Rye 1806–07, Ilchester 1807–12, and Poole 1812–18: he was a Whig and was sponsored by the Earl of Portland.[7] The Bawtry Volunteer Infantry were commanded by Robert Monckton Arundel, 4th Lord Galway, MP for Pontefract 1780–3, York 1783–90 and Pontefract 1796–1802.[8] Doncaster was commanded by William Wrightson, who would be an MP from 1826 for the Whigs.[9] Wrightson, we remember, had backed a call for an immediate peace with France in 1797 and again in 1800–01.

The 'Loyal Leeds Volunteers' was headed by Thomas Lloyd. He owned the fulling mill at Armley and rented it to Benjamin Gott, and made his fortune from selling woollens to the American and Portuguese export market. Lloyd was a member of Leeds' vestry that governed the borough. Unlike his brother Gamaliel, Thomas was a Tory, opposed to pollical reform and religious dissent. He resided at Horsforth Hall, and was considered in many respects the leader of the 'Church and King party' in Leeds. He had left the family merchant house to his brother Gamaliel in 1794, so he could command the Volunteers on an almost full-time basis. Gamaliel had been a keen supporter of reform:, being active at that time in campaigning for electoral reform, and offered help in corresponding with provincial centres of population, and went door-to-door with the Yorkshire Association petition, accompanied by a fluent speaker of the local Leeds dialect.[10]

Lieutenant-Colonel of the 'Loyal Leeds Volunteers' in 1803 was Unitarian woollen merchant William Smithson, who was in business with Samuel Hamer Oates and the Rev. William Wood, as Messrs Oates, Wood & Smithson. William's son, Joseph, was an Ensign in the corps. Smithson was a cloth merchant attending Mill Hill chapel, and had married the daughter of his co-religionist Joshua Rayner and was co-partner with his brother-in-law Milnes Rayner. Remarkably Smithson was Mayor of Leeds in 1781 and eventually succeeded Lloyd as Colonel Commandant on 10 February 1807. Smithson had been Deputy Lieutenant of Yorkshire and had served in the Leeds Volunteers since 1 March 1797 despite being a Unitarian and outspoken Whig and like Wrightson a peace activist.[11] The status from being Colonel and the attendant privileges helped to cement Smithson into Leeds society and shake off any suspicion of disloyalty.

The Leeds 'merchant prince' industrialist Benjamin Gott who was commandant of 'Leeds Armed Association', and others of his class such as Thomas Lloyd and William Cookson, had incomes in excess of £10,000 a year: they were the billionaires of the era. The gulf between the rich, the middle class and the poor, then as now, was staggering. It was estimated in 1790 that in Leeds a woman spinning could earn 2s a week, and a labourer 5s–9s, artisans could earn 15s and the croppers – the 'kings of the working class' who finished broadcloths – the unheard-of sum of 30s a week. A clothier was reckoned to be of the 'good sort' to earn £50 a year, the price of a two-bedroom cottage. In comparison in 1796 a Mrs Arthington sold a pair of houses in Park Place, Leeds for £3,000; John Dennison spent the unheard-of sum of £6,100 on constructing Denison Hall in 1786. Most merchants, who comprised the 'middling sort' had an income of £200–£600 a year: in 1790 the Leeds Street Commissioners noted an income of £400 a year would allow a merchant to rent a town house 'with five servants and a princely table'. The world of the elite is enshrined by Jane Austen: the real world was 'hellish, short, nasty and brutal'.[12]

As well as men of commerce, former soldiers were made Colonels or senior officers. As we have seen, the Pontefract Volunteers was commanded by former professional solider Teesdale Cockell. In Wakefield retired regulars John Tottenham, William Rookes Leeds Serjeantson and David Parkhill all held commission: Tottenham only

110

gained the coveted rank of 'Colonel' by investing time and energy into the 'Royal Wakefield Volunteers'.

Towns frequently had aristocratic patrons: Pontefract had both Lord Galway and the Earl of Mexborough and his son Lord Pollington, the latter dominating the town's Volunteers. Yet such overt elite patronage was unusual in urban corps, as most commanders and officers were solidly middle-class business leaders, their rank giving these men an advantage against the overwhelming weight of aristocratic privilege by superficially making them equals in military rank and also in terms of national defence. Bucking this trend was the Pontefract Volunteers. The officers were appointed on 3 September 1803:

PONTEFRACT VOLUNTEERS. SIR,
I have the Honor to transmit to you by order of the Committee of the PONTEFRACT VOLUNTEERs, the Resolutions entered into at PONTEFRACT on the 3rd instant, and am requested by them, to state to you the Expediency and Necessity of such Exertions being made by Yourself (if you would be good enough to countenance the Measure) among the respectable and opulent individuals in your Parish, in support of the effective Corps above mentioned, which has been accepted by His Majesty, and is now so far constituted as to require a very considerable Sum for its Establishment and Support. The officers already returned to the Lord Lieutenant are:

John Earl Mexborough . . . Colonel Commandant.
William Sotheron, Esq. . . . . Lieutenant-Colonel.
John Cooke, Esq. . . . . First Major.
The Hon. Henry Savile . . . Second Major.

Captains: Sir John Ramsden, Bart, John Viscount Pollington, Edmund Mark Winn, Esq. Robert Seaton, Esq, Christopher Wilson, Esq. Ellis Leckonby Hodgson, Esq., William Lee, Esq., Richard Rhodes Milnes, Esq. The Hon. Charles Savile, Grosvenor Perfect, Esq.
Lieutenants: George Alderson, Henry Taylor, George Pyemont, Thomas Dunhill, John Bowers, William Carter, Josiah Smithson, Richard Horncastle. Thomas Wild.
Ensigns: Joshua Hepworth, James Berry, Richard Wilson, James Muscroft.

I am desired to request you would be good enough to make such Returns as you are prepared with on the same, to me at the Red Lion Inn, PONTEFRACT, before the Sitting of the Committee on Saturday, the 17th instant. I am, Sir, Your very humble Servant,
THOS. MOORE, Secretary.

That it is of the opinion of this meeting that under the Returns of Volunteers already made, by the respective constables of the Parishes and Townships following, viz: Ackworth, Aketon, Badsworth, Brikin, Brotherton, Burghwallis, Campsall, Carlton and Tanshelf, Castleford, Darrington, Elmsall North, Elmsall South, Fenwick, Ferryfrystone, Featherstone, Kirby South, Knottingley, Methley, Norton, Ouston, Pontefract, Pontefract Park, Skelbrooke, Smeaton Church, Womersley, & C, Nostal.

The Committee of the Pontefract Volunteers is justified in offering to the Lord Lieutenant of this Riding, a Corps to consist of Eight Hundred Men, including officers, for the service of government, subject to the conditions originally presented to Lord Hobart and accepted by his Majesty.

That it appears to this Meeting that the Sum already subscribed, is insufficient for the intended Purpose, and that a Circular Letter be written and Copies of it addressed to the officiating Minister, or to some principal Inhabitant of the Parishes and Townships before mentioned, requesting him in conjunction with others of his Parish or Township, to use such Means as they think the most likely to promote an extended subscription to the aforesaid Corps; and that the said Minister or principal Inhabitant, to whom such Letter has been addressed, be requested to transmit the Result of his Applications to this Committee, by Saturday the 17th instant. GOD SAVE THE KING. With Success to the FLEETs and ARMIEs of OLD ENGLAND, May the Pride of France be humbled, And the Spanish Dons to tremble, At the WOODEN WALLS of Great Britain.

For an urban infantry corps – which also recruited from the majority of the former Honour of Pontefract – the number of former and future MPs amongst the officer corps is remarkable, so too its aristocratic nature. Amongst the captains we find, the son or Sir Roland Wynn of Nostell Priory. Others of importance was Richard Rodes Milnes son of the MP for the City of York, two sons of the Earl of Mexborough as well as a man of vast wealth derived from the slaver Ellis Leckonby Hodgson.

The corps was very much the Earl of Mexborough's private army, recruited from his tenants. The town of Pontefract itself was dominated by the Monkton-Arundel family, who owned most of the burgage rights, who were in political opposition to the Mexborough Interest. The Pontefract corps, superficially appears to have 'blocked out' Robert Monkton Arundel's interest by appealing not to the urban base, but to the rural interest. Here we have an ostensibly urban corps recruited from a widely dispersed rural base. This may partly explain Lord Galway's 'Loyal Bawtry Infantry' being formed in Bawtry, near

Doncaster, a case of 'anything you can do I can do better' in a public display of loyalism and militarism.

In many urban centres magistrates were frequently the officers commanding their local units: Robert Athorpe was both magistrate and Colonel in Sheffield, George Armitage magistrate and Colonel of the Huddersfield Volunteer Infantry; J.A. Busfield magistrate and Colonel of the Bradford Volunteers, and Thomas Horton of Halifax magistrate and Colonel of Volunteers. This meant that the magistrates had direct control over the corps which had been raised to aid the civil powers.

Several MPs were Colonels of Volunteer units. William Mordaunt Milner was Lieutenant-Colonel of the City of York Volunteer Infantry: he was one of the two MPs for the city from 1790 to his death in 1811. As a committed Portland Whig, he was still able to speak against the government of William Pitt, and voted consistently against the government's repressive measures in November and December 1795. Indeed, he defended the meetings held across the country, especially the country meeting at York held to oppose these measures. The Seditious Meetings Bill he described on 12 November as 'useless for the object to which it was directed' and 'an alarming invasion of the Bill of Rights, and would destroy the public spirit of the country, which had in cases of the utmost distress been its real support'; in the House he opposed the suspension of habeas corpus in 1800, 'because he was instructed by his constituents so to do. These he considered himself in duty bound to obey.' He declared that Addington's ministry 'should, for having made peace, receive his cordial support and thanks, but in other cases he must be guided by a consideration of their transactions since their coming into the ministry'.[13]

Command of corps in rural areas was largely placed in the hands of the local MPs or gentry. Yeomanry officers by and large formed an exclusive club.[14] Prime Minister (1801–04) Henry Addington, later Lord Sidmouth, was the head of the Woodley Cavalry Volunteers.[15] Similarly, two out of five of the Wiltshire Yeomanry captains were also in the Wiltshire Corporation, namely Dugdale Astley and John Audry.[16]

In the West Riding, Bryan Cooke was named Colonel of the Southern Regiment in 1794. Cooke was MP for Malton 1798–1812 for the Whig Fitzwilliam interest. He had served in the Royal Horse Guards from 1775 with George Fitzwilliam, younger brother of the Earl. In politics he voted against Union with Ireland, voted against renewal of the Seditious Meetings Act on 20 April 1801, opposed peace in 1802, and in his only Parliamentary speech on 20 May 1802, he spoke against the expansion of the Militia as 'a useless expense to the country', and objected to the 'gentlemen of property and consideration in the country' acting as 'drill serjeants'. He was named Colonel of the 3rd West Yorkshire Militia in 1803. He voted against the abolition of the slave trade. He resigned his commission and seat in January 1812 and died in Geneva on 8 November 1821.[17] The Major, or second-in-command, was John Pate Neville of Skelbrooke Park, Badsworth.

The Northern or 2nd Regiment was commanded by Thomas Lister, Lord Ribblesdale, and Benjamin Ferrand was appointed Major. Captain commanding the Agbrigg and Morley Troop was John Lister-Kaye, son of Sir John Lister-Kaye. Lord Hawke commanded the Barkston Ash Troop, Captain Robert Harvey commanded the Tadcaster Troop, and later took command of the regiment from 1812, and Captain William Markham commanded the Skyrac Troop. Robert Chaloner of Netherton Hall, near Wakefield, had volunteered as Cornet in the Agbrigg and Morley Troop, and was named Captain Commandant in 1798.[18] He would be elected MP for Richmond 1810–18, was partner in the banking firm of Wentworth, Chaloner and Rishworth and was bankrupted when the bank failed in 1825.[19]

Francis Foljambe commanded the Rotherham Troop from 1794 and became Lieutenant-Colonel Commandant of the regiment in 1803. He had been MP for Yorkshire in 1784 and was MP for High Ferrars 1801–07. He had been High Sherriff of Yorkshire 1787–8. Foljambe, an ally of Earl Fitzwilliam and supporter of the Earl of Portland, supported war against France and voted against the Treaty of Amiens, and was in favour of the abolition of the slave trade. He died in 1814.[20]

Walter Spencer Stanhope had command of the Barnsley Troop. He was MP for Carlisle 1775–80, Haslemere 1780–4, Kingston upon Hull 1784–90, Cockermouth 1800–02 and then Carlisle again 1802–12. Despite Whig leanings, he supported Pitt and the Tories in the House, yet he opposed Robert Peel's Apprenticeship Bill of 1804 as it discriminated against Dissenters.[21]

Officers of the Southern Regiment of West Riding Yeomanry appointed in 1803 were under the command of Francis Foljambe, with J.A. Stuart Wortley as second-in-command. Wortley was MP for Bossiney 1802–18 and for Yorkshire 1818–26: he backed war and William Pitt, and spoke against Lord Milton and the Whigs at the 1807 general election and was the 'avowed enemy of all Whigs and Whiggism' as well as political reform.[22] In 1803 we find amongst the Captains Hugh Parker, the senior magistrate acting for Sheffield, the Hon. Frederick Lumley, John Henry Smythe the future Whig MP for Cambridge University, and Lord Milton, future MP for Yorkshire from 1807 for the Fitzwilliam Whig interest. Amongst the Lieutenants we

A review of Volunteer cavalry and horse artillery in Hyde Park, London in 1804.

Robert Athorpe, Colonel of the Loyal Sheffield Volunteers, whose blue-faced red uniform he is wearing. As both magistrate and colonel, Athorpe took part in several actions in Sheffield and its vicinity against what he understood to be 'traitors.'

Review of the Dudley Armed Association cavalry and infantry at Dudley Castle in 1798.

Jonathan Atkinson Busfield, wearing his uniform as Lieutenant–Colonel Commandant of the Bradford Volunteer Infantry. He also served as the magistrate for Bradford and environs, and called out his Volunteers to quell riots in Bradford and district.

YORK, *16th April*, 1798.

## To the Gentlemen and Inhabitants of the City and Ainfty of York.

THE General Meeting of Lieutenancy having deemed it expedient, in the prefent crifis of Public Affairs, to raife more
VOLUNTEER CORPS, to ferve without pay, for the internal Defence
of the Country, in cafe the prefent Force of VOLUNTEERS, already trained, fhould be called into actual Service, according to
their refpective voluntary offers——Thofe Gentlemen and Inhabitants of this City and Ainfty, who are willing to ftand forward and
affift the Magiftrates of this Jurifdiction, in the Suppreffion of
Riots, the Defence of Property, and the Maintenance of good
Order, are requefted to meet the Deputy Lieutenants at the Guild-
Hall of this City, on Thurfday next, at Eleven o'clock in the
forenoon, and give in their Names to be enrolled in VOLUNTEER
CORPS of Infantry or Cavalry to ferve in cafe of emergency; fo
that their Names, together with the Names of fuch Gentlemen
as they wifh to command them, may be fent to the Lord Lieutenant at Leeds, for his approbation, on Monday next, to which
day the next General Meeting of Lieutenancy ftands adjourned.

By Order of the Deputy Lieutenants,

RICH<sup>D</sup>. TOWNEND,

Clerk to the Subdivifion Meetings for the City
of York and County of the fame, and Liberty
of Saint Peter in York.

Recruiting poster for the Ainsty of York Volunteers.

Recruiting poster of the Wakefield Armed Association.

## WAKEFIELD

### Armed Affociation.

THE Committee met this Day, (agreeable to the
Refolutions, at the MOOT-HALL, on the 21ft
Inftant) and fixed the ballotting of Members to be
admitted into this Affociation, to be on Monday
next, the 30th Inftant, at eleven o'Clock. In the
mean Time, the Lift of fuch of the Inhabitants of
the Town and Neighbourhood, as have offered
themfelves for Enrolment, is left at my Office, for
the Signatures of fuch other of the Inhabitants as
are inclined to join the Affociation, under the
Terms of the faid Refolutions entered into at the
MOOT-HALL; and in Cafe any Member, who
already has offered, or fhall offer himfelf, is
defirous of entering into a Troop of Cavalry,
inftead of ferving on Foot, he is requefted to fignify
the fame to me before the Time of Meeting on
Monday next.

*By Order of the Committee,*

### EDWARD BROOK.

*Wakefield*, 25th April, 1798.

ELIZABETH WALLER, PRINTER, WAKEFIELD.

Lieutenant James Cave of the Bristol
Light Horse Volunteers c. 1794.

An unknown member of an
unidentified regiment of Provisional
Cavalry. His green dolman with red
facings was a standard uniform.

Front view of officer's coat of the Staincross and Osgoldcross Local Militia. This unit replaced the Pontefract Volunteer Infantry from 1809. (Wakefield Museums and Castles)

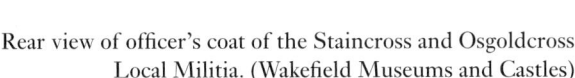

Rear view of officer's coat of the Staincross and Osgoldcross Local Militia. (Wakefield Museums and Castles)

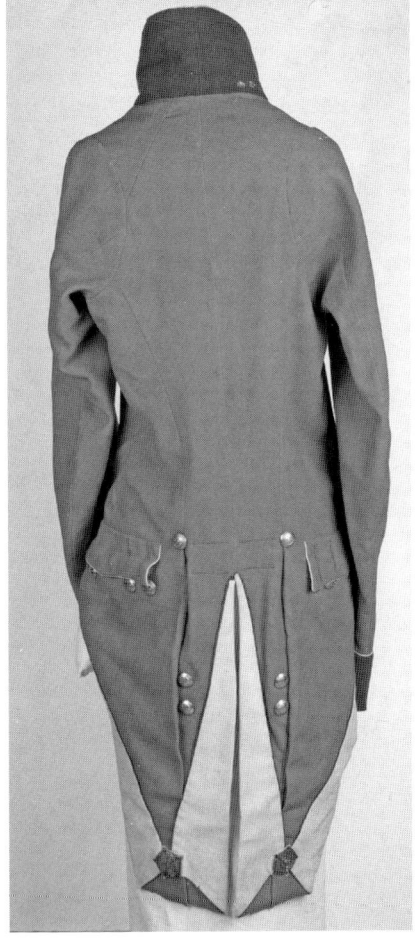

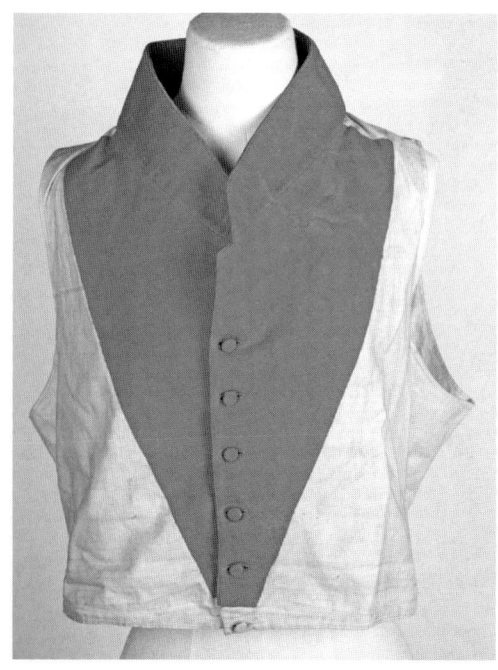

Officer's waistcoat attributed to the Staincross and Osgoldcross Local Militia. (Wakefield Museums and Castles)

Officer's buff leather sabre belt of the Staincross and Osgoldcross Local Militia. (Wakefield Museums and Castles)

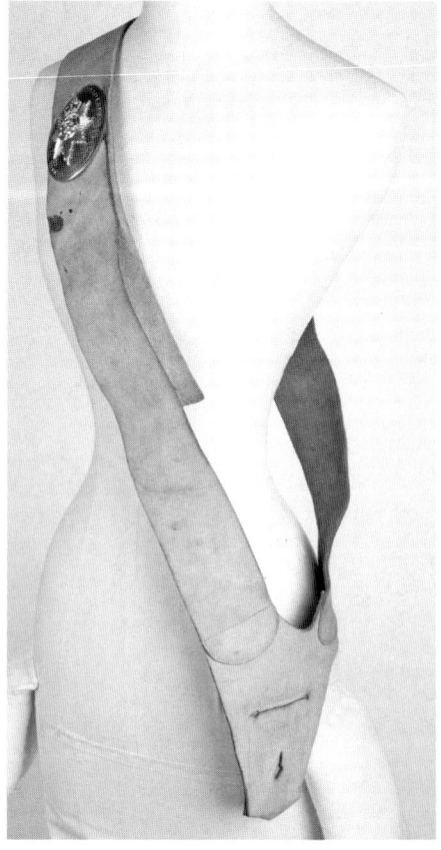

Officer's elaborate belt plate of the Staincross and Osgoldcross Local Militia. (Wakefield Museums and Castles)

Colonel Hanson wearing the uniform of the Manchester, Salford, and Stockport Independent Rifle Corps which was clearly inspired by the 95th Rifles.

Naïve impression of a Volunteer c. 1805. With yellow facings, turned back in imitation of an officer's coat, black leather equipment and clubbed and queued hair, the Volunteer presents a marked divergence from the appearance of a 'traditional redcoat' soldier of the era.

Portrait of an officer of the Loyal Leeds Volunteers c. 1795. The coat, with its waist-length lapels and buttons in threes, is a marked divergence from how we expect an officer's coat to look. Two officers' coats for this unit exist, one in Leeds City Museum and another in the National Army Museum.

find Daniel Gaskell, Unitarian and future Liberal MP for Wakefield 1832–7, and Robert Pemberton Milnes, eldest son of Richard Slater Milnes, Whig MP for York 1784–1802, son-in-law of Robert Monckton Arundel, Lord Galway, named as Cornet, who would be Tory MP from Pontefract from 1806 to 1812.[23]

As we have seen, the officers were by and large, local men of prominence and fortune, but not necessarily 'gentlemen'. Although it is undeniable that Volunteers 'cemented into place' pre-existing lines of patronage, they also allowed for a marked degree of social mobility.

Chapter 11

# THE LOCAL MILITIA

By the end of 1803, the organisation of the Volunteer system was in chaos. Returns sent to the War Office tell us 362 units were serving under the terms of the Defence Act of June: of these 152 served only in their military district, 108 had agreed to serve throughout the country if there was an invasion, 56 agreed to serve anywhere in the country and 46 chose their own terms. Simultaneously, there were 1,165 units under the August allowances, and a further 43 units under concessions granted on 31 August. Furthermore we find eleven units which seemed to be serving under no specified terms at all. Remarkably, it seems despite the reforms of Fitzwilliam and other Lords Lieutenant men were serving in the same corps but under different terms. In the Norfolk Yeomanry, each of the six troops had differing terms of service. In total 342,000 men were under arms, 211,000 serving under the August allowances, 67,000 under the June allowances, and the remaining men under local conditions. To the force, the Crown provided 66,800 muskets, the intention being to arm 25 men in every 100. Allowances provided for 24 ball cartridges and 60 blank cartridges per man per year. To make up the shortfall of muskets, 103,572 pikes were issued. The Board of Ordnance eventually grappled with the shortage of weapons, and authorised 300,000 muskets to be allocated to the Volunteers in December 1803.[1]

To bring order from this chaos, at the close of 1803 the Home Secretary Charles Yorke introduced a Bill to consolidate Volunteer legislation, to limit the autonomy of the various corps, particularly concerning the influence of committees and the way in which officers were appointed, as well as a thorough review of discipline and management. The Act, passed on 20 December, also set the minimum training requirements for exemption from the Militia ballot and the Army Reserve Act as 24 days. At the same time, it was reported from Whitehall that in order 'to secure the regular attendance of the members of Volunteers corps at Inspection' they were to be paid 3d a day.[2] Furthermore, Volunteers attending compulsory training days were not to be placed in the town where they were raised for permanent duty for the purpose of training and exercise. They could be taken into a garrison, if raised in a garrison town, in special circumstances. The Volunteers could be expected to be on duty for no more than two consecutive months and be paid an additional 1s per man per day.[3] The *Leeds Intelligencer* reported in its first editorial of 1804 of the spirit that pervaded the people and of the zeal with which those who took up arms endeavoured to make themselves worthy of the cause they had embraced:

> in every town and village within the circuit of this paper the spirit of Volunteering is carried on with the utmost alacrity, and from the information we can obtain, the progress and discipline is equal to the unwearied exercise by which it is attained. The Volunteer Infantry, both officers and privates, who form two battalions of about 700 men each, are, beyond any previous example, zealous to excel in arms and military tactics. The order just received from Government for a new ballot for the Army Reserve, to attach to all men from the age of 18 to 45, whether Volunteers or not, unless they have attended 24 drills previous to the 1st instant, we are happy to find will lay hold of very few indeed of our officers, many of whom have attended nearly double that number.[4]

The Army Reserve Act was suspended in April 1804, causing Henry Addington's resignation and replacement by William Pitt once more as premier. Passed in June 1803, the Act had sought to provide an additional 30,000 men to the Militia in England, and 16,000 in Scotland. The Army Reserve was replaced with a permanent additional force as a reserve through Yorke's Volunteer Consolidation Act. The Volunteer Consolidation Act of 5 June 1804 repealed all previous legislation. All Volunteers and Yeomanry were now restricted to 24 days' pay per annum. To ensure attendance at training, the minimum number of days training needed to qualify for Militia ballot exemption for Volunteers was also set at 24 days, and 12 days for Yeomanry.

When Pitt the Younger returned to office in 1804 he replaced the Army Reserve with a 'Permanent Additional Force'. Each parish was given a quota of men to raise for locally-based 'second battalions' attached to the regulars. The men were to serve for five years and would receive a bounty if they transferred voluntarily into the regular battalion.

Unfortunately, the Additional Force that had been raised in June 1803 suffered from the emphasis on a quota rather than on a ballot, and most parishes preferred to pay a fine rather than go through the expense of raising the required force. The legislation was suspended in May 1804 and replaced with the Permanent Additional Force Act of June 1804. By the time of its repeal in July 1806 the Additional Force was only 24,000 strong, rather than the hoped-for 34,000. The problem was that exemption from the Army Reserve included poor men with more than one child born in wedlock, all serving Volunteers and Yeomanry who had enlisted before June 1803, and all who had already served in the Militia. This reduced the number of men aged 18 to 40 prepared to come forward.

It was replaced with the Training Act, which proposed that all males between 16 and 40 were to be liable for 24 days' annual training within five miles of their place of abode. A total of 200,000 men would be selected to undergo such training each year with a remuneration of 1s 0d a day and defaulters liable to a fine. The Training Act reflected William Windham's dislike for the Volunteers. Windham became Secretary of State for War and Colonies in the 'Ministry of the Talents'. He found fault with the Volunteer system, and desired a more uniform military system that placed the needs of the army first. He was convinced that that given the unpopularity of compulsion, wider military training and the reduction of the Militia and Volunteers might induce more to enlist in the army.[5]

To do so pay was cut and clothing allowances withdrawn, making Volunteers now increasingly reliant on subscriptions to cover costs. The 'Loyal Leeds Volunteers' protested in print via the newspapers, condemning the fact that no Volunteers were to be enrolled after 14 July 1806, that the men had to find the money to buy their own uniforms and would no longer be paid for the 21 days' active service. They blamed Pitt for 'improper and ill-judged treatment'.[6] This more than anything restricted volunteering to the affluent artisans and middle class who had surplus funds to literally 'pay' for the privilege of serving in the Volunteers. In consequence, 13,000 Volunteers resigned and approximately 10 per cent of all officers as well.[7] Men resigning from the corps could not be replaced: this was the death-knell of the Volunteer movement – perhaps Windham's intention.

We find as a consequence of the Act abolishing the clothing allowance, new appeals for funds to cover these costs. Recruited from a broader base, the men under arms often could not afford to purchase their uniforms and equipment. For example, the Wharfdale Volunteers opened a subscription list in October 1807: Colonel Fawkes himself headed it donating £205, Lieutenant-Colonel Henry Carr Ibbetson gave £21, the captains of the corps between them subscribed £105,

Miss Marshall and Miss Dinsdale of Yeadon Low Hall gave £1 each, £12 was raised in Idle and £65 was given by the Archbishop of York, to pay for new regimentals.[8] The captains made a second donation of £105 in November to ensure sufficient funds were available.[9]

With the reduction of allowances in 1806 many men resigned: they stated that they simply could not afford to remain under arms. In essence, this 'weeded out' the poor and the labourers and left the middle-class gentlemen to play at part-time soldiers. The removal of allowances also resulted in outbreaks of 'munity'. In the Ecclesfield Volunteers, Sergeant English refused to attend two consecutive drill parades because he was no longer being paid to attend and no longer received a clothing allowance. He was dismissed from the corps for disobeying orders following a court martial.[10] Earl Fitzwilliam called this rank insubordination.[11] Yet the episode was not unique, and hundreds of men left the colours across the country.

Uniform allowances and pay was compensation for loss of free time, rather than an attraction to volunteer. This was perhaps the government's intention: to make volunteering more socially acceptable and to remove the danger from radicalised labourers and artisans.[12] To make up the drop in number of Volunteers, Secretary of State for War Windham ambitiously aimed to train 200,000 balloted men in the use of arms through the Training Act. Under the Levy *en Masse* Act, the West Riding was to provide 14,000 men by the end of 1807.[13] Earl Fitzwilliam, as an ardent Portland Whig, felt he could not openly criticise the government as he was a Cabinet member, but even so he called the act 'harsh and oppressive' in a letter to the Home Secretary.[14] It was rapidly replaced by the Local Militia Act.

Membership of Volunteer corps had fallen year on year since 1804, accentuated by the changing ideology of the war, being no longer considered one of self-defence: this made it far easier for anti-war liberals to resign given the prospect of peace was in the air once more with Charles James Fox back in government. The Continental System and Orders in Council which would have a major impact on the economy of the Midlands and the North heralded a new war: a war of attrition by every means possible. The ministry of the Earl of Portland understood the necessity of reviving the Volunteer movement. Viscount Castlereagh sought to reduce the number of Volunteer corps by half and then secure their eventual disappearance by a permanent county-based Local Militia. Permanent country regiments, six times the size of the Militia proper, were proposed, raised by ballot of all able-bodied men aged 18 to 30 for three years' service. The ballot was to only be called if insufficient volunteers came forward. It was the first government Act concerning recruitment for the army that met local defence requirements and also managed to meet both temporary and future needs. It provided for 200,000 men to be balloted to serve four years, and a proportion of them would be encouraged to transfer to the regulars in return for a bounty and to enlarge the standing army. As with Windham's Training Act, Castlereagh wanted to create a trained body of men for the regulars to use as a source of recruits. Short of outright conscription, it was the best way of producing a pool of armed men who could be called on for a variety of purposes at home and abroad. It created a large armed force for domestic defence, and when Britain returned to the offensive in the Peninsula in 1808 it adapted well to the new circumstances of providing trained men, who willingly volunteered. Balloted men, unlike the Militia, could not provide substitutes, but could pay a graduated fine based on income for non-attendance: the concept was to retain the middle class, shopkeepers and artisans actively engaged in national defence as it was felt that these groups would not naturally or willingly join the Militia. Indeed, the Local Militia can be considered the 'first comprehensive attempt to alter national attitudes to military service'.[15] The Tories howled with rage that:

> the opposition with their usual disregard of propriety and of truth, and their accustomed wish to excite murmurs and created discontent amongst the people . . . the opposition crown the whole of the patriotic attempt in this instance, by desiring the people to 'recollect what they have suffered since 1793'. What ever the people have suffered, we are persuaded to proclaim the general sentiment when we declare, that they would suffer much, very much more, rather than give a desperate faction another opportunity of exercising their talents . . . they would annihilate England.[16]

The Whigs were seen as little better than irresponsible French Revolutionaries. For the Tories, then as now, the idea of opposition and views counter to their own was anathema. The thinly veiled reference to Fox and Grenville's ministry in 1806 is not hard to miss. Even amongst the elite of the county Walter Spencer Stanhope called the measure 'a Jacobin and despotic practice' being nothing short of 'French compulsion'.[17] Conversely, Earl Fitzwilliam was an advocate of the new system.[18]

The new legislation envisaged a total of Local Militia and Volunteers of about 309,000 men, equating to six times the 1802 Militia quota. In order to encourage the Volunteers to transfer to the Local Militia, they were offered a two-guinea bounty. Individuals could enlist on the same terms. In addition, provision was made for a 'marching guinea' to be paid for attending the first annual training, which was for 28 days. Enlistment was for four years with annual training. For 'necessaries' 10s 6d was to be paid annually and a further guinea was payable should the Local Militia be mobilised. Shortfalls in men enlisting or transferring from the Volunteers were to be met by a ballot of those aged 18 to 30 with no substitutes allowed and heavy fines for defaulters. Under the Act, only very limited exemptions were granted: just to those who had served in the Militia or Army of Reserve. As an incentive to enlist, Local Militiamen would be exempt from the Militia ballot during their service as well as for two years after completing their term of service. The Local Militia were liable to serve anywhere in the country in the event of invasion or insurrection. Furthermore, men were also liable to be called out for up to 14 days to suppress riots. To incentivise Local Militia transferring to the regulars, the men themselves would receive an 11-guinea bounty for limited service, and 16 guineas for unlimited service. The Local Militia Act was a carefully-crafted piece of legislation which in effect forced Volunteers to sign on as Local Militia. It very starkly said either join the Local Militia or face the Militia ballot and the likelihood of service in Ireland. With rising tensions in Ireland, service abroad seemed a very distinct possibility. As the *Leeds Intelligencer* was quick to point out, Volunteers who did not transfer their service were clearly lacking in loyalty, moral fibre and spirit, and would expose not only themselves but also their neighbours to the threat of the ballot.[19] When spelled out like this in the press, the Volunteers had little choice. The converse was true, and in Leeds 200 men balloted to the Militia joined the Leeds Local Militia, as upon doing so they became exempt for six years.[20]

Officers seem to have been more in favour of the new system than the men: the new forces were wholly government funded, and thus the financial burden of maintaining the Volunteer corps was entirely lifted. At the same time, the chance of promotion was greater in the new system, and the commissions carried more weight than that of a mere Volunteer officer, and transferring meant retaining local influence and status. Lieutenant-Colonel Serjeantson, commanding the 'Royal Wakefield Volunteers', transferred as Colonel of the 4th North Yorkshire Local Militia, being commissioned on 28 February 1809.

The Whigs howled with rage that Local Militia Act was 'conscription' by another name, and gave the state and magistrates a powerful standing army for suppression of 'liberties and rights'. A war of words erupted, the Tories stating 'spacious, deceitful, disloyal' Whigs sought to leave the nation defenceless. The Tories in Leeds admitted that the primary attraction of the Local Militia was the bounty, and by not transferring to the Local Militia, lacked gratitude. Unlike the Volunteer Corps where a member could resign when he so wished, under the new system enrolment was for four years, a substantial change to the terms of service.[21] Volunteers were urged to embrace the Local Militia:

> War Office, August 5th, 1808. Sir, As a considerable proportion of the Volunteer corps which have already offered to transfer their services into the Local Militia have been assembled on permanent duty in the course of the present year, and it is understood that it would be particularly inconvenient to many other corps desirous of transferring their services into the Local Militia to be assembled and called out for exercise during the ensuing Autumn unless in case of absolute necessity, I have received directions to acquaint you that it is not His Majesty's intention to call upon any corps of Volunteers transferring their services into the Local Militia to assemble for exercise until the Spring of the next year. I have the honour to be, &c., JAS. PULTENEY.[22]

The Local Militia was in essence a supplement or reserve for the Militia proper, which after all was the intention of the bill. Call-up to the Local Militia was, in theory, by ballot for four years, and men called up to serve had to attend 28 days training, came under military law and the Mutiny Act.[23] The Local Militia proved deeply unpopular. By the close of 1808, not one of the twenty-two Local Militia units in the West Riding were complete. Sir George Cayley, Lieutenant-Colonel of the Pickering Volunteers, threatened to resign when less than one in four men transferred to the 6th North Yorkshire (Malton) Local Militia. A similar situation arose in Leeds. From the 1,400 men of the Leeds Volunteers, only 274 from the North Battalion and 214 from the South passed into the Local Militia.[24] The Halifax Volunteers, according to the *Leeds Intelligencer*, reported that the corp's 1,100 men transferred totally to the Local Militia in having 'but one common sentiment of devotion to the cause of their King and Country! May the sentiments of the Colonel inspire other brother officers!'[25] The *Leeds Mercury* caustically commented that the truth of the situation was that only 827 other ranks transferred.[26] What we see in Yorkshire reflected national trends. Of the 294,378 Volunteers under arms in 1808, perhaps just 125,000 transferred to the Local Militia, which by the end of 1809 mustered 195,161 men, 100,000 short of the hoped-for establishment. Almost 70,000 men remained serving as Volunteers, much to the government's chagrin.

Unlike previous legislation, the Local Militia Act no longer excused Quakers from service: a diarist tells us that in consequence Quakers were gaoled in Wakefield, Northallerton, Pontefract and Ackworth, with sentences ranging from seven 'days' to one month, for refusing to be called up.[27]

Swearing an oath of allegiance was required on enlistment. Oath-taking was deeply unpopular, as was the ballot i.e., conscription by another name. It was feared that taking the oath would make the men liable for service anywhere in the country. Local resentment of taking the oath and being balloted came to a head in May 1808 when the press reported that:

> the defendant who is a blacksmith and lives in Mirfield, was in the course of last summer balloted to the serve in the Local Militia. He attended at Wakefield accordingly on the day appointed . . . during the oath of allegiance, which the words are – 'I swear to bear true allegiance to his Majesty King George' – at these expression he went on thus – I swear to bear true allegiance to his majesty, DAMNE King George – and the threw down the book.[28]

The balloted man, James Asquith, was put on trial for disloyal words with intent for 'stirring up the King's Liege Subjects to sedition'. To the consternation of Michael Angelo Taylor MP, chairman of the court who placed Asquith on trial, a verdict of not guilty was returned.[29] Clearly, expressing one's anger at being balloted could sometimes get the better of men.

The fears over taking the oath and being bound to serve overseas – notably in Ireland – after being forcibly transferred to the regular Militia were grounded in fact as in October 1809 the *Leeds Mercury* reported that the regulars were to be brought up to strength with volunteers from the Militia for a bounty, and the consequential vacancies in Militia to be filled with volunteers from the Local Militia or by ballot. It was hoped that Local Militiamen would volunteer to reduce the numbers being called by the ballot.[30] The fears of extended service were proved correct. In May 1811 no man from the Wakefield Local Militia offered themselves for general service. In December 1813 the government again appealed for Local Militia to go on active service anywhere in the country: the Wakefield Local Militia agreed to go on six weeks' service.[31]

## Training

Officers were appointed by ballot and were no longer elected by the committee or fellow officers. The Local Militia was in essence a far more professional force than the Volunteers had been, and became in essence the reserve for the regular Militia. One such officer was Joseph Rogerson of Bramley in Leeds who records in his diary '8 May 1809. Very slack work in the mill – I was balloted for the local militia. 13 May. Went to be sworn in for the local militia.'[32] Rogerson has left us his impression of the training weeks undertaken in 1811:

15 May. Pretty well for work this week. Packing my cloths up to send to Pontefract . . .

17. Received a letter from Captain Bischoff[33] saying I was to be at Pontefract by 10 o'clock in the morning.

18. Very fine morning, set from home by 5 o'clock in the morning, got there about 10 o'clock found part officers there before me, they were at breakfast. I rode our horse.

19. Delivering the men their cloths out, gone done by 4 o'clock, did not see Captain Bischoff till 5 o'clock which was our dinner time. Went to the theatre at night – saw the pantomime of Perous most wretchedly performed, came home by eleven & went directly to bed.

20. Parading the men in the Horse fair . . . I lodge at the same place I did last time we were here at Miss Morley, Star Yard – I pay 10/6d per week – Breakfast at the Star along with out 11 officers pay 16fr per head – we are pleasant company.

21. Adjutant Drill at 6 o'clock this morning. I did not get there till 7 o'clock – I had no occasion to go at all. We have been again from ½ past 9 to ½ past 2 drilling the men with the manual exercise; they do remarkable well and improve fast. Writing a new list of the men for the serjeants – 12 o'clock before I got to bed to-night.

22. Fine pleasant day – did not get to field day till I got my breakfast – Grenadiers and Light Infantry gone to fire ball today – the Light Infantry put 150 balls in the target, 5 of them was in the bull's eye. Captain Wormald's company and our company goes today to fire ball on Darrington common; Captain Wormald's company put 92 in the target and 7 into the Bulls eye – Our Co. put 153 into the target, 10 of them into the bull's eye also ten into the Leg – got back by 2 o'clock met at the . . . other companies present in Carlton. At the play tonight.

23. Practicing marching in open column.

24. was to have gone to Darrington common to fire with ball but turns out a very rainy morning . . . went in the afternoon to fire 10 rounds.

25. Firing blank cartridges in the park.

26. Marching in open column.

27. Many people here from Leeds.

28. Rainy morning – not in the field till 4 o'clock in the afternoon.

29. Rainy morning – ordered to go to the field at 1 o'clock. Colonel Ilkin drilling the subalterns in the Star room.

30. At the field this morning by 6 o'clock. Marching with the men round the race course at ordinary time got home about ½ past 8, went there again at ½ pas 9. Firing blank cartridges.

31. Went to the field ½ past 9; met Mr Hodghson & Mr Bushby preparing the men for to morrows inspection – did not fire today, got back by 1 o'clock.[34]

Rogerson left a vivid picture of the life he led away at the camp in 1812:

25 May. Walk'd down to Leeds this afternoon to prepare a few things ready for going a soldiering.

27. Preparing and packing my cloths for Pontefract to be sent by trunk down to Leeds.

29. Set off this morning for Pontefract on permanent Duty, I hope for the last time in my life – set off at ½ past 6 in the morning, I arrived here near 12 o'clock after a pleasant ride – Delivering the men their clothing. Rainy afternoon. No Parade.

30th. Fine pleasant still morning – Did not go to the field till 8 o'clock got back by 10 – many of the men missing. Dinner today at half past 4 at the Starr. Practice the men with the swinging step and salutings. Fast how to spend time – Recd my commission today to be Lieutenant in the first regiment . . .

1 June. Orders to go to the field at 8 o'clock but too rainy and unpleasant; hopes it will be better in the afternoon as I am tired of the idle life. Drilling the men after it was fair in the street till 3 o'clock in their manual exercise. Dine at 4 o'clock at New Elephant – got to bed by 11 o'clock.

2. Got up at 7 – went to the field at 8, men gone ½ an hour before. Fine pleasant morn – Got from the field a little after 12 o'clock, had to get our breakfast when we came back. Recd a letter from home – Drilling men in manual & Platoon. Playing at cricket in the park with the Major & several more of the Officers. Came to dinner at Red Lion at 5 o'clock. Began to rain at the evening parade when the men had just got on, Adjutant order'd to dismiss them. Stop'd drinking our wine till after 10 – part of the officers got as much as they cd carry, got to be by ½ past 10.

13. we were throng in taking in the arms and accoutrements at the Black Moor's Head – hard day at it: got off from Pontefract at ½ past 3 and arrived home by ½ past 7 – had a pleasant ride.[35]

Rogerson evidently left the Militia in 1813 as he did not attend the field days in 1814. It is also clear that the men only received clothing and equipment and arms on field days, and only attended two weeks' training a year. With some pride, the *Leeds Mercury* reported in 1810:

that the whole of the Local Militia having now completed the annual training required by the Act, the present seems a very convenient opportunity for remarking on the exemplary and undeviating subordination to their officers which has been manifested by all the corps of the Yorkshire Local Militia, and particularly those of this Riding. And we believe the reason is, that the common people in this district are in general better informed than in most of the other parts of the Kingdom, for it is an undoubted fact that in proportion as men are ignorant, they are rude, disorderly and unmanageable, and the general instruction of the people would do more than 10,000 prosecutions for libels to secure the peace and good order of the country.[36]

## Demise of the Volunteers

Despite official utterings to do away with the Volunteers, when asked to transfer again to the Local Militia in November 1811 the officers of the 'Royal Wakefield Volunteers' sought to join the Local Militia, but the men were uncertain.[37] With the creation of the Local Militia, it the need for the Volunteers was precluded, and clothing allowances had been removed in 1809, yet by March 1812 68,643 remained under arms. Just four Volunteer units remained in the West Riding: 'Skyrac Volunteer Infantry', the 'Loyal Bawtry Infantry' commanded by William Monkton Arundel, 5th Viscount Galway, Wharfdale headed by Colonel Walter Fawkes and the 'Royal Wakefield Volunteers'. During the Luddite troubles in 1812, the Wakefield corps had been unable to assist the as its clothing was in poor condition; some uniforms were 16 years old. Yet at the review on 22 June, Colonel Pulliene noted the men were 'very good' in drill, cleanliness of uniforms and equipment and bearing.[38] Henry Addington, Lord Sidmouth, ordered on 17 March 1813 that the Volunteers were to be stood down, 'that as the establishment of the Local Militia precludes the necessity of continuing' adding that 'the Volunteer infantry of the West Riding of Yorkshire, should, after the 24th instant, be released from their military engagements'.[39] Units like the 'Royal Cheltenham Volunteers', 'Gloucester Loyal Volunteer Infantry' and the 'Loyal Berkswitch Volunteers' amongst others were stood down. The Yeomanry remained as a volunteer force, and the Local Militia was now filled by balloted men, the last of the Volunteers being discharged in 1812 after their four years' service.

Disbandment of the Volunteers was very unfair on the men, as on dismissal they became immediately liable for balloting to the Local and regular Militia. Colonel Serjeantson of the 'Royal Wakefield Volunteers' noted to the War Office that a member of his corps who had served for 10 years and on discharge was immediately balloted to the Militia. He called the episode 'exceedingly bad treatment in return for long and faithful service'. The colours of the 'Royal Wakefield Volunteers' were hung in Wakefield Parish Church.[40] They were inherited by the Wakefield Rifle Volunteers who carried them for the last time to mark Queen Victoria's birthday on 6 June 1880 before that corps was disbanded.[41]

Almost simultaneously with the disbandment of the Volunteer infantry came a missive from Whitehall on 29 October 1813 to encourage recruitment of Volunteers into the Yeomanry. The Act also sought to consolidate the Yeomanry much as had occurred to the Volunteer infantry. Many counties – the West Riding being an exception – had no higher-level formation for the Yeomanry troops, which operated as independent commands. The Act forcibly brought into existence regional or county-based regiments of Yeomanry. Each county or riding was to furnish six troops, which were to be formed into a regiment. If a county did not have six troops, their troops were required to be brigaded with neighbouring regiments on forfeit of losing their allowances.[42]

On 2 May 1814, Addington ordered the Local Militia to be stood down, and it was officially disbanded on 24 April 1816:

> the arms, drums, clothing and accoutrements were to be sent into the public stores, but should there be any sorts of clothing belonging to men enrolled before the 17th March, 1812, they were to be delivered to the men to whom they belonged. The non-commissioned officers and drummers were to be discharged on the 24th inst., unless the packing, &c., should not be completed in the time, in which case two sergeants might be retained for the completion of the business 14 days, but no longer. The Adjutant was to be the only officer to be placed on the reduced pay of 4/- per diem.[43]

The Local Militia would not reappear. The Yeomanry by and large continued to serve till after the Napoleonic Wars were over, some units being stood down in 1816, others in 1817 or later still. The Barton-Le-Street Troop of Yeomanry, raised in 1803, disbanded in 1825, likewise the Helmsley Troop. The Scarborough Troop, raised in 1798, was stood down in 1828, the same for the Kidderminster Troop and those at King's Norton and Stourbridge.

It has been argued that the Volunteers were 'volatile and politically subversive' based on the idea that no more Volunteer corps were formed till the 1850s.[44] This is categorically not the case as Richard Warren remarks that the Bath Riflemen existed from 1815 to around 1825, the Retford Volunteer Infantry were attached to the county Yeomanry; the King's Cheshire Volunteer Legion existed from 1819 to around 1825, likewise a comparable force in Newcastle-under-Lyme, the Newcastle Volunteers. Indeed, the Leeds Volunteers were organised in January 1820 and consisted of three line companies, a grenadier company and a light infantry company, with colours being presented in 1821. The 'Huddersfield Riflemen' were formed in April 1820, dressed in dark green with black facings. Both units were disbanded by 1825. The Yeomanry made a resurgence in 1817: with an increase tide of popular unrest and agitation for political reform, units like the 'Manchester & Salford Yeomanry' re-appeared, which galloped to infamy at Peterloo in 1819. In Oldham, the Yeomanry did not re-appear in 1803, but re-emerged in 1817, and likewise the Richmond Foresters which was wound up in 1828. The Huddersfield Armed Association Cavalry of 1798 re-appeared in 1817, still commanded by a member of the Atkinson family. In response to Peterloo, the Wirral Troop of Yeomanry was raised, and stood down in 1825. As Austin Gee points out 'the Yeomanry cavalry survived the war largely because it had never become a mass force like the Volunteer infantry; being small and more closely identified with the landed classes'.[45]

We therefore have to look for other explanations: the truth probably is, the compared to the Local Militia, the Volunteers were inefficient, undisciplined, and for the officers, lacked the social cachet of the Militia and cost the officers and towns they were raised in money. They were a drain on the middle class and wealthier artisans' incomes, which was not sustainable in the long term, given the economic realities of the period. The decline in volunteering from 1804 was ultimately terminal. The Local Militia, having weaker local bonds, and not intimately attached to the towns in which they were raised due to a far larger recruitment base, meant that they were more reliable, and could be used more readily outside of their military district and with troops of the line. The Local Militia was a professional force, the Volunteers were not.

Chapter 12

# DEFENDING HEARTH
# AND HOME?

As our previous chapters showed, a desire to defend the nation led men to join the Volunteers. Yet we ask was it purely nationalism and hatred of political reform that drove enlistment? The next few chapters explore the various reasons which drove men, who came from a broad spectrum of backgrounds (as our previous chapter has explored), to volunteer. Again because of the wealth of material, Yorkshire predominates. Volunteering was the mark of the loyalist, the Anglican and sedition-hunter, which were religious duties as the Rev. Munkhouse commented from his pulpit at St John the Baptist Parish Church in Wakefield:

> Loyalty, in the West Riding of the County of York, is, with but a few solitary exceptions which form the rule, AN UNIVERSAL SENTIMENT. The numerous addresses (expressive of the unchanged resolution of its Inhabitants of all descriptions to stand or fall with the present Government) now circulating, and preparing to be presented to their beloved Sovereign for his gracious acceptance, will best speak the sentiments, and most unequivocally convey to their fellow-citizens at large an accurate idea of the zeal, and magnanimity, and true allegiance, of this great County. YORKSHIREMEN ARE A HOST OF THEMSELVES. And, in the full pride of their Patriotism, without the least distrust of the prevalence of sterling British valour in other Provinces without disparagement to any, so great is their confidence in their own powers; such are their wealth, population, spirit, and exertions; that, in contemplating their conduct and character at this critical juncture, one might be led to suppose, that they could presume, even upon their own unassisted strength and efforts, to guarantee the safety of their Country.[1]

At times of national crisis oppositional patriotism was marginalised through 'Church and King' mobs and government repression. However, these marginalising effects would not end the contestation of national identity. National identity was a politically-fractured concept, heavily fought over by rival groups who gave it their own distinct interpretations. Patriotism has to be understood as a multi-vocal entity, carrying a plurality of different meanings and, as with all political discourse, intimately connected to the context in which the competing patriotic rhetorical narratives are expressed. In this war of words, terms such as 'patriot', 'liberty' and 'constitution' became highly contested and therefore had meanings which were in perpetual flux and constant redefinition. The attachment of the Volunteers to their locality helped to foster an idea of national unity regardless of political persuasion. The Crown, in witnessing the civil war in France occasioned by the Revolution, had sought to control such activities by binding the people to itself through loyalist activities, volunteering being the primary means from 1794 to do such that. Yet, we ask, was there more to volunteering?

Volunteer units created in 1794 were, as we touched on earlier, formed in the West Riding in centres of radical unrest by largely Anglican Loyalist property owners. These units were a natural extension of the groups that met to burn effigies of Thomas Paine in December 1792, and supported the Gagging Acts. Thus, it is hardly surprising, that the Volunteer infantry was an overtly political and religious force. The Volunteers were the willing accomplices of the state in the crackdown on 'the other' and political opposition. The *Leeds Intelligencer* carried an editorial written in November 1792 by the 'True Blue Club' of Birmingham which had grown out of the Priestley Riots, as a tool for recruiting for the Leeds Volunteer Corps for:

> opposing the pernicious doctrines of Paine and of preserving internal tranquillity, at a time when seditious writings were crammed into every hole and corner of the kingdom . . . threatening with desperate frenzy . . . to plant by force in this happy island, their accursed Tree of Liberty, more baneful in its effects than the poisonous tree of Java . . . it having now become the indispensable duty of ever Briton, who has the least veneration for his ancestors, the least sense of religion or allegiance, the least consciousness of the numerous blessings we enjoy, or the least stake in the country in the shape of property, possession or trade, immediately start from their lethargy, and unit every effort and body and mind . . . in erecting the standard of unshaken Loyalty and Constitutional Freedom. Convinced that nothing would more effectually intimidate our enemies . . . than the decided and artful plan of a whole nation rising in a mass of Volunteers.[2]

Containing sedition and cowing the opposition and anti-war liberals was the *raison d'etre* of the Volunteers, as was made clear in the formation terms for the West Riding Yeomanry, who purpose was:

> in the first place, for that of strengthening the means of national defence against foreign invasion; and in the next, for that of giving additional energy and effect to the constitutional authorities of the Kingdom, towards the suppression of Riots and Tumults that may arise in consequence of the dangerous machinations of audacious and designing men, tending to subvert our present happy constitution and thereby to destroy those beneficent laws and liberties which have so long afforded the inestimable blessing of equal protection to every rank and description.[3]

Magistrate Beckett from Leeds explained to Earl Fitzwilliam about the meeting that:

> a day or so ago the inhabitants of the Borough were convened for the purpose of considering the propriety of an armed force for the defence of the Borough – we immediately voted the measure to be expedient – we subscribed upwards of £3000 [illegible] which 100 Volunteers [illegible] – men of property – men who have something to defend, enrolled themselves as Volunteers & more are daily doing the same – it is by measures like this my Lord that the Government of the Country is to be supported & our necks kept from the Guillotining party – notwithstanding that their cause runs high.[4]

Furthermore, the Pontefract Volunteers were formed specifically to guard against home-grown Jacobins, to protect private property and in times of peace to be a bulwark of the Church and State.[5] Indeed, in Pontefract, a broadsheet reported that 'When the laws are outraged and the Civil Power is trampled upon, it becomes necessary for the magistrate to call in the military to support him in the discharge of his duty'.[6] The Bradford Volunteers were formed at the suggestion of and by the members of the Bradford Constitutional Society; the Loyal Sheffield Volunteers were created by the magistrates to opposed the radical artisan grouping gathered around Joseph Gales; the Royal Wakefield Volunteers were funded by the Wakefield Pitt Club, the 'Loyal and Patriotic Club of St George' which gave an annual donation of £10 10s. Indeed, the leading lights of the Royal Wakefields were correspondents with John Reeves. In Bradford 'The Union Society' gave a subscription of £20 a year.[7] The link between the groups that organised the burning of effigies of Thomas Paine in late 1792 and those who formed the Volunteer corps is overwhelming, especially when we consider nearly all the corps of the West Riding sent proclamations to the Crown backing the infamous Gagging Acts in winter 1795.

As can be clearly understood from the preceding section, the goal by and large was repression of radical associations. 'Church and King' magistrates and manufacturers saw the potential for using the institution of Volunteering both as an extension of the loyalist associations and as a means of inculcating loyalism among the rank and file. We note furthermore that the Loyal Sheffield Volunteers' enrolment terms stated that the corps was to 'co-operate with the civil magistrates in enforcing obedience to the Laws, in apprehending all disturbances of the Public Peace, and, at his requisition, in preventing or suppressing all riotous, disorderly and unlawful meetings or assemblies'.[8]

However, it is also clear that the reasons for joining the Volunteers were far more complex than repression, as has been made out by J.E. Cookson with the creation of the idea of 'National Defence Patriotism'[9] as opposed to the narrow nationalist confines postulated by historian Linda Colley.[10]

Primarily, enlistment in the Volunteers allowed one to show your patriotism and serve one's country without the danger of actually being killed or endure the hardships of campaigning – you could wear your red coat and still live in comfort at home! Furthermore, by volunteering you escaped the hated Militia ballot, and for the working poor, you got paid and a brand-new pair of shoes. The Volunteers undeniably harmed the Militia and by inference the regulars, as they drew in men who would have been balloted and likely also men who could have joined the regulars. No doubt for the officer class, national defence did play its part, but largely a variety of pragmatic reasons drove men to Volunteer. Volunteering, ostensibly – if not overtly – in very simplistic language said to the wider community 'I belong' and 'I am part of this nation'. In saying 'I am part of this nation' the Volunteer said above all else, 'I support the war and the goals of the Crown'. Saying 'I belong', however, has markedly different connotations.

## Localism
At its most basic level, volunteering allowed the aspirational middle class to emulate the nobility and oligarchy: local elites cemented their position in society by commanding Volunteer corps and gaining military rank and all the associated privileges of title and prestige it afforded. Loyalist associations and Volunteer corps were little more than the tame servants of the state; so too were huge swathes of the press, in the 1790s and beyond. Localism allied with the Volunteer movement

allowed the largely urban elites to act independently of the 'country gentlemen'; providing the officer corps with a conspicuous part in the public life of a town reinforced the power the local elites wielded in their communities and declared to the wider nation loyalty to 'Church and King'. Men joined the Volunteers ostensibly to defend their 'hearth and home', and their town or village or area rather than any notion of wider nationhood. These men were invested in their local community, and were prepared to defend this against external aggression.

Furthermore, localism threw down the gauntlet from one town to another: through ever increasing numbers of Volunteer units, towns and villages sought to 'outdo one another' with virtuous patriotism. The *Leeds Intelligencer* trumpeted 'The subscription for raising a Volunteer Corps within this borough fills most rapidly; and the number of gentlemen who have already enrolled themselves amount to upwards of 200'.[11] In Wakefield, the Rev. Munkhouse proclaimed:

> the truly loyal and patriotic Town of WAKEFIELD has to boast its Corps of Volunteers; and one Troop and two Companies of ARMED Associators. There is also at present quartered upon it more than two-thirds of the Fourth Battalion of West-Riding Militia; whose uniformly sober and orderly conduct is highly creditable to Discipline, reflects great honour upon their Officers, and has justly endeared them to the different ranks and descriptions of the Inhabitants . . . this blaze of patriotism diffuses light and warmth to distant regions.[12]

Across the West Riding we see an initial phase of volunteering that began in 1794 in urban centres, like Leeds and Wakefield. Virtue signalling by raising a Volunteer corps allowed a town to say to others 'we are more loyal'. Pontefract, with two MPs and a full corporation – the sole town in the West Riding to have direct political representation elected by under 500 voters! – did not raise a Volunteer corps till summer 1797. Knottingley had relied upon the Royal Wakefield Volunteers for riot suppression in 1795, so it is surprising that no move to raise a Volunteer corps took place in the immediate aftermath of that event. Nor was the corps raised to guard against the French, it was to guard against local 'insurgent' Jacobins: when we look at the Quarter Sessions, a case of seditious libel was held in 1798 in Pontefract for favouring an invasion by Bonaparte aligned with the request for raising Volunteers.[13] The two instances are inextricably linked. Issues faced by magistrates at local level required a local response. In addition, the voters of the borough could also declare to Wakefield and Leeds 'we are as loyal as you!'. Yet Doncaster, after an initial flurry of activity

133

in May 1794, never formed a corps of Volunteer infantry. The York Volunteers paraded in January 1804 at All Saints Pavement in their new uniforms, a sermon being preached by the Rev. William Flowers taking as his theme 2 Kings, Chapter 19 verse 34 'For I will defend this city to save it, for mine own sake and for my servant David's sake'.[14]

## Town verses Country

Localism also had other pitfalls. As we have seen, localism and civic pride crippled many proposed units or Armed Associations; other, more pressing needs emerged. Rural-based units had other issues: recruited from farmers and farm labourers, demands on the men's time at harvest crippled the unit's efficiency.

Proposed in May 1798, to be raised within the wapentakes of Osgoldcross & Barkston Ash, the first commissions being issued 25 October 1798, the 'Barkston Ash Volunteer Infantry' was commanded by Lieutenant-Colonel Sir Thomas Gascoigne, a recusant Catholic. Gascoigne informed Earl Fitzwilliam that nothing could be expected of them during the harvest, as the men were farmers, and, because the companies were so far apart across the vast recruiting area, the entire unit could not meet up to train.[15] This effectively meant that the corps only existed on paper and could only drill outside of ploughing, sowing and harvest time. The bulk of the men forming the Skyrac and Barkston Ash corps were the tenants and tenants' servants of Sir Thomas Gascoigne.[16] More worryingly, Lieutenant-Colonel Gascoigne reported to Earl Fitzwilliam that serious problems had developed in the Barkston Ash and Skyrac corps during 1799 about the extent of the military district in which they were to serve. In April 1799 a major disagreement broke out over the terms of service. The York Military District was expanded to take in part of Lincolnshire and many Volunteers took this as a prelude to being forced to serve in any part of the country. The enrolment terms of the unit stated that it would only serve in the West Riding of Yorkshire; however, the officers discovered that in order to get pay and uniforms, the corps would need to be willing to serve in a more extensive area. This caused considerable discontent in the corps: some men resigned and the officers were divided over changing the enrolment terms. Several Volunteers withdrew, and during a field day Lieutenant Edmonson harangued the men of Captain Fox's company, in front of other officers, encouraging them to leave the corps. Edmondson declared that if the men would not leave the corps, they were to refuse to serve outside the area agreed to in the original terms of enrolment.[17] How this was resolved we know not as no further archive papers can be located. It was a major breach of military etiquette, however, and showed the strength of local feeling amongst officers and men, who were prepared to defend 'their hearth and home' but not those of their nearby neighbours. The unit was stood down in June 1802, but was accepted back on the muster lists on 17 May 1803. Again, as the men were primarily agricultural labourers, due to the lack of training time, the corps was considered fit for duty only at the end of 1804, the inspecting officer remarking that he was obliged to regret 'their want of arms'.[18] Harvest season was 'off limits' which meant the summer months, with long warm days, were not able to be exploited for training. Recruited from farm labourers, the men's priority was their farm and not the Volunteers. In pursuance of Fitzwilliam's goal of larger corps, the Barkston Ash and Selby Volunteers were amalgamated in 1806 by which time the drill of the corps still had 'great room for improvement'.[19]

In nearby Skyrac, the Volunteers who came forward in 1803 were again recruited from agricultural labourers. Their Colonel, Michel Angelo Taylor MP, noted the men were widely dispersed across the wapentake, and he had 'the devil's own job' getting them together to drill. He further informed Fitzwilliam that because of the difficulties in assembling his men to train, he had had to organise two consecutive training days with pay to make it worth the men's time to travel to the allotted training location.[20]

In Rutland, the 'Belvoir Castle Volunteers' faced the same serious obstacle. Organised into four companies, recruited from twenty-six different villages, in order to drill the men, the corps was broken down into eight regional groupings, each with its own local assembly point and drill instructors. The corps was stood down in September 1806.[21] The reason given for disbandment was 'the great extent of the country over which they were scattered' which 'rendered assembling together, even for the common purpose of exercise extremely difficult'. Again, for the same difficulties of training, the Shepshed and Garendon Volunteer Infantry and the Donnington Park Volunteers as well as the Lutterworth Troop of Yeomanry all stood down.[22] Loyalism was no match for the widespread recruitment bases of these units, which prevented them being effective formations.

In rural Beaminster in Dorset, the Volunteers exempted men from parade and drill training if their business or place of work was six or more miles away from home and it was furthered order 'to dispense with the regular attendance of any member employed in agriculture during the Harvest months'.[23] In Oldham, which was then rapidly industrialising but had a rural hinterland, the same issues which beset the Volunteers and Yeomanry impacted on the Local Militia when organising field days. The commanding officer related 'my reason for making the choice of the 7th August as the commencement of service' was to 'avoid interfering with the conveniences of agriculture'. The date picked was after the hay harvest and before the corn harvest began, which left a period of three or four weeks in the summer.[24]

Forming units in rural areas from agricultural labourers was never going to be straightforward, and the units that did exist were far from well-trained or cohesive formations, and were paid to serve. Indeed, in the West Riding at the close of 1803, it was reported that Volunteers who were farm labourers, increasingly found themselves put out of work, because of the time they needed to be away from the farm to carry out their duties.[25] Volunteers in rural areas had a stark choice: defend the nation or be unemployed and unable to feed their families. Finding suitable men to engage as officers was also an issue in rural areas. The Allexton Infantry, commanded by George Cramp and recruited from rural Leicestershire, were wound up in 1805: finding officers and men had always been problematical, the corps never mustering more than 30 men out of the intended establishment of 120. Also disappearing were the Appleby Volunteers commanded by George Moor, which never mustered more than 60 men; likewise the East Stilton Volunteers and Kirkby Mallory Volunteers were all wound up in 1805. In Leicester and Rutland the Lord Lieutenant created parish-based units: but when faced with a plethora of small, rural parishes it was inevitable that many units would suffer from their recruitment base among agricultural labourers. Thus four units all disappeared within two years of being founded.'[26] Yet urban corps faced similar issues as one commentator noted because they 'are in general so much composed of men particularly engaged in trade & business of various kinds' the men could not be expected to assemble quickly or 'be expected to march from home and engage in actual service',[27] the inference being the men's livelihoods prevented them from serving beyond the immediate area in which they resided.

Nor was this just a northern phenomenon. The annual four weeks training of the Buckinghamshire Yeomanry were postponed due to a late harvest in summer 1795 and, again, in September 1797 due to wet weather. In April 1798, it was reckoned that the Buckinghamshire Yeomanry could only go on active duty during 'the season of the year at which it would be the least inconvenient to them to be'.

Recruitment for the Yeomanry, raised in predominantly agricultural districts, faced the same issues in assembling men to drill. Unlike the infantry in urban centres, the rural Yeomanry relied upon the goodwill of farm workers. Worse still recruitment was slow as Thomas Tew, a banker in Pontefract, lamented to Earl Fitzwilliam:

the subscriptions are liberal, the enrolments nothing – I suppose Mr Frank would inform you the meeting at Doncaster was respectably attended, the subscription liberal, headed by the Corporation with 500 guineas, the enrolment consisted of 3 persons, to whom the example was set by Mr Copley of Nether Hall – at Halifax not a farthing subscribed or a men enrolled – at Huddersfield the same – at Leeds one handsome subscription amounting to £1025, to which Lord Harewood made a part by subscribing 500 guineas, the Enrolment consisted of two persons – at Knaresborough a subscription of about 400 guineas to the Riding, but not a man enrolled – at Tadcaster a subscription of upwards of 300 guineas, 2 persons enrolled – Rotherham, Sheffield and Barnsley I have had no report – Tomorrow I go to Wakefield. It is my private opinion that there wants the Exertion of the Country Gentlemen among their Tenantry to make the present or future plan for raising a Corps of Cavalry Successful.[28]

Clearly 'joining up' was not the will of the people, nor was it a spontaneous outpouring of loyalism when it came to the Yeomanry. About the reasons for lack of response from rural communities to join up – largely those we have discussed earlier that prevented training – Magistrate Bacon Frank felt one reason was that:

the farmers do not feel the necessity to national defence, they are afraid of being called from home – they are afraid that if once embodied they may be kept on during the war as the militia are, some of them carry their fears from farm to farm as to [illegible] pretends they may be sent out of the Kingdom – others and with reason – use the inconvenience of being called from home who is to manage their farms for them? . . . it is hitherto held out to them is there loss of both of time and money, therefore no wonder they should hang back . . . I find there are people who make it their business to discourage the farmers by throwing obstacles in their way . . . believe the disaffection to the government of this country is strongly rooted in the minds of the common people and more so than we are aware of I fear.[29]

Farmers were unwilling to give up free time from their day-to-day work, which the magistrate conflated into disloyalty. Frank was very much 'Church and King' and was at pains to inform Fitzwilliam that broadsheets were being distributed that stated 'as was as a man enrolled himself, he becomes a solider and not only liable to be sent to any part of the Kingdom but even overseas of it'.[30] Such broadsheets were clearly designed to hamper enrolment as it raised the prospect of service outside their district which was a perennial fear of those who enlisted. Many of these broadsheets had been published in the early 1790s, most notably by the Sheffield Constitutional Society to encourage townsfolk not to join the regulars, or later the Volunteers. The Society campaigned actively for peace, the abolition of slavery, religious toleration and political reform, ideas that were anathema to many 'Church and King' supporters. Political identify was increasingly reactionary and based on opposition to the Whigs' ideals for a fairer and more equal society, and making a compromise with Napoleon. We must also imagine a degree of war weariness, and also fears of economic recession and a return of rioting over food. The experience of war on the home front perhaps explains the Rev. Joseph Hunter reporting to Earl Fitzwilliam:

> the Rotherham Volunteers amount to 31. And on or before Monday next it is hoped that a troop may be completed . . . Rotherham is the only place I know at present, that presents any flattering prospect of success in the present business.[31]

Raising money to form a Volunteer unit was far easier than getting to men to commit time and a loss of wages to being a Volunteer soldier. This is one of the reasons why the Local Militia was raised by ballot and it removed the major hurdle of apathy to the perceived danger of invasion and fear of service beyond the district.

As with the infantry Volunteers, recruiting from farmers and agricultural labourers into the Yeomanry suffered from the same major drawbacks as Lieutenant Richard Medley of the Pontefract Troop explained: as harvest season approached his men would not assemble with the Rotherham troops for training because his 'troop in greater part consist of farmers, the present time would be exceedingly inconvenient to them'.[32]

The dispersed nature of rural corps also made them being assembled for active service problematical. For example, the Skyrac Troop of Yeomanry, it was reckoned, needed 24 hours to be called to a muster because of its dispersed disposition. The Leeds Cavalry was again almost useless. Being based in the Town, it could be expected to muster in shorter time, but overall, both troops of cavalry were of little use as they were not immediately to hand:

> It is necessary that I shall here state to your Lordship, what Volunteer Establishments will be forthcoming within the district in question, in aid of the Magistrates upon emergency. There are two viz: 1st the Leeds Volunteer Cavalry, an excellent troop, but officers included, is consist of 38 only - & 2ndly the Skirac Troop of West Riding Yeomanry, which I expect will continue its service, if its numbers can be made up to 40, but

as yet I have no heard that they are so . . . I fear none but Regulars will answer and effectually. I feel it therefore my duty in transmitting the inclos'd memorial to your Lordship, to add my request to the opinion of the magistrates, that Troops be quartered in the large manufacturing districts.[33]

Fitzwilliam identified the Achilles heel of these part-time soldiers. Both urban and rural units took time to muster: regulars marching from a barracks could respond immediately, unlike their part-time colleagues in the Yeomanry or Volunteers.

Opposition to the war, the loss of money and time, and fear of being enrolled in the hated Militia were all factors against joining up, and runs contrary to the notion that the country was 100 per cent behind Pitt, the government and war. The Volunteers were a reflection of the national mood: some wanted war, others wanted peace combined with political, economic and religious reform. The strength of anti-government and anti-war feeling impacted on the formation of Volunteer units from a broader base than middle-class, loyalist, Anglican Tories. It is notable, that the West Riding clothing districts were the least well represented in the Southern Regiment of Yeomanry. We note 119 enrolled in Stainforth and Tickhill, 42 in Staincliffe, 26 in Barnsley, 30 in Barkston Ash, and 26 in Staincross, which were all rural and largely agricultural centres, whereas Agbrigg and Morley (Wakefield) and Osgoldcross (Pontefract), which were more urbanised and increasingly industrial, contributed very few men to the regiment.[34] This may be due to these areas being more urban, and the men already being committed to the Volunteers. Yet the villages in the hinterland of these towns, which should have been recruitment areas for the Yeomanry, contributed very few men indeed. More research is needed to look at motivations for volunteering between town and country.

It is undeniable that urban areas – Leeds, Sheffield, Wakefield, Halifax, Huddersfield – greatly facilitated the training of Volunteers, as the men all lived within a few miles of the orderly room and could rapidly assemble as a complete force, and conduct company- and battalion-level drills several times a week, which were essential if the corps was to take the field and be able to operate as effectively as the regulars. Although rural units often united parishes, it seems captains would often assemble their company, or even the sergeants to drill their sections from men gathered locally: the rural corps usually trained as independent companies, and so were unable to attain the urban units' level of training beyond the basic rudiments of drill to load and fire their muskets, and be able to march. In the West Riding, therefore, it was often more than not the larger corps based around the principal towns that were often reported as suitable to fight alongside regular troops, whilst the more rural units only reached a standard suitable for garrison duty. This no doubt reflected national trends. More research is needed to assess how these problems were overcome outside of Rutland and West Yorkshire.

Chapter 13

# CIVIC PRIDE

For urban centres, the Volunteers became an extension of civic pride and the growth of an urban consciousness, and a symbol of municipal authority and communal unity against 'the other'. York was not part of the West Riding, but was grouped with it: to this end, Fitzwilliam always had to ensure that York had a separate Volunteer corps. The other Parliamentary boroughs in the Riding, notably Pontefract, Knaresborough and Ripon, also required similar management so as not offend local sentiment.

Civic pride blossomed with the presentation of colours and church parades, as well as events to mark victories and local celebrations to mark the birthday of the King. For example, in Leeds in 1794 for the King's birthday, we note that:

the morning was ushered in with the ringing of bells; at Ten O'clock the Leeds Gentlemen Volunteers assembled in the White Cloth Hall yard from whence they marched through the principal streets of the town, attended by an immense concourse of people and a most excellent band playing 'God Save the King', 'Rule Britannia', 'Britain's [sic] Strike Home' & C . . . the officers provided an elegant cold collation, of which the whole corps partook as well as a great number of the gentlemen and corporation . . . Dinners were provided for the Volunteers at the Old King's Arms, the Hotel, Rose-and-Crown and the Three Legs Inns, where every rarity of the season were served up . . . in the evening there were bonfires, a most brilliant ball at the assembly rooms . . . At Bradford the Volunteers assembled in the forenoon and went through various evolutions, four six pounders were fired three rounds amidst general acclamations, the band of music belonging to the corps playing 'God Save the King', 'Rule Britannia' & C. At three O'clock a number of the Volunteers met the gentleman of the town and neighbourhood at the Sun Inn, where an elegant dinner was prepared... the day was concluded by a ball, where many gentlemen of the corps appeared in uniform, and the ladies, ever ready to display their loyalty to the King and attachment to our glorious constitution, joined the gentlemen in singing 'God Save the King' and requested they might present the corps with colours. At Pontefract in the evening about thirty young men headed by Lieut. Norton paraded the principal streets and fired their pieces at intervals. They were preceded by a band playing 'God Save the King' . . . nothing could exceed the loyalty shewn by the inhabitants.[1]

In October 1794 Sheffield was the scene of a great military procession combining the new levies of the Royal Wakefield Regiment or 132nd Regiment of Foot commanded by Colonel Cameron, the 'Loyal Sheffield Volunteers' and the Rotherham Troop of the West Riding Yeomanry commanded by Captain Foljambe:

at the close of the procession, each of the commandants of the cavalry and infantry made a short but manly and spirited address to the spectators, declaring it to be the firm determination of their respective corps, to protect, at the hazard of their lives and fortunes, their King and Constitution, and to preserve the peace and good order of society.

The cavalry afterwards partook of a dinner which was given by Captain Foljambe at the Angel Inn; the gentlemen of the town joined Colonel Cameron at the Tontine; and the Sheffield Volunteers dined at George's Coffee House.[2]

Early in January 1795, the 'Royal Wakefield Volunteers' were reviewed on Heath Common: their drill and volleys of musketry 'would have done honour to any veteran regiment'. To mark the Queen's birthday the Loyal Leeds Volunteers fired three volleys, followed by a reception hosted by the Mayor and Corporation.[3] Such events to mark coronation day and the King and Queen's birthdays as well as inspections, punctuated the social year, and provided a focal point for civic and local pride in the achievements of their fellow townsmen. The winter season of 1795 also witnessed the premier of the 'Royal Wakefield Volunteers March' between the acts of a benefit concert given in the Old Assembly Rooms at the White Hart Inn, Kirkgate, Wakefield.[4]

For loyalists, marking the King's birthday was an important moment in the year. In 1796, the 'Loyal Leeds Volunteers' fired three volleys in Park Row to mark the event, followed by a public dinner for the Volunteers and corporation in the Music Hall. In the evening the Theatre put on a special performance and ball was held in the Assembly Rooms.[5] The 'Halifax Volunteer Cavalry' colour was presented by the daughter of the Captain Commandant, William Ingram, to mark the King's birthday in 1799.[6]

Such events were not spontaneous displays of loyalty. They had been prepared weeks or months in advance. These events were social occasions, which like charity balls for the aid of the House of Recovery in Leeds or Wakefield Dispensary: such spectacles were an accepted part of the normal social life for the urban middle and upper classes. Attendance at these functions owed more to societal norms than loyalism or patriotism. The sentiment may have been to show loyalty, but attendance and participation was 'part and parcel' of the social contract of the era; it was the done thing to attend these functions in a display of localism and class recognition/belonging rather than higher-level notions of loyalism. On 10 March 1797, a benefit concern was given at Leeds Music Hall under the patronage of Colonel Thomas Lloyd of the Leeds Infantry and Cavalry Volunteers.[7] Localism and civic pride were foremost in the mind of Colonel Thomas Lloyd of the Loyal Leeds Volunteers when he presented £14 15s 6d arising from fines from men defaulting on attending drill parades to the Leeds General Infirmary.[8] Such actions strengthened bonds between the Volunteers, the town corporation and increased the social standing and prestige of the corps in the sphere of public imagination and perception. In 1798, Colonel Lloyd opened a subscription to raise donations from the people of Leeds 'anxious to show their loyalty' to gift to the Bank of England to help pay for the war: some £761 was raised.[9] Such collectivism fostered both a sense of local pride in that Leeds could raise such a sum; a sense of collective responsibility in fighting the war as well as attachment to the nation as whole.

Other displays of civic patriotism included:

> A loyal and public-spirited innkeeper in Sheffield, has not only subscribed £50 towards raising a subscription for the Loyal Independent Sheffield Volunteers, but has also sent his son as a Volunteer in the cavalry under the command of Earl Fitzwilliam; and he has agreed to build a riding school in Chesterfield, on his own premises, for the use of exercising the Cavalry raised in Chesterfield and its neighbourhood, under the command of C H Rhodes Esq.[10]

The Rotherham Volunteers had been formed in April 1798 as an Armed Association, to bolster the number of troops in the Sheffield area. It was linked with a troop of Yeomanry cavalry and the Sheffield Association infantry. The first presentation of colours to the Rotherham Volunteers was by the Countess of Effingham on 20 December 1798. On that day the 'Rotherham Volunteer Infantry', under Joshua Walker, Esq., Lieutenant-Colonel Commandant, assembled in a field near that town, attended by two troops of the West Riding Yeomanry cavalry, where they were presented with a pair of elegant colours by the above-named lady. The Rev. T. Bayliffe, vicar of Rotherham and chaplain of the corps, began the ceremony with a spirited exhortation, and afterwards offered up a prayer. The Countess of Effingham spoke as follows:

> Colonel Walker, I feel most sincerely gratified in having been called upon to have the honour of presenting the colours to you this day, for Rotherham Volunteer Infantry, and beg leave, in common with the rest of our neighbours, to bear testimony to the ready zeal your corps has manifested in their standing forth in defence of our religion, our King, and the happy constitution of our country; trusting such general exertions at home, united with the great successes with which his Majesty's arms have been blessed abroad, can alone enable us to look forward to the pleasing hope and expectation of an honourable peace.[11]

In reply, Colonel Walker addressed the regiment at some length, after which the colours were brought forward to them, first under a general salute, a *feu de joi*, and a discharge of one-and-twenty pieces of cannon. The regiment was then reviewed by Colonel Athorpe, attended by Major Fenton, of the Sheffield Association. Afterwards, a dinner was given to the regiment, and to the two troops of Yeomanry cavalry. At the close of the day, there were fireworks, and on the following evening, a ball was given by the officers of the regiment, attended by Lady Effingham and a full company. Such displays of loyalism bolstered civic pride and no down local patriotism. The colours were re-presented on 28 December 1803, again from the hands of the Countess of Effingham. The Colonel, in acknowledgment, observed:

> at the close of the late war, these colours were entrusted to my care by the late regiment of Rotherham Volunteers—untarnished, unsullied—they are now again unfurled as banners under which we may probably soon fight in a cause dearest to every Englishman—the defence of our country: they are now placed under your protection, and I confidently trust under Divine Providence, that our determined exertions will ever nobly defend them unblemished.[12]

The regiment was inspected by Colonel Gooch, who, with the Earl of Effingham and Bacon Frank, Esq., Deputy Lieutenant of the county and chief magistrate, as well as 'a very numerous assemblage of military officers', 'expressed the most unqualified approval of the forwardness and discipline of the men. The skill and promptitude with which they performed their various field exercises was deservedly praised.'[13] Indeed, Walker's regiment was on parade at the end of 1804. On 8 October 1804, Brinsworth Common was the scene of a grand review by Earl Fitzwilliam of the Sheffield, Rotherham, Ecclesfield, and Wath Wood Infantry, and of eight troops of the Southern Regiment of Yeomanry Cavalry: an estimated 2,000 Volunteers were present. This no doubt through down the challenge to other towns to receive similar plaudits.[14]

Indeed, in May 1804 after three weeks' service at Harrogate, when the Royal Wakefield's return to Wakefield:

> they were met at the extremity of the Parish by Sir Ed Smith's troop of Yeomanry Cavalry, commanded by Sir Thomas Pilkington; by a considerable number of special armed constables, most of the respectable inhabitants of the town and many of the neighbouring gentlemen on horseback, and by an immense concourse of people, who occupied the road from Lofthouse in one unbroken line of more than a mile in length . . . the Corps was very handsomely received in Westgate with presented arms by Col. Walker's regiment of Rotherham Volunteers; and previous to its being dismissed, Mr Naylor addressed the Commandant, Officers, non-commissioned officers and privates in terms strongly expressive of the high sense entertained in the town and neighbourhood of their truly meritorious conduct and service . . . the whole population of the place welcomed them with their cordial congratulations . . . an excellent dinner was served at the White Hart for the officers . . . and good dinners were also provided to the Corps.[15]

Volunteers also gave to charitable causes, as the press was at pains to point out to their readership:

> Before the Craven Legion left York, Lord Ribblesdale with his accustomed beneficence, gave a second donation of £10 to the poor of Acomb. His Lordship and Officers of the Legion also gave five guineas to the debtors in the Castle, and give guineas to the debtors in Ousebridge Gaol.[16]

Following the battle of Trafalgar in 1805, a subscription was opened in Leeds to aid the widows and orphans via a Patriotic Fund; to this the Leeds Volunteer Cavalry gave £120 10s, and we note Mill Hill chapel gave £22 15s and nearby Call Lane £16 11s 8d, both being Unitarian Chapels. Samuel Hamer Oates the leader of the Mill Hill Congregation, and officer in the Leeds Volunteers, gave £5 5s.[17]

Pomp and ceremony through military spectacles, volunteering and ostentatious displays of loyalty to the monarchy and state, opined the *Leeds Intelligencer*, would have a 'beneficial effect . . . on the minds of the rising generation, who may perhaps one day be called to the defence of their country at a similar crisis'.[18]

However, civic pride and localism had their dark sides as well. In the *Leeds Mercury* of 16 May 1812, we find recorded a quarrel between members of the Agbrigg Local Militia and the Wakefield Regiment of Local Militia 'respecting the superiority of their corps'. Words led to blows and 'the town was thrown into a good deal of confusion. Sir George Armytage ordered the drums to beat to arms and the streets were scoured by a horse patrol. Shortly after 10 p.m. the streets were cleared and tranquillity restored.' Some men of the Wakefield regiment were confined to barracks for a few hours and then, as the newspapers express it, ' the incident closed'.[19]

## Women

We should not assume that supporting the Volunteers was merely a masculine activity: as well as presenting colours, women across the West Riding gave money to the cause. In Halifax Jane Caygill gave £100,[20] Mary Wadsworth contributed £10 10s, Miss Wetherhead £10 10s and Mr and Mrs Simpson £21. We also note Mary Haigh gave £30 to the Halifax corps.[21] She was likely to be related to the Haigh family who attended Northgate End Unitarian Chapel in the town.

In Bradford, Ann Rookes gave £50, as did Jane Stansfeld, Susanna Storr gave £40, Widow Hodgson £21, Jane Thornton £10 10s and Mary Hodgson £5 5s.[22] Mrs Richardson gave £40 in July 1794 to the Bradford Corps.[23] Sarah Nichols gave £50 to the Huddersfield Corps, which qualified her as a committee member, Mrs Burnam gave £ 10 10s. In Leeds Alice Scott gave £30.[24] Women are notably absent in Wakefield. In York, Mrs Catherine Cappe, widow of the Rev. Newcome Cappe, minster of St Saviourgate Unitarian Chapel, headed the lists, donating £10 to the Volunteer Fund. Excluded from the state by her faith and her gender, clearly Mrs Cappe found other means of showing 'loyalty' to stave off attacks on her faith and her husband's reputation as being anti-war, by public displays of gift-giving. We also find others from the York Unitarian Congregation: Mrs Salvin gave £5 5s. Further north Mrs Merritt is noted as giving £25 to the Teasdale Volunteers.[25] A week later two more Unitarians gave money to the Volunteers to mark their localism and also loyalism, Miss Bellwood giving £3 3s and a Miss Hotham £5 5s to the York Volunteers.[26]

Buying or making 'comforts' for the soldiers is a timeless occupation: 'The Ladies Committee for Flannel Clothing' in York reported at New Year 1804 that they had provided to the York and Ainsty Volunteers 886 shirts, 598 flannel caps, 60 pairs of stockings, 123 pairs of gloves and 113 pairs of socks.[27] We also note that the 'Ladies of Rotherham' provided flannel waistcoats for the Rotherham Volunteers and Lady Mary Foljambe, subscribed 120 guineas to the Ladies' Subscription, to provide the South Regiment of West Riding Yeomanry with similar garments.[28]

As this chapter has demonstrated, volunteering was closely aligned with the concerns of the urban elites and the growth of an urban consciousness. The Volunteers' presence at significant events in the life of a town strengthened the link between the town and the Volunteers, but also the significance of the event. In broad terms, the Volunteers' attendance at civic ceremonies was to, in essence, strengthen local elites' power and the distribution of power amongst the elite and consequential status of both the Volunteers and the elite. The Volunteers made civic events into colourful pageants, which were therefore more likely to gather to them more spectators, establish or reinforce meaning of the event and evoke a stronger response through a communal display of solidarity, be it a church parade for the death of Nelson or the presentation of colours.

# Chapter 14

# VOLUNTEERS AND THE 'MORAL ECONOMY'

We looked at the relationship between the Volunteers and the moral economy earlier in where the officer class was drawn from. We now explore how the Volunteers cemented local and regional ties as well as the moral economy of the era. The war gave urban elites an ideal opportunity for aggrandisement and imitation of the county gentry, making the urban bourgeoisie firmly part of the loyalist establishment. William Ingram, the son of a slave trader and grandson of the steward to the Earl of Strafford, had made a fortune in the slave trade, and thanks to his fortune had become the leader of the 'Church and King' faction in Halifax. In raising the 'Halifax Volunteer Cavalry', he added the cachet of 'Captain' to his name: a term of status beyond being merely 'Mr' William Ingram. John Naylor, son of a cloth merchant in Wakefield, rose to social prominence through his vocal loyalism, also adding 'Captain' to his name. We see in the urban Volunteer units a mobilisation of merchants into the officer corps: men of trade and therefore no fortune suddenly found a new opening in society in which to advance themselves. Being an officer and especially a commandant became a prestigious honour in the associational world in which local elites mixed. A Volunteer officer could flaunt the trappings of a military career but did not need to participate in it full time, or face the risks of active military service. So too for the artisans, tradesmen and middle classes who formed the bulk of the manpower of these regiments.

Localism, as we touched on earlier, further cemented the social contract and moral economy of the eighteenth century. The appointment of noblemen to positions of command in urban and rural corps reinforced traditional lines of patronage and deference due to men of pedigree. The Earl of Mexborough and his brothers all held officer rank in the Pontefract Volunteers. This confirmation of deference to the nobility is reflected in the grand entertainment given by the nobility to 'the common people'. The Hon. Charles Saville, son of the Earl of Mexborough, gave a grand dinner at the Red Lion Inn, Pontefract, for 300 Volunteers, and hosted a ball and dinner for the officers at Methley Park.[1] In the moral economy of the eighteenth century, it was customary for landlords to generate bonds of loyalty with their tenants through providing meals and distributing gifts of food at times of hardship: estate banquets carried on into the early twentieth century. The 'pub lunch' given to the Volunteers is no different to these events. The exclusive social status of the officers is further cemented by their presence at Methley Park: for an urban unit, the Pontefract Volunteers was remarkably aristocratic in the make-up of its officer corps. Richard Ingram, Captain commanding the Halifax Troop of Yeomanry Cavalry, gave a dinner in the Assembly Room, Halifax, for his troop and:

> all the military gentlemen of the neighbourhood were also present, with a considerable number of officers of the Volunteer Infantry corps and the gentlemen of the town. The dinner consisted of all the delicacies of the season. Many loyal and spirited toasts were given. Messrs Robertson, Wrench and other gentlemen, enlivened the company with a display of their musical talents, in a variety of loyal and harmonious songs, and the meeting broke up at a very late hour.[2]

Those Volunteer officers who could afford to, gave grand banquets as conspicuous displays of wealth and loyalty, and no doubt to reinforce their position in society. In Leeds:

> Colonel Lloyd with that liberality which ever marked his character, treated his corps, the gentlemen and corporation, and all the officers stationed in the town, with wine and other refreshments in the Cloth Hall Yard where his majesty's health was drunk three times . . . Captain Rhodes of the Volunteer Cavalry, with equal liberality, gave a sumptuous dinner to the whole of his corps, the Volunteers officers &c . . . Joshua Field . . . captain of a troop of the West Riding Yeomanry Cavalry, ordered them to assemble at Harewood . . . he treated them with an elegant dinner.[3]

The Volunteer Corps represented the eighteenth-century moral economy of master and servants writ large:

ON Thursday Last, the Wakefield Yeomanry Cavalry, commanded by Sir Edward Smith Baronet, had a field day at Heath, after which they partook of a most excellent dinner at the White Hart Inn, given by their commander.[4]

Sir Edward Sylvester Smith resided at Newland Hall, where he was squire. When the Skyrac Volunteers returned from 21 days' duty in Doncaster, their Colonel, Michel Angelo Taylor MP, gave the NCOs and men half a crown each and 'a very handsome breakfast'.[5]

## The Middle Class
Volunteering gave the local elites the same status as the nobility and country squire: it put the urban elites to the fore in the cause of national defence: it gave the Volunteers a 'purchase' against aristocratic privilege and allowed these men to differentiate themselves from the middle classes and forge a distinct identity. James Milnes of Wakefield, by virtue of his heterogenous faith, was an outsider, but his displays of patriotism in donating funds to the Yeomanry and raising his own troop of cavalry gave him the same social cachet of 'commandant' as Colonel Wrightson, Thomas Lloyd and others. Public displays of virtuous loyalism were liberating: it gave the middle classes confidence and assertiveness at local level to take part in national affairs. The 'Grand Review of Volunteers' at Leeds in 1795 demonstrates this: the urban Volunteer corps from Leeds, Halifax, Wakefield, Bradford and Huddersfield took centre stage whilst the aristocratic Yeomanry were literally on the sidelines:

On Tuesday, the 26th May, 1795, the Military Festival commenced at 3 o'clock, the Halifax Corps of Volunteers, commanded by Colonel Hamer, arriving at the Head-quarters, the old King's Arms, attended with two brass Field pieces, one in front, the other in the rear, each piece drawn by two grey horses. The greatest concourse of people ever known on any former occasion assembled to welcome them as they entered the town, and the streets through which they were to pass were crowded many hours before they arrived. At half past six the Bradford Corps, commanded by Colonel Busfield, arrived at their headquarters, Crosland's Hotel. The concourse of people was then so great as nearly to prevent their marching up Boar Lane into Briggate. They had also two Field pieces, one in front and the other in the rear, each drawn by two grey horses. At half past seven the Wakefield Corps, commanded by Major Tottenham, arrived at their headquarters, old King's Arms. At 8 o'clock, the Huddersfield Corps, commanded by Major Sir George Armytage, arrived at their headquarters, Crosland's Hotel.

On Wednesday morning, at half past eight, the different corps assembled near the Mixt Cloth Hall, and marched from thence to Chapeltown Moor, where they had a Field Day and went through their different evolutions and firing with the greatest exactness. They returned to town again about 4 o'clock in the afternoon. In the evening there was a concert at the Music Hall, in Albion Street, by desire of Colonel Lloyd.

The concert was numerously attended and the Theatre was also uncommonly crowded.

On Thursday (the Grand Review Day), the different corps assembled near the Mixt Cloth Hall, and at half past ten o'clock marched up Boar Lane, Briggate, and by the Market Place to Chapeltown Moor . . . Having grounded their arms for about 20 minutes they went through the following manoeuvres in a soldierlike manner equal to the most experienced troops of the line: -

1-General salute and marched round in slow and quick time.

2-The manual exercise. 3-Primed and loaded with cartridge. 4-Fired one round by companies from flanks to centre; began at the right.

5-Advanced in line and fired one round by companies from flanks to centre; began at the left.

6-Advanced in line and fired one round by companies from centre to flanks.

7-Formed a new line in the rear.

8-Formed a close column in the rear of the right division. 9-The column advanced in ordinary time.

10-The right division formed the line and fired one round by companies from right to left of the line.

11-Formed a close column in the rear of the left division.

12-The column advanced in ordinary time. 13-The left division formed the line and fired one round by companies from left to right of the line. 14-Formed a new line in the rear. 15-Advanced by wings from the left and fired one round from left to right. 16-The right wings advanced into a line. 17-Formed a new line in the rear. 18-Fired by regiments one round from flanks to centre; began at left. 19-Advanced in line. 20-Fired by regiments one round from flanks to centre; began at the left. 21-Advanced in line. 22-Fired by regiments one round from centre to flanks. 23-Retired in line. 24-The right line advanced, at the same time opening ranks. 25-The line halted and gave the grand salute, the colours dropping.

After which the whole corps left the Field in the same order as they took it, and arrived in Briggate about four o'clock in the afternoon.

The great concourse of people and number of horses and carriages assembled in Chapeltown Moor exceeded all conception.

The forenoon was uncommonly fine, but about 1 o'clock a little rain came on, when the spectators began to disperse in all directions.

151

On Thursday evening there was the most brilliant assembly ever known in this town. Yesterday the different corps of Volunteers returned to their respective homes, much satisfied with the civility they received.

Notwithstanding the mass of people assembled in Leeds, on Chapeltown Moor and in all the roads leading from Chapeltown, on the Wednesday and Thursday, it is recorded that not even the most trivial accident occurred.[6]

Such a spectacle was a visible display of patriotism, as well as something exceptional to take part in: it fostered localism through shared experience and pride in the West Riding and the individual units. Spectators may not necessarily have been driven by spontaneous outpouring of loyalism, more of a desire to see the spectacle and get away from the everyday.

The Volunteer movement transformed the relationship between the middle class and the armed forces: it ended the stranglehold on the nation's officers corps by the aristocratic oligarchy: indeed in 1808 the state largely supressed the opportunities for middle-class participation until the 1860s. The Volunteers were a wider reflection of society, and seems to have superficially cut across political and religious divisions, in reinforcing the moral economy and at the same time it provided a degree of urban middle-class solidarity and broader understandings of class and rights consciousness. The period 1790–1820 witnessed the rapid development of the urban middle class: the Volunteer corps welded these disparate identities into a cohesive social class. This was a process begun in the 1770s with the American Revolution and the petitioning of 1775 for peace. The Volunteer movement was a mass participatory 'patriotic' mobilisation of the middle class, driven by 'la patrie en danger'; the fear of social change and revolution – social conservatism protected their business interests and property; the resentment of aristocratic patronage blocking their route to political and social advancement – very Jacobin principles which ran counter to the previous ideals of social conservatism; differentiation from the propertyless and powerless working class; and lastly the desire to form a new social identity outside the remits of the then current moral economy. For the middle class, the Volunteer corps allowed them to be citizens of the nation and protectors of their own interests as they alone possessed the means to mobilise their local communities through their wealth, local influence and middle-class assertiveness. In this sense, the Volunteer movement was deeply subversive: in creating a middle-class solidarity the local elites were challenging the moral economy whilst at the same time wanting to maintain that moral economy: here was the beginning of a dramatic shift in power that would be manifest in the Reform Act of 1832. The seeds of middle-class rights consciousness were sown here. The increasing demands of the middle class in wanting the same political rights as the urban elites and aristocracy made them a formidable political force, which would come to dominate the politics of the country from the 1840s: this was a slow revolution by other means as middle-class confidence sought to exclude aristocratic privilege. In this regard the Volunteer movement was dangerous and may explain why appeals to the middle class for national defence were small and reluctant in the early 1820s and no mass participation took place till 1859 and the threat once more of *'la patrie en danger'*. Indeed, the Local Militia can be argued as a response by the aristocratic elites to put an end to middle-class *petit bourgeois* military power, albeit in the name of efficiency.

## A Political Force?

The reasons for volunteering were many faceted: one man's reasons were different to the next. However, behind the multi-vocality of reason, it is undeniable that the 'first flush' of volunteering was primarily urban, to guard against the perceived threat from the largely urban reformist societies, such as the Manchester Constitutional Society and similar societies formed in Norwich, Nottingham, Derby, Sheffield, Leeds, Birmingham and across London. In nearly all cases in a town where a reformist society existed in 1794, the loyalists would form a body of Volunteers. The reasoning was primarily to defend private property from the mob as the Mayor of Richmond, North Yorkshire, explained: 'Leedes and such places have laudably and as a self defence against disappointed workmen, embodied the respectable inhabitants' in calling a town meeting to form a Volunteer unit in his town.[7]

For this reason, urban corps outnumbered their rural counterparts, possibly by ninety-six to thirty-two by 1795. In this regard Nottinghamshire was typical with all but four of its twenty-two corps confined to the vicinity of the larger towns: Nottingham, Bunny, Southwell, Newark, Mansfield, Worksop and Retford. The predominance of urban corps was more marked in the rapidly industrialising North of England. In the West Riding of Yorkshire, Halifax, Bradford, Leeds, Wakefield, Sheffield, Rotherham, Doncaster and their vicinities dominated almost to the exclusion of the north of the Riding. This dominance of volunteering by urban corps would be reinforced by the government's invitation to form specifically urban Armed Associations in 1798: we remark that two-thirds of the new corps outside the south-west were based in towns, despite a restriction

153

on infantry companies in the smaller inland towns. In the south-eastern and coastal counties most exposed to invasion, Volunteer corps were formed by 1800 in nearly all the ports and larger towns. The defence of London resulted in mass participation in Volunteer infantry and cavalry corps beginning from 1794. In the defence of the Kent coast and London, it was quite common that Volunteer corps would be formed in the rural areas immediately adjacent to the urban centres. Yet this still left huge swathes of the country with no Volunteer force.

For many civic leaders the need for the Volunteers was self-evident and contained in the articles of association for these new units. In Huddersfield the Volunteers were formed 'for the protection and defence of the West-Riding in the County of York' as well as 'the Suppression of Unlawful Meetings in this and Neighbouring Parishes' whilst in Wakefield, the Volunteers were for 'Internal Defence of this Town and Neighbourhood, and against any Insurrection or Commotion'.[8] In Sheffield, similar views were expressed as to the need for Volunteers. According the Rev. Russell, Vicar of Dronfield, the *raison d'etre* of the Volunteers was to 'oppose Jacobin principles so prevalent in Sheffield' which were 'disseminated by a seditious printer Joseph Gales'. By 12 May 1794, the Rev. Russell reported that he had enlisted 100 'patriots' to 'oppose the designs of the Jacobins'.[9] The goal was repression of radical associations, as Rev. James Wilkinson the vicar and magistrate of Sheffield commented:

> a considerable number of the most respectable young men of Sheffield having agreed to enrol themselves to act as a military corps for the defence of the Town and neighbourhood held a meeting yesterday at which Mr Athorpe, Mr Stoum and two other JPs and I attended: It is the opinion of the Justices, that the appearance of this Body of young men in Arms will probably have a good tendency towards repressing the insolence of the disorderly, turbulent and seditious spirit apparent in some people among the multitude.[10]

It should not be surprising then that the membership of these Volunteer corps had a degree of overlap with membership of local branches of the Pitt Club and Reeves' Loyalist Association. When we look at the 136 Volunteer corps formed by January 1795, Austin Gee reports that 54 corps were formed in locations which had a Reeves Loyalist Association where members are known. Of these fifty-four, forty-one, or three-quarters, had officers who had been members of loyalist associations when muster lists and membership lists are compared. In total, 72 out of 136 Volunteer corps seem to have originated from

Reevite associations![11] Thus it is no surprise many of the Volunteer corps that emerged in 1794, primarily in urban centres, shared the counter-revolutionary concerns of Reeves.[12]

In Birmingham, it was the Loyal True Blue Society, whose members it seems had participated in the Priestley Riot, headed by the staunchly conservative Justice Joseph Carles, which oversaw the formation of an Armed Association in the town.[13] Up north, Robert Athorpe JP was the darling of the Sheffield Loyalists, and like many other 'Church-and-King' loyalists, including magistrates and manufacturers, saw the potential for using the institution of Volunteering both as an extension to the loyalist associations and as a means of inculcating 'loyalism' among the rank and file. Athorpe pledged himself 'to oppose every effort' made in the cause of political reform.[14] Indeed, the Loyal Sheffield Volunteers' enrolment terms stated that the corps was to 'co-operate with the civil magistrates in enforcing obedience to the Laws, in apprehending all disturbances of the Public Peace, and, at his requisition, in preventing or suppressing all riotous, disorderly and unlawful meetings or assemblies'.[15] The Rev. James Wilkinson, magistrate and Vicar of Sheffield, opined that: 'the late very alarming appearances and extravagant behaviour of the lower classes of people here by tumultuously expressing their joys on the success of the French Armies and their rich applause of French Principles'.[16] He added that he hoped that the Volunteers would assist in 'repressing the Insolence of the disorderly, turbulent and seditious Spirit apparent in some People among the Multitude'.[17] Both government and civic leaders believed that only through repression and the militarisation of society at large could England be saved from French invasion and the internal threat of home-grown dissidents.

The formation of Volunteer regiments in the West Riding as well as Lancashire represented not the will of the people to defend 'hearth and home' from French invasion, but as we noted earlier, but from the supposed threat of industrial unrest and 'home-grown' Jacobins. The arrest of reformist leaders such as John Thelwall, John Hardy, Horne Tooke and Henry Redhead Yorke and the resulting Treason Trials provided the Crown with solid facts that reformist groups were a threat, and the volunteers were part of the Crown's response in 'closing down' the reformist space of debate. By and large, in the Midlands, London and the West Riding were the main focus of Volunteering in 1794, formed by Anglican elites to guard against local unrest to support the magistrates. As we noted earlier it was these areas that were most affected by food rioting in 1795, and were major centres of anti-government working-class agitation. Certainly, across the West Riding the Volunteers received their baptism of fire during months

155

of food rioting which began in April 1795 and lasted throughout the summer months until September 1795. We are seeing here a force for internal defence and not primarily against invasion.

Into this world of 'them and us' between Whig, Tory, and Foxite, the Volunteers became useful tools in the corrupt politics of the pre-Reform Act era. Colonels now wielded considerable influence in local affairs. Volunteering was a political act by loyalists, as before in the 1790s. Its recruiting base was primarily from Anglicans, and those who sympathised with the ideals of Pitt. Therefore, we are seeing not a national identity being forged, but men reacting to economic necessity, and also, we suppose, from peer pressure, and no doubt downright intimidation. The state, as we mentioned earlier, through its broadsheets and caricatures by Gillray and others of Napoleon, fostered anti-French sentiment. The press with editorials printing anti-Napoleon and anti-democratic propaganda played its part in whipping up public outrage against France. The *Leeds Intelligencer* remarked:

> That the man who is backward in coming forward in volunteering his services at this critical juncture, deserves neither the blessing or protection of the land he lives happily and securely in – participating the glorious and much envied privileges, we as Britons enjoy – May such be speedily roused to a sense of their duty.[18]

Basically, 'you are with us or you are against us' thundered the Leeds Tories. As an ephemeral and transient political force, this nascent national identity was however subject to strong external forces over the nature of the Napoleonic Wars that have seldom been commented upon. It was a fleeting phenomenon. Volunteering was not a nation-building force: men volunteering received pay, a decent pair of shoes and clothing and, above all, exemption from the hated Militia ballot. It was not driven by patriotism, or if it was, it was opportunistic. The reasons behind the willingness to volunteer arose from numerous sources beyond patriotic loyalty to the state: we shall never truly know what drove men to 'sign up', for the answer lies within the psychology of the individual Volunteer and his local community. Wearing a red coat and attending drills was a shared experience that bolstered a sense of class identity amongst the largely middle-class participants, who were on the whole, Anglican or Methodist and largely Tories or Old Whigs. It created a sense of purpose, of belonging and created a new identity of participation.

The Whig party, if such a thing ever existed, had fragmented in the 1790s between one-nation conservatives or 'Old Whigs' lead by the Duke of Portland, and in whose ranks Earl Fitzwilliam, Lord

Lieutenant of the West Riding, could be found, and the 'New Whigs' of Charles James Fox. The 'Old Whigs' sat on the government benches, were pro war but by and large stood opposed to the ideology of the Tories and the undue influence of the Crown. Volunteer unit Colonels wielded considerable political influence, especially if the officers were landlords. Through their officers, the Colonels could therefore exert political influence to ensure the 'right man' was elected MP.

For example, in Pontefract, since the 1770s the Monckton Arundel family had been the owner of the burgess rights and sat as the MP: Robert Monckton Arundel, 4th Viscount Galway, a gambling addict and drunk, had sat as MP since 1796 and stepped down in 1802 in favour of his nephew Richard Benyon for the 'Fitzwilliam Interest'. Galway, sometime Tory and sometime Whig, controlled 150 electors out of 550. Benyon stood against William Wrightson of Cusworth Hall for the Portland Whigs. Lieutenant-Colonel Teesdale Cockell, reported to Fitzwilliam that Lord Galway had successful canvassed the town noting:

> the majority of the inhabitants was so much in his lordship's interest that it was almost impossible to overthrow it. In the case of another candidate being offered it is impossible to know how popular opinion may change—I hope with spirited exertion one of the family may be returned. However, this cannot be certain.[19]

To achieve this, Cockell told Fitzwilliam he would use his influence amongst his corps to ensure that the electors amongst them voted for Richard Benyon, and to canvas the town on the behalf of Benyon, to ensure that he would be elected for the Fitzwilliam Interest.[20] Basically, to ensure Benyon was elected, the voters amongst the Pontefract Volunteers were given the stark choice to vote for Benyon or resign. In the corrupt world of eighteenth-century politics, no doubt 'strong-arm tactics' were used to get as many votes as possible in Benyon's favour, who was duly elected Whig MP for Pontefract with 484 votes out of a total of 550. How much of this was due to Cockell's 'gerrymandering' is not known, but we assume Cockell's coercion played a major part in the outcome of the election.

Cockell was a 'fully paid-up member' of the English exceptionalist xenophobic racist view of the war with France commenting that he:

> would wish to see our children reared up with a greater abhorrence of a Frenchman than of the devil himself, and I do not think, odd as it may appear, that this would be going too far . . . Always keeping in

157

mind how inferior they are to us in real courage and generosity. At the same time do not let us rob them of one superiority which they possess over the whole word, I mean in lying, bragging, intriguing, in hypocrisy, treachery, impudence, and all other vices that are yet unknown to the rest of mankind. — But I beg your pardon for this digression; though I do not think you will be the worse for attending to it, and thinking of those hell-hounds the French as I do. I am sure you will be the better Christians for so doing . . . Our motto is for our King and Constitution, and the loyal sentiment has taken root in the heart of every Pontefract Volunteer. Was there one that had a different opinion, I know you so well, that such a character would not long disgrace your colours; that spirit of unanimity and friendship which is so conspicuous in our regiment, I hope will ever be its character.[21]

Cockell's racism knew no bounds, and he refused to use French words in his day-to-day speech and in his military instruction. His nationalism was based on opposition to France, rather than a sense of any pride in the British nation. Cockell was exactly the middle-class 'hot-headed hawk' that championed war that the Crown's propaganda machine appealed to, much as modern right-wing newspapers do concerning BAME, BLM and immigrants. Cockell despised anyone not like him. Indeed, he reported to the Home Office that he had 'kept sedition and treason in terror and silence'.[22] Cockell's sabre, which he carried when his men marched out against food riots in 1801, is in the author's collection: 'I trembled at the idea of marching out against the starved poor. I really felt myself a coward, & yet it was a Duty I must display energy in. I was only out twice and thank God the appearance of the Corps threw a panic upon the poor starved people!'[23] Cockell clearly had no qualms about killing French soldiers, but does seem to have questioned his role in policing his town. Localism would have a hugely detrimental effect on the effectiveness of the Volunteer corps in their role as police.

Cockell's use of the Volunteers for political ends became almost 'traditional' when election time came. The Pontefract Volunteers were embroiled in the 1806 general election. One of their officers, John Saville, Viscount Pollington, stood to replace Richard Benyon, against Lord Galway's interest. Robert Pemberton Milnes, whose brother was a fellow officer of Saville's, had married Galway's daughter Pollington came third in the election: John Smyth of Heath was returned so too Robert Pemberton Milnes. A year later, all this changed. The Earl of Mexborough ensured that his son Pollington was elected alongside Milnes, and ousted Smyth. The volunteers again were told who to vote for or face dismissal. For his father's interference, Pollington was reviled by the townsfolk of Pontefract, one observed saying that voters were 'heartily ashamed of having chosen such a mountebank, such an ass!'.[24] Lord Galway died in 1810, and his trustees, rather than pass the burgage rights to his 'kith and kin' – Robert Pemberton Milnes married his daughter, we remember – put' them on open sale. In 1812, after spending £40,000 to buy the Galway Burgage and Tenant rights in Pontefract in 1810, thus securing a guaranteed 183 votes, Milnes was returned on 6 October 1812. Milnes, however, was unseated on 22 December by John Saville who had been made Lieutenant-Colonel Commandant of the Pontefract Volunteers in 1808, largely through bribery and open corruption, about which a complaint was lodged in new year 1813. The investigation held Saville duly elected, and he chose to sit for Yorkshire, leaving Ellis Leckonby Hodgson, an officer in the Pontefract Volunteers, to sit as MP for Pontefract: Hodgson, a major and notorious slave trader, sat until 1818.

In Knaresborough, when the town's two MPs came up for re-election in 1804, rioting broke out when the officers of the Volunteers endeavoured to prevent the voters in the corps from casting their ballots. Knaresborough was a 'rotten borough' with two MPs returned by just ninety-six electors. Lord Cavendish, the Duke of Devonshire, sought to protect the 'ancient constitution of the Borough', yet he stepped down to contest Aylesbury, young Viscount Duncannon, John William Ponsonby, being offered in his place. The townsfolk objected to his nomination, and sought to change the voting rights of the borough. An effigy of Ponsonby sat astride an ass labelled 'Ponsonby Pinchgut' was paraded through the town. What was described at the time as 'a riotous mob' hindered the election, forcing the burgesses, who almost to man supported Ponsonby, to retreat. The bailiffs, unable to obtain due protection from justices or constables, made no return of a member and could report only their failure to do so. The magistrates could not call upon the support of the Volunteers, as many were actively involved in the protest against the interest of the Duke of Devonshire, which was led by Joseph Mossy Allen, an attorney. The involvement of the Volunteers on the side of the 'mob' is understandable as the Colonel of the Knaresborough Volunteers ordered officers and men who were burgesses to vote for Ponsonby or not at all.[25]

A year later, once more the Knaresborough Volunteers became embroiled in a riot over the right to vote: the free burghers of the town, and independent householders technically had the right to vote, but this had been consistently been withheld by the Duke of Devonshire. The disfranchised residents were reported to be culpably encouraging 'a very large body of Irish mechanics and labourers' to 'raise hell' on their behalf to press the issue forward. Rioting broke out. When returning from voting, Sir John Ingleby, the commanding officer, was pushed down stairs and 'beaten black and blue'; the same fate befell Lieutenant Dewse, because they had publicly spoken out against against reforming the borough's constitution. One member of the 'mob' who assaulted the two officers was Corporal Whitehead of the Knaresborough Volunteers![26] Political division ran deep in the unit. On 25 February 1806 Lord John Townshend, seeking re-election, was stoned, and saved the situation by a timely speech; and at the general election, on 4 November 1806, the populace dispersed 300 lead miners sent by the Duke of Devonshire as special constables who again sought to interfere in the election. The 'mob' then took on the Scots Greys who were called in to quell them, the Volunteers being incapable of acting.[27] The 1807 election pitted Tories against Whigs in one of the most violent contests of the period. Rioting again broke out between the two diametrically opposed camps: the Tories screamed the Whigs were Jacobins and wanted to make peace with France. Earl Fitzwilliam noted in a letter of 25 May 1807, opined that:

> the rioting over the previous two years had prevented any returns being made. 1807 was no exception. The Magistrate, Mr Knowlton swore in 200 special constables in case of a breach of the peace: Coming polling day, a mob drove off the constables, the riot act was read, a troop of Dragoons from Harrogate dispersed the mob.[28]

The Knaresborough Volunteers, as could be expected from the riot of 1806, took a leading part in support of the 'mob' and political reform against the views of the Duke of Devonshire. Fitzwilliam in a letter to Lord Pelham at the Home Office that:

> one half of this corps are inhabitants of this town of Knaresboro' and suspected in their individual character to have form'd on every occasion, a great part of the strength of the rioters at the same time I beg to be understood as distinctly exculpating them from an ever official information that has reached me, from having ever put themselves in any military order, as to have appear'd to act together on an military principle: if making part of the mob, they acted merely as mob. I state their suppos'd dispositions for the purpose of shewing that great reliance cannot well be plac'd in that corps as an aid to the Civil Powers, indeed their commander Sir John Ingelby lost greatly his influence over the corps, in consequence of the part he took as a Magistrate in one of the elections & of the steps he took as the commander of the corps for the prosecution of mischief at the last General Election.[29]

Rioting was part and parcel of the political process, yet a food protest or a political rally to demand political change was illegal! The hypercritical double standards of the era – corrupt politics was fine, but seeking political reform was bad – are all too obvious in Fitzwilliam's letter. He was also conscious to downplay the Volunteers' mutiny, and direct involvement in the rioting. As In Pontefract, the Volunteers were told who to vote for by their officers in an audacious demonstration of the moral economy and the influence the senior officers had at local level. The Volunteers were a potent force in local politics. How far this was just a West Yorkshire issue is hard to assess without more research being carried out in regional archive offices. It seems likely, however, that the actions in West Yorkshire were not unique, especially when we consider the Volunteers in the light of the moral economy and the influence of the officer class in town and country.

Chapter 15

# CHURCH AND STATE

For men like Edmund Burke, the Anglican Church was the bedrock of the constitution and thus supporting 'Church and State' was a key component of the moral economy of the late eighteenth and early nineteenth century. Indeed, the Anglican Church fought off all attempts to give Dissenters, who were excluded from political life via the Test and Corporation Acts, the same rights as Anglicans from 1774 to 1828. Anglicanism was the bedrock of the nation and non-attendance at the parish church was seen as little better than atheism and Jacobinism. After Waterloo, Lord Liverpool would spend millions building parish churches to bind the working class to the state and to hold back the tide of Nonconformity. The trumpet of state nationalism, according to historian Linda Colley, was the Anglican Church and its clergy, a view with which I agree. Moreover, Colley stressed the role of the Anglican clergy in promoting a sense of national 'patriotic consensuses among the civilian public'.[1] Attendance at church parades along with presentations of colours aligned Church and nobility to the Volunteers, and the Volunteers with the national church. The Church emphasised that the war against France was a war against atheism, blasphemy and democracy. The Stoke Newington Armed Association was told by the parish vicar that the atheist French state mocked religion and had declared a war of extermination against England. In Hackney, French ideals of democracy were considered more dangerous than the French themselves in a vitriolic sermon from the pulpit of the parish church and the Rev. Sandilands exhorted the Volunteers to be bulwarks against democracy and were thus 'friends of peace and order'.[2] Perhaps the vicar of Hackney was thinking of the Unitarian congregation which backed democratic ideals when he told the Volunteers they had to be unified in their action against external and internal threats.[3]

By 1803 government policy was not to grant commissions to clergymen, but the attitude of the church authorities varied between dioceses. The Archbishop of Canterbury in April 1798 stated his opposition to clergymen joining military forces, as he believed that it would interfere with the proper duties of the profession. Moreover, he felt that clergy learning the use of arms and enrolling as Volunteers would not add materially to the defence of the kingdom. Tellingly, the Archbishop felt the clergy should, however, assist in repressing rebellion or insurrection at home, and if and when the time came fending off the French if they landed.[4] Therefore, the clergy were emboldened to take action against those they considered to be Jacobins and thus traitors. It comes as no surprise then, given official sanction, that clergymen played a very prominent part in promoting and organising volunteering. Despite professing to be men of peace, some went as far as to join corps themselves in positions other than that of chaplain. Ralph Fletcher, the Tory magistrate of Nolton-Le-Moor in Lancashire, was also the incumbent at St Peter's Parish Church and Lieutenant-Colonel of the Volunteers. He led an active spy ring that sought to crush Jacobinism and political reform. He was violently anti-Catholic and was a key member of the Orange Order in Manchester. He used his position as magistrate, parson and colonel to enforce his views on the local populace, and was sitting as a magistrate when the 'green light' was given to the Peterloo massacre. Although not a Volunteer, the Rev. William Robert Hay, vicar of Ackworth in the West Riding, acting as a Justice of the Peace, was active in persecution of reform groups and sought to close down public expressions of disaffection. Hay, like Colonel Ralph Fletcher – who was also a parish priest – was a key person in the Peterloo massacre in 1819 who permitted the Yeomanry to charge the protestors. Hay commanded Volunteer troops in West Yorkshire 1801–03 in hunting down Jacobins.[5] For example, on Sunday 24 May 1801, Hay commanded a force of 40 regulars from the 11th Light Dragoons and 250 men from the Huddersfield Fusiliers into action near Saddleworth 'to show the disaffected a ready and formidable appearance of the military . . . by way of intimidation'.[6]

Being a parish priest, as with the case of Hay and Fletcher, did not always equate to being a man of peace. So common was the local parson heading the Volunteers, Henry Redhead Yorke commented pithily in 1794, that far from being men of peace, clergy were warmongers, observing on a recent trip to Bolton that he had encountered a parish priest 'marching at the head of a recruiting party, with a cockade in his hat, and his gown and cassock on him, and so drunk, that it was with some difficulty he could keep in time with the fife and drum'.[7]

Thus it comes as no surprise that we record that five clergymen were officers in the Derbyshire Volunteer corps. In Belper, a town dominated by the Unitarian Strutt family, the Reverend Joseph Bradshaw was Major of the Belper corps which became dominated by Anglicans in opposition to the Belper Constitutional Society centred at the Unitarian Chapel and led by the Strutts. History suggests that Rev. Bradshaw reputedly would read prayers to his troop in uniform from horseback at Sunday morning musters, having held a service an hour earlier than usual in order to attend.[8] Rev. John Langham Dayrell of Lillingstone Dayrell in Buckinghamshire recorded in 1797 that 'no County can boast of a more active Lord Lieutenant . . . he is a great encourager to the learning the use of arms, and even that the Clergy should do so, who in some parts of the County have enrolled themselves'. The Rev. John Kipling from Shabbington, whose services as an officer had been initially declined in 1798, joined the Yeomanry in 1804.[9] In the West Riding parish of Horbury, the Armed Association was to be headed by the curate, the Rev. John Raynor. Stopping 'home-grown terrorism' was the *raison d'être* of the Horbury Armed Association, as the good reverend opined to Earl Fitzwilliam:

> in the present juncture of public affairs, it becomes the indispensable duty of every lover his God, his King & country to exert himself by every means in his power, against the avowed insolence of foreign invasion & the secret plots of internal Jacobinism.[10]

So important was allegiance to Church and State, that the Loyal Leeds Volunteers' first major public event was a church parade:

> Yesterday the Volunteers of this borough assembled in the Cloth Hall yard, and from thence went to the Parish Church, attended by the Mayor and Corporation, where they heard a most excellent sermon from their Chaplain, the Rev. P Haddon, the vicar: his text was the XIV chapter in the 1st Corinthians, and part of the 33rd verse 'For god is not the author of confusion but of peace' – The Corps made a very martial appearance in their new cloathing, scarlet faced blue, and were accompanied to and from the church with several thousands of spectators![11]

As with Leeds, the Halifax corp's first public appearance was church parade on 17 August, the slave-owning vicar of Halifax Rev. Dr Coulthurst being both subscriber to the corps and was its chaplain. The press reported that:

the Halifax Gentlemen Volunteers made their first appearance in their full and elegant uniform, and marched in procession to church to hear an excellent sermon that was delivered to them by their chaplain, the Rev. Doctor Coulthurst, the Vicar, which was couched in terms, at once nervous, impressive, and elegant and which will be speedily published. A temporary gallery was erected in the choir of the church – in which all the Volunteers were regularly seated in companies and made a striking and pleasing appearance.

On Monday last they proceeded to the consecration of a set of beautiful and most elegant colours given them by the Ladies of the town and neighbourhood, which were presented to the Volunteers by the Rev. Dr Coulthurst, in their name attended by a deputation from the Committee in the Piece Hall, – after which they marched to the moor and fired several excellent vollies, amidst the unbounded shouts and acclamations of an immense and applauding multitude.[12]

In the prayers given after the presentation of the colours, Coulthurst gave thanks for the Seditious Writing and Meeting Acts in safeguarding the nation, and remarked that 'laws are not strong enough' to 'restrain infidels and atheists' and 'our own disaffected countrymen'.[13] For Coulthurst, atheists were those who denied the 'revealed religion' of the Trinity and therefore he was aiming 'four square' at Unitarians, as well as Jews. No doubt he also had issues with Catholics.

The Huddersfield Volunteers' colours were presented in May 1795 by Lady Armitage, following a parade and field day. After the colours had been consecrated and presented the officers dined at the George Inn, followed by a ball 'attended by all the principal families in the neighbourhood'.[14] The colours of the Leeds Volunteer Cavalry were presented in November 1797 by Mrs Peter Rhodes, wife of the captain commandant, who on delivering the standard to Cornet Rimington spoke thusly:

> Sir, I have the honour to present you with this standard, our Moto [sic] Our Country Our Laws, in defence of which, should the service of this troop be required, I have no doubt but you and your companions will acquit yourselves as men, zealous for your country's honour, and the preservation of our liberty and laws.[15]

The Rev. Miles Atkinson, vicar of Bradford and leader of the pro-war faction. who was chaplain of the Braford Volunteers offered the following words when the units colours were presented: 'you stand here as men armed for the battle, and before you is the ensign of war . . . the enemies that whom you are preparing to go against are not only enemies to you but enemies to God'.[16]

Perhaps the most significant colours presentation of the 1790s was that of the 'Sheffield Volunteer Cavalry', presented by Earl Fitzwilliam, in what can only be described as a conspicuous display of 'shock and awe' through a marked display of militarism conjoined with church and state to suppress and intimidate the Sheffield radicals, and foster a sense of achievement and patriotism among the 'Church and King' supporters:

> the Inhabitants of the town and neighbourhood of Sheffield were gratified with one of the most brilliant spectacles that was ever presented to the public eye in this part of the country – It consisted of an assemblage of different troops of the West Riding Yeomanry Cavalry, of five troops of the Somersetshire Fencible Cavalry, at presented stationed in the barracks there; of a very numerous corps of the Loyal Independent Sheffield Volunteers and of the two new raised levies of Cavalry and Infantry for the defence of that town and neighbourhood consisting in the whole about a thousand men; this meeting having been occasioned by Lady Fitzwilliam having agreed to present the standard of the new raised corps of the Sheffield Independent Voluntary Cavalry.[17]

On presenting the standard, the Rev. J. Lower of Brotherton, Earl Fitzwilliam's chaplain, declared:

> I have great pleasure in coming forward . . . to exhort you to perseverance in the loyal and patriotic cause you have commenced . . . your voluntary services, at a period so critical to your country, fully envice the public spirited principles on which you have acted . . . we have nobly stood in the breach, repelled the inroads of Barbarism, impiety, and Anarchy, and preserved to Europe, perhaps to the world, the blessings of Religion, good government, social order and rational liberty. . . . this standard consecrated in the name of Jehovah, may point the way to Victory over the enemies of God and Man.[18]

These events were public spectacles and ostentatious displays of loyalty. William Ingram at the presentation of the colours to his troop of cavalry in Halifax in 1799 remarked that 'a well-grounded faith in the Christian religion' was the 'surest shield against the arms of our inveterate enemy . . . the tyranny in France' and that the goal of the war was to conjure up a New Jerusalem 'to make Great Britain the chosen land of old, the deposit of True Religion, the asylum of Balanced Liberty . . . '.[19] Yet Ingram was a slave trader – what of the liberty of the slaves he transported? What of non-Anglicans? Clearly for Ingram and others of his ilk, 'Liberty' was white, middle class and Anglican.

What the Unitarian congregation at Northgate End in the town felt is not known. They had been intimidated by the mob in 1792 with threats to burn down the chapel, and the minister, the aged Rev John Ralph, had fought for reform and peace throughout his life. Clearly, the town was polarised between Whig and Tory, Anglican and Dissenter. Ingram had marked out dissent from Anglicanism as little short of treason, yet Ingram was not the first to articulate these thoughts. As historian Dr Susan Loughlin writes, the great innovation of Henry VIII was to assimilate loyalty to the Crown with loyalty to the Church of England. Loyalism and nationhood was bound to religious identity. Dissention from the Church of England meant in very simple terms disloyalty and therefore treason. We look at loyalism and Dissent in a later chapter.

The blessing of the colours sanctified the agreement between the Volunteers, 'Church and State' and the Moral Economy or in layman's terms, the rest of society, in a very public manner. The elaborate ceremonies to present the colours were in direct imitation of established military conventions, in form and appearance, with local dignitaries standing in for the monarch. They were exclusionary acts, that as we have said several times before, aligned Loyalism with Anglicanism and said that Dissenters were not welcome.

The omnipresence of the Anglican Church and clergy, and Edmund Burke's identification of democracy as a threat to the Anglican Church, its theology, doctrine and dogma, made it a powerful anti-revolutionary force, but also by 1799 an enemy of the people which in part led to the Nonconformist expansion of the 1790s. The growth of political and religious dissent led in 1792 to the Lord Mayor of Liverpool writing to the Home Office urging the Government to build churches in the numerous towns and villages that had sprung up with the growth of manufactories, giving as his reason, not the advantage of spiritual provision but for the danger of leaving these places to the Methodists and 'to keep in touch with families of labouring classes, and so strengthen a link in society almost broken in some districts and which has by its want of support enabled the Dissenters to extend themselves as then have done'. The view that that the absence from Anglican worship amongst the working class and urban poor lead to the growth of anti-establishment activities was so prevalent in government that when the loans to Austria and Prussia were called in after Waterloo, the money was spent building Anglican churches! It happened to be mostly true: the Millenarianism and social divisiveness of Nonconformity – particularly middle-class Anglican-minded Wesleyans against the Tom Paine Methodists of the New Connexion, or hatred of Unitarians who were marked down as

Jacobins and blaspheming heretics as well as the Ezekielites – were fundamentally destabilising ingredients in the social milieu of the period. The socio-religious element has been largely ignored in the driving force of opposition to Burke and the war. Opposition to the war was not solely based on ideological support and sympathy for French Jacobinism: undoubtedly such sympathy played a huge part in anti-government politics 1789–93, but from 1800, opposition was rarely due to support for Napoleon, but on the grounds of morality, religion and crucially on the opinion about the Revolution in France as an ideological struggle between contrasting ideals of 'Britishness' and 'Frenchness' in relation to property, law, democracy, and the rights of man. This battle of ideology, more than anything, defined the conflict.[20]

Chapter 16

# LOYALISM AND DISSENT

As our previous chapter started to explore, Volunteering was a largely Anglican phenomenon, with members by and large being Tory: this is not surprising as approximately 80 per cent of the country was Anglican in 1800. The remaining 20 per cent were Dissenters, who were politically Whigs of one sort or another. The leaders of the Whig movement in Yorkshire were wealthy Unitarians, who were by and large members of a new merchant-gentry elite that dominated towns such as Hull, Leeds, Nottingham, Derby, Belper, Sheffield and Wakefield. Outside the West Riding, Unitarians wielded considerable economic power in Liverpool, Bristol and Manchester by 1800, and were conspicuous for civic leadership and political influence. Unitarians figure large in the making of provincial middle-class culture across the country.

As we noted earlier, in her seminal work *Britons* historian Linda Collepostulated that membership and development of the Volunteers witnessed the creation of a new national identity, which understood Volunteers were defenders of the nation against the foreign enemy and overrode previous political and religious identity: historian John E Cookson described this phenomena as 'National Defence Patriotism'.[1] Such a cover-all term explains how political and religious differences could be overcome, or at least set aside, at crisis points. Indeed, over 100 years later in 1914 the Suffragettes supported the government's war effort, and a similar mind-set laid aside political differences in 1939–45. Yet as in 1914, did such an identity develop spontaneously, or was it created by an effective propaganda machine?

In a largely post-religious world, it is hard to imagine a period where religion played a leading part in society, personal identity and politics. The prominence of religious issues in eighteenth-century British politics, most gratifyingly, is beginning to gain increased recognition in recent years. The debate over the doctrine of the Trinity was central to both the theological and the political rhetoric of the era. Then as now, the term 'orthodoxy' referred to one's position in this debate and concept of the state, and how it wished to be perceived. Unitarianism, both political and religious, was an explicit critique of the existing regime, especially after 1775. For religious Dissenters, who by and large drove the desire for political reform and the ending of the perceived injustices of the Test and Corporation Acts – symbolic and psychologically exclusionary legislation which excluded Catholics, Unitarians and other Dissenters from taking part in public life – led to an upsurge in opposition to the status quo: when Americans began to speak out against injustices metered out to them by English tyranny, the Dissenters understood their rhetoric, and took up the cause as their own. From 1799 Catholics no longer had to swear an oath of allegiance to the Church of England, whilst Methodists and other Dissenters such as Baptists and Independents appear to have been free to associate and worship together throughout the period. These Trinitarian faiths were within the remit of 'revealed religion': for those who denied the Trinity, the law was much more inflexible. Furthermore, in denying the Trinity and divinity of Jesus, Unitarians disavowed the Bible as divine revelation and the notion of original sin. Not only was this blasphemy for most Christians, but it gave Unitarians a differing world view. Rather than seeing humanity as damned and unredeemable, Unitarians believed – and still believe – that mankind could be redeemed, and that all in society had the same human rights, that education had the power to lift the poor out of poverty, and to allow humanity to grasp its full potential. This led Unitarians to champion women's rights and electoral reform.

Unitarian worship was illegal till 1813. Despite the illegality of their faith, Unitarians were the leaders of religious Dissent: in general terms, Unitarians were the wealthiest 'sect', largely being urban merchants, and thus often highly educated. Business links and political patronage gave some congregations a high degree of influence. Westgate Chapel in Wakefield, thanks to the Milnes family, was as influential as any London congregation. Religious Dissent offered the merchant and working class and artisans an attractive and contrasting vision of society to that harboured by the Anglican elite, and to distrust and resist the influence of their superiors: for the artisan and merchant the goal was ending the stranglehold of church, king and aristocracy over local and national government to create a society of free citizens. This was incompatible with the creation of a strong, stable – conservative – state founded on 'Britishness'.

This struggle for equal rights set Unitarians on a different political path to that of Edmund Burke and William Pitt. Unitarians were increasingly despised by the Tories since the Rev. Dr Richard Price issued his famous sermon in defence of the French Revolution in 1789: Unitarians became increasingly persecuted. The Priestley riots in Birmingham in 1791, where two Unitarian chapels were burned to the ground, followed in 1793 by the Manchester riots which witnessed two more chapel-burnings, showed the degree of hatred that existed against Unitarians. Edmund Burke set the stage for national attitudes by the state, and the Tory Loyalist mobs, by calling Unitarians in the House of Commons:

> insect reptiles, whilst they go on caballing and toasting, only fill us with disgust; if they go above their natural size, and increase the quantity, whilst they keep the quality, of their venom, they become objects of the greatest terror . . . What would they do if they had power commensurate with their menace? God forbid! . . . I would rather have Louis the Sixteenth than . . . Dr. Priestley . . . their cabals . . . and 'low-bred' insolence.[2]

To be a Unitarian meant to be a Jacobin, to be an enemy of the state. So, what was the position of Dissenters with the formation of the Volunteers? The open Anglicanism of volunteering we discussed in the last chapter. In Dorset, when it was proposed to form a Volunteer corps in Swanage, one writer commented 'Presbyterians, who are very numerous here, are the principal cause' for the failure to form a corps, because 'they take every opportunity of representing this, (and every other mode of supporting government) in a manner that may be injerous [sic] to the People'.[3] No doubt the 'Presbyterians' the writer spoke of were supporters of the Rev. Joshua Toulmin, a Unitarian divine, who had backed the Colonists against the Crown during the American Revolution and supported the French Revolution, in whose congregation could be found the poet Coleridge.[4] Unitarians, with their support for the opening stages of the French Revolution, for religious toleration and freedom, for widespread political reform and a restriction on the power of the monarchy and Church, shared differing world views to Anglicans and orthodox Dissenters. Their disavowal of original sin, the denial of the atonement of sin by the crucifixion of Christ and the denial of his divinity placed Unitarians at loggerheads with the society around them. The open hostility towards non-Anglicans is exemplified by a letter from George Dyson, a Baptist living in Gledhow. He reported to a friend that 'at Halifax a company of Volunteers was drinking and the first toast was Damnation to all Dissenters and Methodists. The second toast, Down with all their meeting houses, chapels and conventicles . . .'[5] Such views were preached from largely Anglican pulpits and spread by loyalist media. The Wakefield Armed Association and 'Royal Wakefield Volunteers' were urged from the pulpit to:

> boldly dare to oppose yourselves to this torrent of iniquity and licentiousness, and narrow the circulation of those noxious Publications so notoriously hostile to the Cause, – which such numbers of you are ready to maintain at the hazard of your lives. They have too long been the successful vehicles of Sedition; and, with unmerited impunity, have insulted your attachment to the Religion of your Ancestors, (all heavenly as it is) your Patriotism, and your Loyalty, by their avowed contempt of whatever bears the name of Truth, Honour, Honesty, and Decorum . . . As Subscribing Members of News-Rooms, and Public Libraries, exclude or expel them. To Provincial Booksellers—to such more especially as I know to rank with the most Virtuous And Patriotic of their fellow-citizens, who (many of them) whilst they hold themselves in readiness to repel, by Dint of Arms, any open attack upon the Rights and Liberties, would shrink with horror from the bare idea of becoming accessory in corrupting, to any degree, the Morals of the People—to these I most earnestly address myself, and presume to suggest the Expediency of their exercising their own Private Judgment, in every possible instance, on the Contents of all those Volumes, which are unceasingly poured from certain Marked Metropolitan Presses, previous to the giving any order to have them transmitted to them, and for the honest and conscientious purpose of obviating by this precaution the evils, which must otherwise inevitably result from the wider dissemination of the most pernicious opinions through the Medium of their Circulating Libraries. They are of a nature, the tendency and design of which cannot be misunderstood. They are 'a scandal to any Christian Country;' and having once unhappily been permitted 'to pass through the Press', ought instantaneously to be made 'to pass through the Fire'.[6]

Clearly, the Volunteers were being exhorted to burn books and libraries that were critical of the war and the government! We note that in Wakefield the news room in the town was funded by Unitarians, as was the circulating library, and the publications that Monkhouse censored were primarily written by Unitarians who had a virtual monopoly on the anti-government, pro-peace and pro-reform press. It is very easy to see that the Volunteers were an ex-officio extension of the Church and State militant in fighting a war against political and religious dissent. Thus, it is no surprise that Unitarians and radicals were 'not welcome' and seen as 'part of the problem'. Direct evidence of this 'war' against reform and the threat posed by religious dissent as espoused from Unitarian pulpits is best demonstrated by the views of Teesdale Cockell, the commanding officer of the Pontefract Volunteers, who no doubt cultivated his views amongst his fellow officers and men. Cockell sought to blame Unitarians for food riots, and wrote to Earl Fitzwilliam in April 1798 expressing his concerns about:

> the increase of disaffected people in this town & neighbourhood, which of late years had most rapidly spread amongst the lower orders, that have become Dissenters & from the indefatigable attention of the sect to make new converts, it was thought necessary to fall upon some means of checking the spirit of Disloyalty.[7]

Six months later, following widespread food rioting, Cockell stated to Earl Fitzwilliam that he had raised the Pontefract Volunteers 'not merely for the purpose of being ready on all occasions of Riot, but to remain permanent after the war, on account of the increase in the Presbyterian sect in this town & neighbourhood; it is well known that every convert is an Enemy to the constitution & established religion . . . '.[8] For Cockell, supporting the Established Church and controlling, if not ending, religious dissent was key to keeping the peace. Writing once more to Earl Fitzwilliam, Cockell expressed his fears about 'fifth columnists' in the West Riding who met under the guise of religion, admitting he had:

> great apprehension from the vast increase in the Presbyterian sect who are indefatigable in making converts: every Priestleyite becomes a Republican, a leveller & an innocuous enemy to our Established religion. I am about my Lord to advance a bold operation, but I can support it. After this, that what are called the well educated & higher classes of the Presbyterians are not Christians. They deny his divinity & in so doing they must deny his veracity in which case my Lord, what opinion can they form of our Saviour & his revealed truths . . . I don't hesitate to say that if this turbulent sect of infidels continues to gain strength in other parts of the kingdom as in this neighbourhood, they will (unless properly looked after) plunge the nation very shortly into the most imminent peril – they Divest the lowest order of the people of a belief in the Revealed religion & other sacred truths & I will venture to assert that land of Happiness will speedily become the same chaos of horror, slaughter & misery that France has & still groans under.[9]

Cockell is clearly describing the Unitarian congregations (i.e., denying the divinity of Jesus, the Trinity and the Bible which under the

Blasphemy Act of 1689 made Unitarians heretics and not Christian, despite denials of this by Unitarians who considered themselves nominally Christian) in Wakefield and Pontefract and making references to Rev. Dr Priestley: perhaps the most famous, or infamous Unitarian in the country following the Priestley Riots and his flight to France in 1791. Cockell and the 'Church and King' mob's hostility resulted in the Unitarian chapel on Newgate, Pontefract, being closed down. The rump of the congregation built a new chapel on Finckle Street, the trust deed stating no Unitarian was to preach or be a member of the congregation. Unitarian historian John Goodchild M.Univ comments that this was not a unique event: the minister at Wakefield had been arrested in 1792 for sedition; the minister at Derby was reviled for supporting the ideals of Thomas Paine; Belper Unitarian Chapel was attacked in winter 1792; and the Bristol congregation was likewise a victim of violence. Across the Pennines, Rev. Thomas Bancroft informed the Home Office that in Bolton, the active Jacobin club was 'almost exclusively composed of Dissenters they gather in two meeting houses, one is Unitarian and the other Presbyterian'.[10] This was a war of ideology and religion.

Yet despite this intolerance, as we noted earlier, the West Riding was dominated religiously and politically by the Unitarian congregations in Halifax, Leeds (Call Lane and Mill Hill), Sheffield, Wakefield, York and to an extent Holmfirth, Rotherham, Selby and Bradford. It was here in Leeds and Wakefield that the 'wealthiest merchants in the county' worshipped.[11] Nor was this just a Northern phenomenon. The Earl of Warwick expressed doubts in September 1803 that a 'proper Corps' could be established in Warwick, as the 'few gentlemen of the town would not take any lead and the Volunteers would be entirely under the guidance of Dissenters and manufacturers'.[12]

Katrina Navickas argues that the levy *en masse* had allowed for any urban or rural elite to establish their own force, so the new corps founded from 1803 represented a broader community base, and allowed Dissenters to serve, both as rank and file and as officers.[13] She is correct that 1803 marked a watershed for Dissenting participation. Given the degree of animosity and downright sectarian hatred shown to Unitarians for both their faith as much as their politics, it is easy to understand why, to use a modern phrase, 'community leaders' made ostentatious shows of loyalty by volunteering when given the opportunity to do so. Yet the situation is not as clear cut as Navickas makes out. As we have seen with the 'Royal Wakefield Volunteers', many who were Unitarian Whigs became 'Church and King' loyalists and ultimately Anglicans. The impact of the French Revolution on Dissenting communities, though fascinating, is beyond the scope of this work, but does warrant further study. Not all Unitarians who volunteered before 1803 changed their religion and politics to suit the times: the Naylor family and the aforementioned David Parkhill both left Unitarianism to conform to Anglicanism by 1795. At the time of the invasion scare of 1798, we find that Unitarians attending Westgate Chapel were the core around which the Wakefield Independent Cavalry was formed, headed by James Milnes, future Foxite MP for Bletchingley in Surrey. He was a member of the Wakefield Constitutional Society, and challenged the government's Seditious Writing Act, narrowly escaping gaol.[14] Clearly forming his own troop of cavalry removed all suspicion from him for being 'disloyal'. Loyalism in the case of James Milnes was pragmatic. He had much to lose from revolution at home – he led out his cavalry in 1800 against a food riot – yet barely six months later he was heavily involved in the 1801 Peace Petition. The editor of the *York Herald*, Alexander Bartholoman, made much of the fact that the 'High Sherriff of Yorkshire James Milnes, and Richard Slater Milnes as MP for York had signed the Wakefield Petition'.[15]

Also involved in the peace movement were other members of the corps: John Pemberton Heywood was 'a Cromwellian and leveller' according to slander he reported to the Marquis of Rockingham in 1784; Thomas Lumb would lead the anti-war protests of 1801 and 1808 and was a committee member for the Whigs at the 1806 and 1808 general elections. Indeed, sixteen of the fifty troopers in the unit can be identified as attending Westgate Unitarian Chapel in Wakefield and supporting anti-war liberalism.[16] In May 1803, Milnes gave £1,000 to clothe and equip the Wakefield Troop of West Riding Yeomanry, amongst the officers of which was his nephew, Daniel Gaskell.[17] Barely six months later, at the end of 1803, James Milnes feared that in order to pay for the huge expansion of the Army and Navy, taxes would increase which would result in rioting breaking out. Milnes feared that the war would cripple the economy, and moreover, given the failure of the Flanders Campaign, the war was 'as good as lost'. He opined to Rev Wyvill:

> We shall engage in continental expeditions, in which if we are unsuccessful, we may be ruined, then we will be easy prey to invasion – Indeed which either way I cast my eyes, I can see little else but ruin before us. If Providence should again interfere on our behalf & secure negotiations for Peace we shall have great reason to rejoice.[18]

Milnes' participation in the Yeomanry was, we suppose, to present an outward display of loyalism, whilst privately hoping for peace and a Whig administration.

Milnes was clearly a complex character. He neatly shows the complexity which abound about being able to neatly define participants in the Volunteering system into 'Patriots' as Linda Colley and others suggest. Far more research is needed on the officers and men and their motivations before we can pigeonhole them as Patriots cum Nationalists.

In Bolton, a town with both a parish church and Unitarian chapel, John Pilkington of the latter place cooperated with the Anglicans and members of the Orange Order in the locality – the Rev. Ralph Fletcher being centre stage here – to set up a Volunteer corps. Pilkington would command the cavalry contingent.[19]

As we noted earlier, self-made man John Buddle, who would command the Wallsend Volunteer Rifles, attended Hanover Square Unitarian Chapel in Newcastle. His congregation had been attacked in 1792 during a 'Church and King' burning of an effigy of Thomas Paine, and was fire-bombed in the spring of the following year for the minister Rev. William Turner junior's support for peace and the ideals of the French Revolution. Buddle would have been very aware of the social stigma he faced for being a Unitarian, considered something of a Jacobin and as a self-made man and not 'establishment' or even a gentleman. His participation, like his loyalism, was clearly pragmatic.[20]

In Leeds, the 'Loyal Leeds Volunteers' formed two battalions, one for Anglicans and the second for Unitarians and other Dissenters. The Dissenters' battalion was headed by Samuel Hamer Oates, a stalwart of Mill Hill Unitarian Chapel:[21] as with James Milnes, his 'joining up' was fuelled by patriotism as well as an ostentatious display by Leeds Unitarians, to show that they too were loyal, brought about by the need to get the 'Church and King' mob off their backs. Leeds was unique in having a battalion specifically raised for Unitarians and Independents lead by men from Call Lane Independent Arian Chapel, which was nominally Unitarian. As a leading cloth merchant, along with fellow trustees at Mill Hill like Abimelech Hainsworth, Milnes Raynor and others, Oates had a huge degree of influence over the cloth merchants and croppers in Leeds and its environs.[22] The firm of Messrs Oates, Wood & Smithson linked the families of Samuel Hamer Oates, William Smithson and the Rev. William Wood, who were related through marriage, and the firm of Thursby, Hainsworth and Dunn brought together three chapel trustees![23] At a pro-peace rally held in Leeds in 1801 Oates remarked that the current war, like the American War which he had been a vocal opponent of, would lead to total ruin of the manufacturers, and hoped to live to see public opinion change to be against the war and was 'glad to see the time was come when the friends of peace whom he considered as the best friends of the country, dared assemble to petition their sovereign without the dread appellation of Jacobins'.[24] Yet, in a letter to veteran radical reformer Rev. Wyvill – an erstwhile Unitarian – the Rev. William Wood, the minister at Mill Hill, remarked that the petition had done great harm, and the 'Church and King' mob had renewed their attacks on his congregation and that at nearby Call Lane which were defamed as 'Republicans and Traitors'.[25] Despite this, Mill Hill and Call Lane men took the lead in showing their patriotism: John Bischoff, William Glover and Arthur Lupton of the latter place being officers. From Mill Hill we find Josiah Henry Oates, Benjamin Wilson jnr and George Stansfeld. Thomas Woolwrich Stansfeld took command on the resignation of Oates. In the first formation, it seems the Leeds Volunteers had excluded Unitarians and Dissenters. This is perhaps not a surprise as the Tory–Church of England *Leeds Intelligencer* went as far as to denounce Whigs as being Jacobins, and labelled their supporters as 'free thinkers, rabble rousers and Presbyterians'.[26] The Oates, father and son, resigned in 1807, so too Arthur Lupton and George Stansfeld – all anti-war liberals and Whigs. Participation of Unitarians was clearly transitory.

In Belper, the Strutt family, who dominated the Unitarian chapel for over three centuries, came forward in 1803. Joseph Stutt was nominated Lieutenant-Colonel and his son Captain, with the Rev. Bradshaw, the perpetual curate of Holbrook, as Major, and his son Joseph as clerk. We met the Rev Bradshaw earlier. Commissions were signed 31 October 1803. The Strutts' coming forward was an act of 'realpolitik'. Joseph and William Strutt of Belper Unitarian Chapel, aided by Ward and Darwin, had formed the Derby Society for Political Information, its membership being drawn largely from the middle class, and the Derby Literary and Philosophical Society, which included the radical Henry Redhead Yorke. In a repeat performance of the Priestley Riots, loyalist opposition to reform burned the library and home of William Strutt in November 1792. The loyalist mob blocked up the waterwheel so that the mill race overflowed and virtually destroyed the family-owned mills. By May 1793 the Strutts had withdrawn from radical politics, such was the backlash from loyalist mobs.[27] By being the leading light in the Belper Volunteers, Joseph Strutt showed that he too was patriotic and loyal, and no doubt get the mob off his back and his congregation before the troubles of 1792–3 could happen again.

A similar story is true of Halifax, where in 1792 the Unitarian congregation had been over-awed into supporting Loyalist burnings in effigy of Tom Paine.[28] In 1803 we find the General Committee to form the Halifax Volunteers included Dr Disney Alexander, Rawdon

Briggs, Robert Swaine, William Kershaw and John Priestley.[29] These men were all trustees of, or attended, the aforementioned Northgate End Unitarian Chapel.[30] Indeed, nominal Unitarian Law Atkinson was Captain Commandant of the Huddersfield Armed Association cavalry. As a Unitarian supporting abolitionism – the former slave Olaudah Equiano was a personal friend – and democratic ideals, he was also a proponent of laissez-faire economics and the end of restrictions on the use of machinery. Despite his undoubted display of loyalism, at the height of the invasion crisis of 1803 he was denounced as a traitor and spy.[31] Clearly, the doctrine of Burke that said 'Unitarians are traitors' was alive and well in 1803, even when Unitarians had made conspicuous displays of loyalty through the Volunteers! By simply not being 'good Anglicans', Unitarians would never be accepted by 'Church and King'.

Ostentatious displays at times of national emergency and the emergence of 'National Defence Patriotism', ironically never really dissipated the charges levelled at the start of the decade that radicals and Unitarians were 'traitors' and akin to 'fifth column collaborators' especially when espousing peace. Conflicting visions of 'Britishness' between Unitarians and Church of England Tories within the sphere of Volunteers could be hugely problematical.

On the morning of 28 July 1804, the radical politician Joseph Hanson met John Leigh Philips at Kersal Moor for a duel. Philips commanded of the First Regiment of Manchester and Salford Volunteers, while Hanson led the Manchester, Salford and Stockport Independent Rifle Corps. Hanson's corps mustered two companies more than Philips, and thus he obtained the rank of Lieutenant-Colonel, and claimed authority over other commanding officers in Manchester. Pride and politics were at stake. The Philips family were supporters of the Pitt Club in Manchester and 'pillars of the establishment'. The officers of the First Regiment of Manchester and Salford Volunteers included four borough reeves, who like the Philips family were supporters of the Reevite Association for the Protection of Constitutional Order and Liberty against Republicans and Levellers. Hanson was a Unitarian attending Stand Chapel, had backed petitions against the Gagging Acts in 1795, and was suspected of providing funds to the United Irishmen and their English counterparts. Hanson was a wealthy member of the local elite and was challenging the Anglican Tory monopoly on Mancunian affairs since the riots of 1793 which witnessed the burning of Cross Street and Mosseley Street Unitarian Chapels by 'Church and King' mobs. Hanson was hostile to the elites, and favoured a meritocratic society. The duel reflected the tensions between 'the two sides', with

Hanson being dubbed a 'Democratic Tyrant'. Clearly Volunteering was 'Church and King' only. Hanson, like other Unitarian Volunteer officers, would lead peace petitioning from 1807 into 1808 and back workers' rights over the business owners. Ultimately Hanson was arrested at St George's Fields on 25 May 1808. Hanson's arrest and with memories of the fate of Thomas Walker, many Unitarians chose to 'keep their heads down' through the fear of 'Church and King' violence.[32] As can be easily understood, any societal consensus over 'Britishness' with the invasion scare of 1803 was rudely shattered with the resurgence of 'Church and King' over the 1807 general election to oust the Whig party from power – which sought an immediate peace with France and could have been achieved had it not been for the untimely death of Charles James Fox in September 1806 – which turned to violence in Leeds and Ripon. We are dealing with a short-term sense of 'Britishness' which runs counter to Colley's thesis: she excludes the minority in creating a vision of Britishness based on conservative, Anglican values.

Dissenters and radicals had hoped through conspicuous displays of patriotism by Volunteering to 'pull the rug from under the feet' of the loyalist mobs. For their part, Whig and Unitarian alike felt that they could volunteer to defend one's country and still demand political change and religious freedom, and that, they like loyalists, were patriots. The 'Church and King' loyalists never understood this: one could not be a loyalist and support reform. Yet for many, reform was seen as nothing short of irresponsible Jacobinism. The predicament faced by Unitarians across the country is neatly summed up by the Rev. Charles Wellbeloved, the minister at York Unitarian Chapel:

> we are classed with levellers and regicides, blasphemers of God, and revilers of kings, madly bent upon the destruction of regular government, ready to become plunderers of the property of others, and secretly endeavouring to bring upon our country all those evils which have desolated a neighbouring nation, Good God! to what will not religious bigotry impel men! How does it either darken or destroy the understanding, or sanction the most gross and palpable falsehoods. Have Unitarians then alone no interest in the peace and prosperity of their country? Have they no property to lose? Have they not among their number manufacturers and merchants of the first name and credit, whose whole substance depends upon the preservation of public tranquillity and subordination, and who have, therefore, as powerful motives to support the constitution of the country as any who sits on the episcopal bench? In our sentiments concerning the person of Christ, what is there which necessarily leads us to adopt political opinions, or to engage in political practices, hostile to the peace and welfare of our country?[33]

No doubt Wellbeloved was thinking of the Atkinsons, Milnes, Oates, Woods, Stansfelds, Swaines and Wedgewoods when he spoke of manufacturers and merchants. He continues:

in any other article of our religious faith, what is there that pervert our understanding, and corrupts our hearts, so much as to cause us to prefer violence, tumult, and rapine, to the enjoyment of personal liberty and security, and the unmolested possession of our property Nothing surely in the eyes of the sober-minded and candid. No article in our religious faith produces that depravity which rejoices in the sufferings attending all political convulsions; – nor are we of that needy class which subsists upon the spoils of others. They who have avowed principles at all tending to anarchy, have been neither Unitarians nor Churchmen; – they have been persons of no religion, – persons removed from the influence of that doctrine, which breathes good will to all, and instructs us to live peaceably with all men, we may have had intemperate men amongst us, and their language may, in many instances, have been misapplied and misunderstood; so, it has happened to other religious denominations. We may have had, and still may have amongst us those, who, in their closets, have conceived that the most perfect theoretical form of government is the Republican: – the Church of England has, in her own bosom, persons of exactly the same description. The sentiments of the majority are not to be taken from these; nor can it be decided from the speculative principles, even of such persons, what their political conduct, when tried, would prove. It is certainly possible to consider a Republic as the best form of a government, so far as theory is concerned; and yet to be very sincere friends, and steady supporters of a limited monarchy, which meets the approbation of the majority, and is productive of happiness and security to those who live under it. But whatever may be the speculations of a few individuals amongst them, as a body, I feel no hesitation in affecting, they are firmly attached to that form of government under which this nation has been so long prosperous and happy, And should occasion require it, notwithstanding the unjust suspicions of many of their countrymen, they will be found as ready as any other class of the community in giving it effect, and in warding off the evils of anarchy and levelling principles. Protestant Dissenters have served their country in times of great necessity and danger, and all denominations of them are ready to serve it again.[34]

Wellbeloved was trying to find a middle ground between the likes of the radical Milnes family and also the much more moderate Unitarians who no doubt made up the backbone of most congregations the length and breadth of the county. Yet it was not just Unitarians who were opposed to the war, although they played a prominent part. Independents and Baptists in Leeds, Halifax, Bradford and Huddersfield were also opposed to the war.[35]

So yes, as Cookson argues, 'National Defence Patriotism' was a real force for those excluded from British Liberty, to show they were loyal and to endeavour to remove the stigma of 'Jacobinism' and end attacks on their homes and chapels. However, it was a transitory phenomenon: as soon as the war was seen to be being lost, we find that Unitarians backed the call for peace that began in 1806 with the return of Charles James Fox to government with the death of Pitt, and returned once more to Foxite politics and harsh critique of the government. Prominent leaders of the peace movement included Thomas Lumb who had served in the 'Wakefield Independent Cavalry', and Lieutenant-Colonel Oates of the 'Loyal Leeds Volunteers'.

The Foxites, along with elements of the emerging Industrialists, the urban middle class, Unitarians and some other Dissenters were largely of the same mind about the war: it was unnecessary, morally wrong, economically unsustainable and was causing real suffering at home. The war showed starkly the gulf between the haves and the have notes and the war and peace factions. The idealism of the peace agitators did overlap with working-class agitation against the Crown and elites, and both urged peace on Christian and economic grounds.[36] Unitarians David Hartley and Benjamin Vaughan, urged peace, and understood the war to be 'a crusade of Kings in the cause of despotism'.[37]

The limited participation of Whigs prior to the Levy *en Masse* Act, other than in 1798 which was a crisis point in the war with invasion seeming imminent, was due to a fundamental difference of opinion over the rights and wrongs of the French Revolution. The Act made participation by non-Anglicans and non-Tories inevitable, and therefore the shape and nature of volunteering had to change to accommodate the greatly altered recruitment basis.

Whilst the war was seen as defensive to protect 'hearth and home' these men stood in the ranks alongside their political and religious opponents. loyalism and radicalism were vital parts of the political culture of early nineteenth-century Britain. New Whigs, Unitarians and other Dissenters in supporting the Volunteer movement were 'behaving so ostentatiously . . . as a way of challenging the official description as being traitors and seditionists'.[38] Such participation was fleeting.

Pragmatism was the key for anti-war liberals and Dissenters. In July 1798, the *Leeds Intelligencer* ranted that any men professing Whig tendencies were supporters of a:

a creed well adapted to Republican Government; and essential to the evidence of Democracy, the majesty should be the people . . . is wholly incompatible with Monarchy . . . the annihilation of our present constitution . . . originated in the inflammatory outpourings . . . of Mr Fox and his party made such declarations that sowed the seeds of discontent in every cottage and secretly fanned the flame of faction in every cottage.[39]

With such hatred towards Whigs shown by the Tories and 'Church and King' mob, one can see why some Whigs simply 'kept their heads down', or made ostentatious shows of patriotism.

By joining Volunteer forces, anti-war liberals and non-Anglicans sought to display their patriotism to end persecution by the mob. It was politically expedient when the country was felt to be in danger to 'defend the nation'. Any such concept quickly evaporated when it became clear the war was being lost after the battles of Austerlitz and then Jena, and the economic collapse brought about the Continental blockade and the Crown's own trade embargo with America through Orders in Council which destroyed the economy, resulted in Whigs, radicals and Dissenters stepping back from supporting the war and put their energies into a renewed democratic offensive to bring about peace and reform starting in 1806 with the death of Pitt. We see across the West Riding the resignation of Unitarians from Volunteer units and their return once more to be community leaders agitating for peace. 'National Defence Patriotism' as a unifying force that cut across political and religious boundaries was fleeting and existed for perhaps no more than 18 months.

With the end of consensus over the war, and open criticism by Foxites and Unitarians, the *Anti-Jacobin Review* and the other Tory press began a campaign against Unitarians participating as Volunteers, because in spite of their public shows of patriotism, their opposition to the Anglican Church by seeking to abolish the Test and Corporation Acts as well as supporting democratic ideals, undermined the moral of Volunteer corps.[40] Basically, Unitarians were not welcome to join because they were not loyal or British as they questioned the rationale for war. Whigs and any who opposed the government were branded Jacobins and therefore disloyal.[41] Indeed, Lord Milton, Whig MP for Yorkshire, was slandered as 'the King of Jacobins' by the Tory Press.[42]

The peace petitions of 1801, 1808 and 1813 were the largest mass-participation democratic movement in the country. In 1801 ultimately, over 42,000 freeholders of the West Riding of Yorkshire signed the petitions for peace out of approximately 50,000.[43] In 1808, the three petitions in the West Riding generated 60,000 signatures, with some 28,268 in Leeds alone.[44] On 1 March, 10,000 people assembled at the cloth hall in Huddersfield, the meeting being chaired by Thomas Haigh, with addresses given by John Platt, a woollen manufacturer from Saddleworth, and Ben Ingham, the leader of Lockwood Baptist Church. Some 20,000 signatures were collected for peace.[45] In Bingley, out of a population of 2,580 people, the petition attracted 2,542 signatures and from Liverpool headed by William Roscoe came a petition of 15,000 signatures. Iron founders in Yorkshire and Derbyshire submitted a petition that had gathered 29,000 signatures on 20 June 1808.[46] A petition started in January 1808 at Bolton Unitarian Church amassed 17,000 signatures in favour of peace.[47] In Rochdale and Oldham the petition gathered 36,000 signatures, Manchester 50,000 and Bolton 18,000.[48] Over 200,000 signed petitions for peace (more than double the number of Volunteers and Local Militia under arms that year), gave up a day or two of work to attend rallies and to get their voice heard for peace. Without shadow of a doubt the war was hugely unpopular, but being 'anti-war' was seen as treasonable by many.[49] The Tory press in Leeds argued that the people were loyalists or traitors, there was no middle ground, and any subject of the Crown who was found to be supporting the peace petitions should be imprisoned.[50] Local leaders of the petition were all Whigs and predominantly Unitarian or Independent, and included former Volunteer officers like Thomas Lumb.

In 1812 and 1813 mass petitions for peace generated a similar level of support. The war was hated by a broad cross spectrum of society; it had flung countless hundreds of thousands into poverty and destitution. The petitions represented the moral feeling of the country, rather than the political differences of the great men of state. The war was a crime of a corrupt government, yet the end of the war seemed at hand along with a general European peace.[51] Whatever notion of a sense of national unity that had existed had evaporated, and the country was divided in a war of ideology.

It is wrong to assume, however, that all Unitarians were anti-war liberals with the resumption of war in 1803. Their anti-Bonapartism, as much as desire to defend the nation, contributed to their change of heart over participation in volunteering and also commitment to Whiggism, or at least Foxite ideals. The Bischoffs of Call Lane, Leeds, are notable in their absence from Whig politics, so too the Luptons, Bywaters and Lucocks; in Sheffield, headed by the loyalist Rev. Benjamin Naylor, the Shores, Staniforths, Palfreymans and Nansons are absent. Indeed, the minster at Upper Chapel, where Joseph Gales and Henry Redhead Yorke had been members, the Rev. Naylor, preached and published a sermon in defence of volunteering in 1803.[52] However, Naylor's loyalism perhaps owed a lot to 'realpolitik' following the arrest of several members of his congregation in 1794 and 1795, and was no doubt assuaging local fears that the congregation were not 'rabid Jacobins' but good 'loyalists' at a time of national emergency. In Wakefield the Naylor family, as well as the Parkhills, drifted to High Anglican Toryism from Whig Unitarianism, over the support for the events in France starting from 1789 shown by Unitarians nationally. Members of the influential Milnes family also distanced themselves from Fox. If anything, as we have observed in an earlier chapter, localism was more important to the country than any overt sense of national unity. The United Kingdom of Scotland, Ireland, England and Wales was not yet 20 years old when Waterloo was fought: no sense of nationhood existed; it came later under Victoria.

The 'national consensus' on Dissent, loyalty and also political reform was markedly different in 1794 than in 1803. The perceived threat from internal dissidents, led primarily by Unitarians, Catholics and men of no faith like Marcus Edward Despard, was by and large removed with the latter's execution for treason in February 1803. Whilst the threat to the nation was seen to be external, internal differences over politics and religion could be overcome, but when that threat as seen to be internal or have dissipated, then old animosity between 'Church and King' and Dissenting Whigs became all the more apparent. As John Cookson notes, the 'National Defence Patriotism was atavistic in its origins, and was 'opportunistic, interested, and conditional' in nature.[53] Volunteering as a nation in arms did not lead to a long-lasting broad consensus and the creation of nationhood: violence over religion and politics broke out in 1807, and culminated in Peterloo.

Chapter 17

# A PUBLIC NUISANCE?

As our chapters have shown, volunteering was for multiplicity of reasons. The Volunteers' use as an armed extension of the law in summer 1795 had proven their worth. Indeed, the 1795 food riots had been a baptism of fire for the Volunteers and Yeomanry, who had done their duty. Recruited from the middle class and the better-educated working class, the Volunteers, as had been the government's intention, were embedded in the moral economy as property owners. In theory, this made the Volunteers 'immune' from working class rights consciousness, and with property to defend, would stand forward against their own townsfolk: this was not always the case, as we shall see later. In comparison, the Militia, drawn from the urban and rural poor, shared the sentiments and concerns of their class: men from the Gloucestershire, South Hampshire, Northampton and Hereford Militias took part in the food riots in sixteen different locales. The Oxfordshire Militia court-martialled two of its members who were summarily executed by firing squad for mutiny. Class consciousness knew no boundaries, whether being a part-time soldier or not. With the expansion of the Volunteer system from 1797, the changing nature of volunteering and its recruitment base deeply affected the efficiency of the various corps.[1]

The expansion of the Volunteer forces in 1797 and the consequential changing demographics of the corps, demonstrates the complexities of volunteering, beyond the simple hypothesis that the Volunteers represented the patriotic will of the nation. Being paid to be under arms allowed the urban poor to participate: it broadened the recruitment base from a narrow property-owning middle class. The working class brought with them their culture and ideology which differed from the property owners: by and large the working-class soldiers joined up for pay, a pair of shoes, and a shirt and trousers as our previous chapter explored. These men carried with them a developing sense of 'rights consciousness' and class solidarity, which included the idea of a 'moral economy'. From the sixteenth century, riot and crowd protest was one of the few ways in which the majority felt the political elite would listen to their demands. Thus, it should be no surprise that the working-class members of the Volunteer corps carried with them their 'rights consciousness' to use protests and riots in order to regulate and protect what they saw as their rights as volunteer part-time soldiers. The Volunteers and their actions are thereby representative of a larger set of working-class ideas and practices that might otherwise remain hidden to historical inquiry. The ideals of the illegal combinations – prototype trade unions – were carried over into the Volunteers. It is notable that in May 1800, several members of the Bilston Armed Association said that they had joined the corps in order to protect their King and constitution, and not 'to give Security to the inhuman Oppressor, whilst the Poor are starving in the midst of Plenty'.[2] In Staffordshire, one Volunteer unit disbanded at the height of the food riots in 1800, rather than participate in a persecutory fashion.[3]

Not every Yeoman was 'respectable' or 'middle class'. Sergeant Crossley of the Wath Wood Squadron of the West Riding Yeomanry Cavalry was tried by court martial for the theft of a silver spoon from the Red Lion Public House in Rotherham, the theft of a hat and stealing coal and in consequence the 'forfeiture of the character becoming a British Volunteer and the associate of men armed for the defence of their country'. On 21 January 1808, the court found Crossley not guilty on all charges but, disgusted at his victimisation by the officers, he resigned from the troop the same day.[4]

## Jacobins

The fear of an English revolution was writ large in 1797 with the Spithead and Nore munities in the Royal Navy. The United Irishmen and their English brethren had some degree of involvement. The leader of the Nore mutineers, Richard Parker, was in contact with the United Englishmen and delegates from France. The Crown feared that the land forces were similarly infected with Revolutionary and Jacobin intent. It would be foolish to imagine that Volunteers, in essence armed civilians, were immune to the Rights of Man, as well as to the aims and objectives of the radical movement the United Englishmen or the reformist politics of Major John Cartwright.

These fears were not groundless. For many radical groups, the 'call to arms' issued by William Pitt in raising Armed Associations and additional Volunteer corps was a golden moment for the United

Englishmen and those of a similar mindset to join the Volunteers, arm themselves and learn how to drill and 'bring about a revolution', according to Samuel Patterson, an informer for the Manchester magistrates.[5] His fears were echoed by Earl Fitzwilliam and proven correct during the course of 1812.

In March 1798, Colonel Athorpe in Sheffield had concerns regarding the men he commanded, and he warned the Lord Lieutenant that the men felt themselves 'above the command of the officers'.[6] Jacobin sentiments were being spread by propagandists for the London Corresponding Society – a radical republican group seeking constitutional and political reform – who were allied with the United Englishmen, an underground secret organisation collaborating with the French to invade England and Ireland. History tells us that two of the propagandists were Robert Watson and Henry Fellowes who, with French gold, began an active campaign of subverting soldiers along the south coast. Watson and John Bone also made contact with the mutineers at the Nore.[7] A year later, the Home Office had received alarming reports from across the North of England: members of the republican society in Sheffield had established like-minded groups in Leeds, Bolton, Manchester, Stockport and Bury, members of which were reported to have enlisted in the Volunteers to learn how to handle a musket, how to drill, and gain access to firearms.[8] An officer proposed to command the Leigh Armed Association was discovered to be a member of the United Englishmen when it was formed in 1798.[9] In the following year, a member of the Battersea Armed Association was convicted of likewise being a United Englishman.[10] William Moores and three others in Manchester were arrested following receipt of secret intelligence that they were to 'debauch the minds' of employees of a large factory and of the Little Lever Volunteers.[11] In 1802 one radical 'publically boasted that 100,000 of the military have promised to join them – alluding more particularly to the disbanded Volunteers and the disbanded Militia . . . and that everything thing is perfectly rife for a rebellion in Leeds, Halifax and Wakefield'.[12] Nevison Scatcherd, of Morley in the West Riding of Yorkshire, reported 'It appears that there are frequently nightly meetings of considerable numbers of people on which occasions they are marshalled in military order' and added that they 'have manifested a person taking command and are appointing inferior officers to drill by squads . . . '.[13] In a letter to Earl Fitzwilliam, magistrate and Colonel of 1st West Riding Militia John Dixon informed the Earl that he was convinced that ex-soldiers, or serving Volunteers and Militiamen, were in charge of the Black Lamp insurgency.[14] In August 1803 Earl Fitzwilliam informed the Home

Office of men taking unlawful oaths to join the Black Lamp movement, including some members of the army, Militia and Volunteers.[15] In Bradford it was reported by Magistrate Busfield that the 'disaffected' were avidly volunteering to learn the use of arms.[16]

It seems undeniable that the Volunteer corps gave basic military training to would-be insurgents. Clearly, recruiting the urban poor into the Volunteers was dangerous, and as in 1800 could potentially backfire. The fears that the Volunteers were a training ground for radical groups was a consistent worry for the Crown. The Volunteer force was an 'accident waiting to happen'.

## Class Solidarity.

Successive bad harvests meant that in November 1798 the cost of a loaf of bread was at an all-time high of 1 shilling 9d. Bread price rises were always likely to cause riots – and prices did depend on the quality of the harvest. A bad harvest was a harbinger of social disorder. Nationally, government policy was generally to allow market forces to regulate prices, and by 1800, the Assize system was being abandoned in many areas, including London, though other local authorities continued to attempt to keep bread prices down for several decades into the nineteenth century. Many blamed publicly 'Billy Pitt' and 'that old 'ellborn tyrant the King' for the scarcity and dearness of corn.[17]

Huddersfield was the scene of a riot led by women in November 1799: the magistrates called out the Huddersfield Volunteers who arrested two people who were later sentenced to three months imprisonment.[18] It later emerged that the Huddersfield Fusiliers had held a ballot about attending the riot; those that obeyed were called 'the Scum of Country' by their colleagues.[19] Recruited from the working-class, the Volunteers' class loyalty overrode orders from their officers. Members of the Huddersfield Volunteers were publicly expelled and shamed:

Huddersfield, November 26th, 1799.

The Undermentioned Privates of the ROYAL HUDDERSFIELD VOLUNTEERS, not attending PARADE, when, by desire of a MAGISTRATE, the Drums had beat to Arms on Tuesday 19th Inst, (a MOB having seized some corn, which they were selling to the public at reduced prices) were personally applied to by the Officers and refused to attend their Duty.

In consequence of the above Conduct, a MEETING of the OFFICERS has been held, when it was UNANIMOUSLY RESOLVED

To Discharge the Said Privates

As Persons unworthy of Remaining in, or ever after Serving, in the Said Corps.

Benjamin Sykes
Thomas Driver
John Dickenson
Samuel Booth
James Goulter
Richard Gibson
Joseph Lodge.[20]

Sir George Armitage, the Colonel, remarked to Joseph Radcliffe, the local magistrate, that if the corps was called out to act against food rioters in the future, it 'would incur the resentment of the Volunteers,' noting 'he could not . . . be answerable for [their] conduct'.[21]

A similar event occurred in Sheffield in September 1800, but with far greaert consequences, during a food riot in the town. Earl Fitzwilliam notes that on arrival in Sheffield, he found Lord Effingham, Colonel of the Loyal Sheffield Volunteers was:

> already on the spot, and expressing to the magistrates, his great anxiety, that in case they should see occasion for requiring military assistance, the Sheffield Volunteers should be call'd upon <u>first</u>. But already an opinion prevailed among the principal gentlemen of the town and no less among the officers of the regiment that there would found a considerable degree of backwardness among the privates to act on the occasion: indeed it was strongly suspected that considerable numbers of Volunteers, foreseeing the probability of being called out, had purposefully left the town in the morning . . . as soon as the Blues had paraded, Ld Effingham beat to arms: I am sorry to say with little effect during the whole evening, I do not believe above fifty men join'd their colours. Certainly, it would be expecting too much to expect that a muster of a corps of [illegible] suddenly call'd would not be very incomplete, many reasonably would be away from home on their ordinary occupation . . . the danger and difficulties of attending to parade: not a Volunteer could make the attempt without being boo'd and hissed. Three men were most seriously wounded and others escaped by the accidental passing of the parties of the cavalry.[22]

Fitzwilliam felt that circumstances beyond the men's control had affected the muster, but Lord Effingham and the magistrates would have none of Fitzwilliam's conciliatory rhetoric. However, as in Huddersfield, the men had held a secret ballot about obeying their orders. Fitzwilliam informed Portland that according to Lord Effingham, the magistrates and principal men of the town had reported to him that the corps was 'infected with Jacobinism' and had held a democratic ballot about attending the muster. The outcome of the ballot was that three-quarters of the 'Loyal Independent Sheffield Volunteers' agreed that they would not support the magistrates if called out: the main reason for the 'thinness of the muster' was the Volunteers' disinclination to disperse a mob composed of their friends and messmates, even their own families, calling for bread. Despite this, Fitzwilliam remained confident that the Volunteers could still be relied upon to act against Jacobinical or similar risings. He also reports that one of the Volunteers who had reported for duty was subsequently set upon by other workmen when he went to his workshop, with 'his head in a tub of water till he was almost drown'd'. Three workmen had been committed for trial for this outrage.[23]

To try and defuse the situation Fitzwilliam urged the magistrates to listen to complaints about the high price of corn and stressed that it would not be helped by rioting as merchants and jobbers would not attend the market. Fitzwilliam furthermore hoped that the situation would be remedied by the large quantity of corn at Hull.[24]

Fitzwilliam's confidence in the Loyal Sheffield Volunteers was misplaced: a week later he wrote to the Earl of Portland that they 'would be as likely to turn their arms against the magistrates as support them in any disturbance'.[25] He lamented that the Volunteers:

> will not act for us . . . we have to rely upon two troops of the Blues and such of the Yeomanry as I can collect . . . which will be the two Rotherham Troops and in case of emergency, the Barnsley Troop, the whole consisting of cavalry. It would be ample for every purpose, if there was not hanging over us, the possibility of some awkward circumstance arriving from the Sheffield Volunteers. In such case the, the want of infantry might be severely felt.[26]

Fearing the Volunteers would open fire on the regulars, Fitzwilliam ordered the East Norfolk Militia up from Doncaster, leaving a detachment of 200 men at Rotherham. Colonel Walker, commanding officer of the Rotherham Volunteers, pledged his word to Fitzwilliam that his men would muster and act in case of emergency in Sheffield, and if needs be against the Sheffield Volunteers.[27] The Rev. James Wilkinson wrote to Portland to inform him that:

> the bad intelligence rec'd from the Major & some other officers of the Sheffield Volunteers of the express refusal of many of the men of that corps to obey the call of their officers to oppose the mob in such attempt, nay it seems probable that a great part of the light infantry & grenadier

190

companies have held meetings among themselves and have entered into formal resolutions to that effect & from the opinion of the officers who have visited the men at their own houses, I fear there is too much reason to apprehend more violent proceedings will ensue than took place last Tuesday & that they will begin tomorrow unless some expedient can be used to prevent them.[28]

Wilkinson added that a great number of handbills urging rebellion because of the high price of provisions had been posted throughout the town. The commander of the Sheffield garrison was concerned that if his entire force was called out, the barracks would be attacked and burned to the ground.[29] Fitzwilliam wrote again to the Home Office on 10 September remarking that:

Colonel Woodthorpe arrived at Rotherham at the hour appointed with the detachment of the East Norfolk Militia: the Rotherham Volunteers under Col. Walker mustered as strong as the notice would permit, almost universally, there was not a hesitation on the part of the corps about acting in anyway they might be required: all the Yeomanry cavalry mustered.[30]

The overwhelming troop numbers allowed the cattle market to pass peacefully but it had been a 'close-run thing'. The fear that the Volunteers could open fire on the magistrates was real enough. Further undermining the magistrates' authority during the riots, it emerged that the Sheffield Armed Association, formed in 1798, when faced with the spectre of being called out to act against their kith and kin, met in an 'illegal meeting' and voted to disband as there had been 'no symptoms of riot or disturbance'.[31] Nor were the episodes in Sheffield and Huddersfield isolated incidents. In Pontefract when the Volunteers were called out to act against a food riot, Lieutenant-Colonel Teesdale Cockell, the officer commanding, realised he faced mutiny. He reported to Earl Fitzwilliam that the Volunteers refused open fire and act to disperse crowds containing 'their particular friends & messmates, perhaps even of their wives & Children'.[32] Benjamin Gott, the Lord Mayor of Leeds, noted that the food riots that took place in mid-September 1800 had been easily put down by the Militia, but bemoaned that he did not have a reliable military force to hand. He opined that the Loyal Leeds Volunteers had proved unreliable and henceforth he had to rely upon the Huddersfield Volunteers,[33] which as we have seen, were far from reliable! Yet what of Gott's Armed Association, in which he held the rank of Captain?

Mutiny was not just a West Riding phenomenon: in November 1800 Rev. Thomas Bancroft received a letter from the Bolton Volunteers and townsfolk saying that they would destroy all buildings housing corn, flour, meal or any other kind of provisions unless action was taken to relieve starvation in the locality.[34] The Volunteers took the side of the starving poor. In North Shields the Volunteers refused to act against their friends and neighbours when called out to suppress food riots. Lord Clifford complained in 1801 that the members of the 'North Shields Volunteer Infantry' felt they had a right to withhold their service from the magistrates in the execution of duties which they disapproved of.[35] In the West Country, the Volunteers were divided over obeying their officers' orders to disperse food rioters. Some of the Volunteers participated in breaking open shops and selling flour and other goods at the previous lower prices. When challenged, the Volunteers stressed their continuing allegiance to the king and the country, but they asked the magistrates to compel the local farmers to sell their wheat in Sidmouth at lower prices. The magistrates ordered all dissenters to give up their uniforms and the magistrates resolved to act decisively to prevent disaffection from spreading to neighbouring towns.[36] Over half of the men refused to continue their service and gave up their arms and uniforms, leaving a compliant and willing core of men ready to do the magistrates' bidding against 'their kith and kin'.[37] In Honiton in Devon, ten Volunteers were expelled for not attending a muster to disperse a food riot.[38] In North Yorkshire the Whitby Volunteers were accused of being in sympathy with food rioters.[39]

The artisan and working-class mutiny in the Volunteers in 1799 and 1800 should have been a stark warning to government about the indiscriminate arming of the population; yet what other course of action had the government got to provide and 'on the cheap' policing force? The presence of large numbers of former Militia and Volunteer Corps members in the 'Black Lamp' conspiracy of 1801–02 should come as no surprise: we are seeing the creation of working-class solidarity and class consciousness. The government had armed and trained tens of thousands of working-class artisans and radicals in the use of arms and tactics.

## Luddism

As with the threat from the United Englishmen, which culminated with the Despard plot, by 1811 it is arguable that the Volunteers and Local Militia had provided the Luddites with basic military training: prior to the attack on Rawfolds Mill, the men were formed into companies and numbered off in military fashion. The same dynamics that drove the mutinies in 1800 were still alive and well in 1812: in both periods economic slump, famine and pestilence drove the working class to acts of extreme violence. Being recruiting from the working class – artisans and labourers – the Local Militia were vulnerable to the forces unleashed by working-class political unrest and solidarity. Major General Stevenson reported about the reliability or not, of the Local Militia and Volunteers in Halifax and Wakefield:

> the Halifax Regt which I inspected last week, are as firm a Regt & as well disciplined as the Troops of the Line, above 700 of them have served their term, & will not re engage, their Officers have [tried] it, the Non Commiss'd Officers say the Men are all Luddites, & will join those disturbers of the Public Peace, your Lordship will receive some reports from the Neighbourhood of Halifax, of a serious nature — here I am obliged to Barrack Troops in the Villages around this place, my head Quarters here is in the midst of these Redressers — I could have reengaged many of the Local if Authorized to have paid them the £2. 20d on the day previous to the Expiration of their Drill, indeed my Lord it is necessary that Lieut Genl Grey should have discretional Powers, to enable him & his Generals to avail themselves of any favorable occurrences. The Local Militia shd have a longer term of Service, & the Age extended to 45 — the Volunteers shd be disbanded or obliged to do the Duty if Piquit with, the Regular Forces in every Market Town, the late Lord Melville told me that, was their duty, & called them Armed Constables, at present they are useless & expensive &, have only entered into that association to avoid the Militia.[40]

Confirming Stevenson's report to the Home Office, history tells us two members of the Halifax Volunteers, Samuel Hartley and John Baines, were involved in the attack on Cartwright's Mill in Liversidge. We also note three 'militia men' were arrested following the arms raid in Sheffield.[41] Corporal Joseph Barrowclough, of the Upper Agbrigg Local Militia was arrested in the early hours of the morning of Friday 3 July 1812: he was a Luddite also named in attacks on Cartwright's Mill.[42] Thus it is hardly surprising that the Local Militia in 1812 were considered totally unreliable by Magistrate William Dawson for taking action against Luddites and other rioters.[43] As in 1800, the magistrates and oligarchy had lost control of the very instruments which they had created to carry out internal policing duties. Recruiting beyond the 'gentlemen' of a town necessitated that artisans and labourer would take part: it set working man against working man, and when 'push came to shove' working-class solidarity overcame other loyalties. The Yeomanry and Gentlemen Volunteers were not so affected by these mutinies, the Yeomanry becoming the primary tool of the magistracy to put down riots as exemplified their deployment against the Luddites in Birmingham, against the mob in Ely in 1816 and at Peterloo. Yet the democratic aspirations of the Volunteers were more widespread than class solidarity.

Chapter 18

# DEMOCRATIC SOLDIERS?

As we touched on in our previous chapter, rather than supporting the magistrates, Volunteers often directly withheld their service. A similar pattern had emerged with the Militia during the food riots of 1795: Militiamen took a leading part in riots in Devon and Gloucestershire, and later in Kent and Sussex. During a riot in Chichester, the Hereford Militia overpowered the civil authorities, releasing rioters in custody and stoning the windows of a tavern in which the magistrates had taken shelter, to release food to the market at a lower price, a scene repeated with a two-day mutiny of the Oxfordshire Militia. Soldiers, like civilians, were not immune to the suffering cause by a cost-of-living crisis.[1]

The very instability of the corps was based on its members and its organisation. Volunteering provided the chance for low-skilled artisans and labourers to rise to NCO rank, allowing a degree of social mobility. The gaining of organisational skills has been shown to be instrumental in the development of working-class identity, and this can be directly linked to participation in the Volunteer corps. By and large it seems that Volunteer corps may well have aided the development of working-class political consciousness. The use of crowd protest and riot was twofold: the 'mutineers' sought not only to protect and observe the customs relevant to themselves as civilians, but also those that they felt were due to them as soldiers, and in particular part-time soldiers. Volunteer officers and the county Lieutenancies were sensitive to signs of disaffection among Volunteers because of the potential consequences of unreliable armed men facing invasion or insurrection.

This was enshrined in the organisation and governances of the Volunteer units themselves. These 'democratic soldiers' alarmed the commentator William Cobbett who through the pages of his influential newspaper *The Political Register* decried that the Volunteers represented a new order in the country through their handbills, pamphlets, subscriptions and democratic committees that was dangerous to 'Church and King' because of the 'mutinous, democratizing and rebellious tendency of the committees and other deliberative bodies, appertaining to the Volunteer's corps, and consisting of its members or of other persons, having authority or influence in the corps'. Cobbett further remarked that committees 'naturally grew out of the system which called upon the people to assemble, and to form an organise themselves into companies and battalions' and noted 'they have done more harm than good'.[2] He continued that the Volunteers were managed by 'a system of government more republican and democratic never yet appeared in the world', noting that management by committee was 'a completely defective system . . . the current principals of which are indeed, so much like those of the corresponding societies, that one cannot scarcely believe them not have originated with someone, who had been in the habit of perusing the rules and regulations of that dangerous combination'.[3] Cobbett chose the word 'combination' deliberately: 'Combinations' were incipient trade unions, banned in 1799 when radical groups like the London Corresponding Society were made illegal and forcibly disbanded. Here, Cobbett was comparing the dangers of Volunteering to that of trade unionism. Ironically, the very forces that the Volunteers sought to defend against – 'Democracy and French Principles' – empowered the Volunteers and gave them a sense of solidarity, and allowed participation in decision-making by the working class and skilled artisans, often for the first time. Confirming Cobbett's suspicions about the latent radicalism within Volunteer units, these democratic principles came to the fore when changes were made to the way in which officers were appointed. Joseph Farrington, who was briefly a member of the Saint Pancras Armed Association, complained that the committee consisted of twelve privates and only three officers, the chairman always being a private, 'Such is the spirit of equality'.[4]

A key aspect of the Volunteer Consolidation Act was the ending of corps electing their own officers and reducing the importance of the committee. Home Secretary Charles Yorke noted in November 1803 that it had never been his attention to allow officers to be elected and sought to end this practice.[5] Officers in the corps prior to the Act had no more power in the corps than any other committee member wielded. Such democratic participation was a vital element in encouraging the middle class to support the Volunteer movement as a whole, and allowed working-class participation in local democracy for the first time.[6] The ending of this privilege aroused much hostility, and shows just how embedded the 'Jacobin' principle of the men electing their officers had become.

Even before the Act came into force, in Sheffield Colonel Athorpe appointed officers as he saw fit and faced the wrath of his men. He opined to Earl Fitzwilliam that:

> for this month past there has been such a misunderstanding betwixt the officers and men of Sheffield Volunteers, respecting Rank and Promotion of the officers for in consequence of some vacancies that I have been under the greatest anxiety least either officers in general would resign or the men would down their arms.[7]

Athorpe had created the problem, and he endeavoured to resolve the issue, which he believed a letter of 8 March had done.[8] The 'Loyal Sheffield Volunteers' as with many hundreds of such corps, echoed the characteristic form of middle-class voluntary societies that managed lending libraries and the local infirmary, dispensary or workhouse: a subscriber democracy funded by its members and townsfolk, and managed by its elected committee and officers, which can be seen as a direct challenge to traditional military service and which was exported through the rapid expansion of the Volunteer movement from 1803. When new officers were appointed in 1799, the regiment was asked to ballot on the nominations.[9] The Colonel of the North Allerton Volunteers felt that the Volunteers' belief in their power to change their officers was not dissimilar to a desire to change the government through the democratic ballot. Such an alarming tendency, the Colonel believed, would lead to perpetual contention between officers and men.[10]

When the Volunteers were re-formed in 1803, the mode of appointing officers changed: they were no longer chosen by the committee and members, but instead by the commanding officer. In disgust at the change, the men of the 'Royal Wakefield Volunteers' argued the change was a 'breach of faith' and threw down their arms on parade in January 1804.[11] Unsurprisingly, the mutineers were classed as 'corrupted dissatisfied . . . Jacobins'.[12]

Matters escalated, and the officers were rapidly losing control of their corps. In what was considered to be an 'illegal' meeting of the light company, grievances in the management of the corps were raised. The men of the company were united in a single intent and voice, and declared that the committee had overstepped the mark in directly appointing officers without consulting the town or corps. The light company declared furthermore 'That the men refused to obey the orders of the officers appointed by the Colonel, and not chosen by the voice of the men of the Corps'.[13]

Furthermore, in order to get their voice heard, the men of the light company proposed that the committee for the management of the corps was to consist of the field officers, a captain and two private men from each company, the privates to be chosen by their companies through democratic process. The men also raised fears that the 'subscriptions' were being used as a means of purchasing commissions without consulting the town or corps, and went against precedent set between 1794 and 1803. The proposition to add gold lace to officers' uniforms and other embellishments to mark them out as superior to the rank and file, also raised the ire of the men of the corps. In consequence, a request was made for the publication of a subscription list and accounts. The demands were all rejected out of hand.[14]

Questioning the conduct of the officers and their management of the unit was tantamount to mutiny: a court of inquiry was held on 11 January 1804, which condemned the motions of the light company. The court named William Batt as the 'ringleader' and publicly declared that his demands 'were mutinous and of disgraceful tendency, and as such were unbecoming of an Englishman and a Volunteer'. The court, unsurprisingly, found Batt and his two co-accused Timothy Beavers and Samuel Wilby guilty of mutiny:

A court of inquiry was held at the Orderly Room by the officers of the Royal Wakefield Volunteers . . . it was unanimously resolved that William Batt of Wakefield, Maltser should be dismissed from the said corps in the most Public and Disgraceful manner, and that Timothy Beavers and Samuel Wilby should also be dismissed the said corps.[15]

The court was a 'stitch-up'. The men did not attend and were not allowed to offer any defence. On 12 January the three men were publicly stripped for their arms and dismissed from the corps, at a special field day held on Heath Common where a drumhead court martial took place.[16] The court was never going to vote in favour of the men: democratic intent and critique of their 'betters' was to be supressed at all costs. This episode raises the question over who the men understood themselves to be, as opposed to the view of the state: soldiers or civilians? The state increasingly took the line these men were soldiers, and no longer the gentlemen volunteers of the 1790s. Cobbett went as far as to ask how it was possible that 'hair dressers, tailors, shoemakers and pastry cooks could regulate the seniority of their officers'.[17] Committees and democracy were dangerous, and such 'little parliaments' were the root cause of the American and French Revolutions.[18] The Secretary of State for War supported the actions of Colonel Tottenham and his officers, applauding:

> the Conduct of Lieutenant-Colonel Tottenham as well as the officers of the Corps in so steady and decidedly resisting the disgraceful and Mutinous resolutions entered into by some of the Men of the Light Company is highly commended, and the punishment inflicted . . . is to be hoped will serve as a proper example . . . Nothing can be more improper than for the privates of Volunteer Corps to Assemble together in that character, without order or permission of their Officers, and when assembled to discuss and determine upon questions intimately connected to the military subordination of the Corps.[19]

However, the dissatisfaction did not end, and Colonel Tottenham published a reward of £50 for the writer of two letters 'with a view to encourage a spirit of dissatisfaction amongst the Corps'.[20] A matter of weeks later, Heath Common was the scene for the re-presentation of the 1794 colours, when the men were inspected by Sir Edward Silvester Smith of Newland Hall, and were wearing new 'regimentals'.[21] Such working-class political agitation was fostered by the structure of Volunteer units and was a reflection of the tensions in society at large in 1803–04, as warned against by Cobbett. By engaging in a club-like organisation, with a degree of empowerment to all ranks through this structure, as well as lessons learned from the Peace Petition of 1801, acting in illegal trade unions – combinations existed in Wakefield for croppers and shoemakers – as well the experience of participation in friendly societies and the creation of a 'common purse', the working-class members of the corps had found that they had a voice when unified in action, and were prepared to act as one. Without their participation, the 'Royal Wakefield Volunteers' would not exist: the power in the corps was with the hundreds of Volunteers and not the handful of officers. Indeed, such strength through unity had led to a county-wide strike between September 1802 and February 1803 in the woollen industry, where the working men agitated against the business owners and managers. The strikers in Leeds won against the merchants and masters, and we see that same scenario being replayed here in the 'Royal Wakefield Volunteers'. This was a very real, and very subversive, threat not just to the nature of Volunteering, but to society at large. Any such working-class agitation and discontent at the management of a

Volunteer corps, and above all, the working class dictating the terms of service to the social elite, had to be crushed. The men wanted to have a say in how their corps was managed: they said we have a voice, we have rights, we demand our voices are heard, and above all said 'without us, this would all come crashing down'. This was Jacobinism in action. One commentator noted:

> Jacobinism having almost totally disappeared from the educated classes has sunk down into the mob: so that since the year 1793, our internal state has undergone as great a change as our foreign relations . . . young men of ardent mind . . . became enthusiastic disciples of a political faith . . . their talk was not merely of the rights of man, but of the hopes and destinies of the human race . . . the populace were incapable of entering into such views: they beheld nothing . . . finding them hostile to the war regarded them as men who preferred France to England, and therefore as enemies to their country. That this was the feeling of the populace twenty years ago is notorious to every one . . . where riots broke out, Church and King was the cry of the mob, and their fury was directed against whom they considered as the enemies of both. Time passed on . . . Every topic is made subservient to the same conclusion that things are bad and must be changed; that corruption must be cut up by the root.[22]

The same Jacobin or democratic tendency prevailed in the Bingley Volunteers as late as 1807. The corps was commanded by Major Wilmer Mackett Willet, and mustered two companies and had its colours presented by Miss Wickham on 15 May 1804.[23] Shortly after the 1807 general election, the corps company sergeant-major refused to acknowledge the new corps commander, Major Currer Fothergill Busfield, as he had not been 'chosen by the voice of the corps'.[24] The offending NCO and others in the corps with the same mind-set were expelled.[25]

Memories of the mutinies of 1800 would still be fresh, and the fear of large-scale mutinies must have caused alarm, especially as in the same month John Crossley of the Staincross Volunteers was arrested for 'riotous and unlawful behaviour' in encouraging sedition and mutiny amongst his regiment.[26] Several drummers and fifers of the 'Glasgow Highland Volunteers' were charged with 'disobedience of orders . . . with conducting themselves in a riotous and disorderly manner, tending to mutiny', each man being sentenced to thirty lashes.[27] In the Fakenham corps, a private was 'drummed out' of the corps with a 'halter around his neck' for disorderly behaviour.[28] In November 1804, a private man in the Bradford Volunteers was convicted of deliberately damaging his musket and uniform, and fined 20 shillings by the magistrates.[29]

In New Year 1805 when the 'Loyal Ripon Volunteers' were asked to carry out more than the regulation 20 days training as stipulated in the Volunteer Act, the Colonel found himself faced with vocal opposition from the officers, who declared they were 'citizens and not soldiers'.[30] Problems re-surfaced in April 1805, when the offending officers in January 1805 again disobeyed orders from Lieutenant-Colonel Wood. Captain Charnock, and Lieutenants John Charnock and Hodgson were charged by the Colonel:

> for disobeying the orders of Lieutenant-Colonel Wood their commanding officer, & willfully intending & declaring their determination so to do for disrupting the authority of their commanding officer and using improper and unofficier like language to him in the presence of the officers of the regiment and thereby endeavouring to weaken his authority as commander thereof.[31]

Lieutenant-Colonel Wood was happy for Earl Fitzwilliam to act as intermediary to resolve the situation.[32] The accused officers agreed to abide by Fitzwilliam's judgement.[33]

The case hinged on the fact that whilst on parade the three officers refused to accept Lieutenant-Colonel Wood ordering the regiment to undertake more than 20 days service a year, and vocally spoke out against the Colonel in front of the men. The three officers were placed under arrest, and the case was to be heard by a court of inquiry.[34] Whilst stripped of command, the officers were forbidden from wearing their uniforms, until such a time as the court made a judgement, but all three broke the terms of the court and appeared in 'their regimentals' at the next parade. The court found the three officers' guilty of disobeying orders twice, and Lieutenant-Colonel Wood was found to have acted illegally in ordered more than 20 days service and arresting officers without a court martial.[35] They were suspended pending a Home Office board of inquiry, which reinstated all four.[36]

As well as the appointment of officers causing local disagreements, the status of the officers also caused resentment. Tempers flared in the troubled 'Royal Wakefield Volunteers' over uniforms. The corps formed in 1794 dressed officers and men identically, save for rank stripes for the NCOs. Officers' coats were devoid of gold lace and other embellishments except epaulettes denoting their rank. In the re-formed corps, however, officers applied gold lace to their coats in imitation of the Foot Guards. The rank and file were incensed, and

201

demanded that the gold lace was removed. The matter was taken to the Lord Lieutenant.[37] Wealth and social status mattered little in the Lutterworth Volunteers which stipulated 'the Uniform of every Volunteer of whatever the rank be in all respects the same'. The men assumed that enlistment in the corps was a social leveller, and that there would be a certain degree of equality. The matter does not seem to have raised the same degree of objection as in Wakefield.[38]

One of the reasons that the Volunteer system was heavily criticised for its democratic construction and plebian membership, was that the committees, often comprising artisans and tradesmen and not gentlemen, were responsible for admission of members and distribution of funds as well as subscriptions. This took responsibility from the officers and undermined the moral economy and social contract of the era, as it elevated the comparatively lowly to positions where they had as much influence and power as a gentlemen. The Volunteer corps were administered on the very Jacobinical and democratic principles they sought to fight against! Cobbett argued that if 'these democrats' could raise funds and form committees for charitable purposes, nothing stood in their way of petitioning the King to make peace or to change his ministers and generals: such actions were disloyal as they questioned the King, which was sedition if not high treason. These 'seminaries' of high treason had to be contained, otherwise they would heartily join with the clubs in America and France and destroy the government.[39] Loyal Addresses to the King were liable to abuse, it was feared, and allowed the common people to petition the King and have a stake in government.[40] Lord Hobart accepted that when the Volunteer corps were first formed, election of officers was within the terms of the constitution as they were civilian organisations, yet as soon as a corps became embodied, they came under military control and thus elections after embodiment 'were unconstitutional and mischievous'.[41] Critics of the Volunteer movement felt it gave too much power to the committees and private men. The Wakefield mutineers' actions had resulted in official statements from Whitehall that changed the very nature of the contract between officers, men and committees. The Volunteer corps were becoming markedly more military.

Two further examples from the West Riding illustrate this point. In 1804 an alarming incident occurred involving the Halifax Volunteers and a local clergyman, the Rev. Christopher Atkinson, which was raised at national level with the Lord Lieutenant and the War Office. The trouble arose over the Sabbath. Atkinson, the son of the Rev. Miles Atkinson, the founder of St Paul's Church Leeds in 1812, was an evangelical Sabbatarian and declared that no work or similar activities were to take place in his parish on a Sunday. It therefore came as no surprise that he openly condemned the Sunday drilling of the Halifax Volunteer corps: at a meeting of the Elland Parish Church Vestry, he urged those men in the unit who supported his scriptural position to petition their officers not to abuse the Sabbath. When petitioning failed, Atkinson told the men to disobey their officers – an act of mutiny! Handbills were published saying at a future vestry meeting Atkinson would further inform the Volunteers how to proceed against their officers. Earl Fitzwilliam wanted Atkinson indicted for sedition, but the War Office advised against prosecution. Atkinson's action was prompted by his evangelical Sabbatarianism, which to Lieutenant-Colonel Horton, the commanding officer, the priest's conduct was 'highly seditious and inflammatory'. Subsequent to this episode Atkinson preached a sermon which condemned the Halifax Volunteers who partook of drill on the Sabbath and any spectators 'to eternal punishment'.[42] The 'Church and King' mob had turned against the Volunteers in Elland, when they no longer supported the fickle moral economy of the day. Yet in York, it was suggested to move the time of evening service on a Sunday to allow the Volunteers to drill, as a great number of people went to watch the spectacle rather than attend divine service, and the drill time prevented the Volunteers attending church also: if they defaulted on attending drill parade, they paid a fine. Indeed, one commentator noted:

> if the corps were regularly marched after the parade was over to Divine Service (suppose a company to one church, dismissing those who are not of the Church of England, if they request it) it would show such a determined resolution on our parts to put our trust in the Almighty as could not fail of producing beneficial effects; besides many who have hitherto lived totally alienated from public worship, might be gradually impressed with a knowledge of divine truths, rendered better members of society, and being prepared for an happy eternity, would bless the fay which they first took up arms to defend the country.[43]

Clearly, pragmatism was the order of the day in York and not in the Halifax area!

It was at the initial period of formation of any corps when the committee was at its most important in raising subscriptions though combined self-righteous appeals to the public aligned with intimidation: 'if you don't contribute, you're a traitor', one suspects was a common theme in both signing declarations of loyalty and in giving funds to the cause in some cases. Volunteer corps believed they were providing a public service of sorts, the expense of which should not be borne by the Volunteers alone, but by the local area in which they were based. The spending of this money was hotly contested, especially when after the initial flurry of activity, officers tended to dominate the distribution of funds. The onus was placed not on those who donated but on those who did not join up or contribute funds.

Money and ownership of uniform also raised concerns. If a man had paid into his corps subscription to purchase uniforms and equipment, surely therefore it could be reasonably argued that they belonged to he who had paid? In 1806 William Moore, a private in the Pontefract Volunteers, was gaoled for seven days for not handing in his uniform and accoutrements following 21 days' service.[44] In the Sheffield Local Militia the same grievances appeared in 1809 about men having to return to the regimental depot shirts and shoes that they had bought with their marching guinea to replace worn-out shoes the corps had provided.[45]

Grievances over money and how it was spent was the basis for the mutiny of the Halifax Troop of Yeomanry: the complaint raised by the private men was that Captain William Ingram was defrauding the corps of money and presenting false accounts. The troopers also attested that the troop was incomplete, and that in supplying the corps with accoutrements Ingram was selling them on to the troop at a profit. The men of the troop also stated that Ingram had embezzled four days' marching pay. A court of inquiry was set up comprised of Sir John Lister Kaye, the commandant of the Corps, Hall Plummer Esq, Colonel of the Ainsty Volunteers as president, Major Staniforth of the North Yorkshire Yeomanry, Major Hawksworth of the Wharfdale Volunteers, Captain Cockshott of the Craven Legion and Captain Cookson of the Leeds Volunteers.[46] The board of inquiry found Ingram innocent.[47] The following men were dismissed from the troop for misconduct and publicly shamed by orders received from Whitehall dated 18 October 1805: Joseph Walker, Benjamin Milnes, John Hodgson, James Staveley, Thomas Preston, William Ewell, James Goodall, Charles Thomas Priestley, John Matthewman, Joseph Armytage, Joseph Waddington, Joseph Bates, Thomas Sladen, Samuel Crowther, John Swift and John Patchett.[48] The troopers cum private men, in questioning the actions of their superiors, were 'having ideas above their station': the men clearly felt aggrieved and had the power and recourse to issue such a claim through solidarity and idealism of the democratic principle in overturning the moral economy.

The maintenance of discipline was far from easy due to the Volunteer corps' club-like structure and organisation. Officers relied on their social influence to manage their corps, and had few or no penalties available with which to discipline the men. Indeed, Volunteers were not subject to the Mutiny Act unless on active service. The early Volunteers decided for themselves how many drills they had to attend; but as government intervention increased from 1797, new terms were set for them if they were to be able to claim the government's incentive of pay and uniforms. Under the August 1803 allowances, Volunteers could receive pay for a maximum of 20 days' drill a year. Thus, we find in the newspapers posters for men deserting from active service. The nature of the men's employment did not always make it possible for men to attend or pay the resulting fine for nonattendance. Going AWOL was the only solution. A wanted man in the Skyrac Volunteers for desertion whilst on 21 days' active service was Serjeant-Major Robert Adamson, who absconded without permission.[49] Whilst on active service, the body corporate of the Wath Wood Volunteers mutinied. Commanded by Major Francis Ferrand Foljambe and Lieutenant-Colonel Samuel Walker, the corps had been formed in September 1803, and had been armed in New Year 1804.[50] When on the march to Pontefract the recently-appointed regimental colonel, who had not yet built up ties of loyalty with his men and officers and relied on his social position to maintain discipline, realised that he could not keep the men quiet: he had given orders for the men to refrain from talking or singing on the march. So angry at his men refusing to obey his direct orders, he threatened to drill them as a punishment. In response to this threat of punishment, a drill sergeant broke ranks and with great temerity informed his superior that he had overheard some men threatening to shoot the officers if the punishment was applied. The colonel seems to have been something of a 'hothead' with a 'short fuse' and despite the warning went ahead in ordering the punishment. In consequence a mutiny occurred with the men refusing to obey their officers and throwing down their arms. The officers were desperate to identify the ringleaders, but the men closed ranks and refused to name them: 'They'll owe us a grudge for't when we get home'. The timing of the event seems to have been crucial as the men faced no reprisals for their actions: the mutiny occurred when the Volunteers were being encouraged to transfer into the Local Militia. Because of this extenuating circumstance, nothing more was said of the event as the corps was 'on its death bed'.[51] Internal discipline also fell afoul of class solidarity. Officers frequently admonished their men, often resulting in resentment and hostility from the rank and file. In the troubled Sheffield Volunteers, a lieutenant ordered his men to refrain from talking in the ranks. Nearly all the men obeyed. Rather than punish the defaulters, the Lieutenant punished the entire company. Disobeying direct orders on parade was technically mutiny. The men protested at this 'rough justice', and in consequence, the Colonel addressed the men and told them it was improper to disobey orders. The Colonel reprimanded the Lieutenant, chastising him that he would be more esteemed by the company by apologising for confounding the innocent and guilty with the same punishment. Richard Effingham, the Colonel, suggested that the young Lieutenant was to give each man a pint of ale. In recompense, each man received 1 guinea and an apology.[52]

Being placed under military law made members of the Local Militia liable to be tried for desertion if not able to attend the 14 days compulsory service. The Wakefield Local Militia, called to Doncaster in April 1811 for their 21 days' training, reported John Chappel of Alverthorpe, John Clark of Sharlston, David Firman of Soothill, John Hirst, George Oldroyd, and Charles Swithenbank, all of Mirfield, David Hollis and Joseph Kinder of Holmfirth as deserters. They had to pay a £20 fine if caught and be punished as deserters.[53] In December 1811 Stephen Hardy, a private in the Morley Local Militia, was sentenced to 12 months' imprisonment for desertion.[54]

Disciplinary issues affected other regions. The 'Melton Mowbray Volunteer Infantry' raised in September 1803 was dismissed in June 1804 for 'gross misconduct'. A new corps was formed, but it too was dismissed in autumn 1806.[55] In St Albans, 300 members of the Hertford Local Militia mutinied over pay and conditions. This was one of thirteen similar incidents that year.[56]

Mutiny and questioning their social betters made Volunteer units a subversive presence. They fostered democratic principles; yet the force could be, and was, used for intimidation and political ends. Worrying for the authorities was the potential for large numbers of armed and trained men to use their muskets and training against the state for radical ends. After their success in putting down the 1795 food riots, the Volunteers became more of a burden than a help to the magistrates. The loyalty of the men in urban corps recruited from the working classes was to their kith and kin and not to their officers. John Cookson termed this a 'Soldiers Republic':

Wellington's 'scum of the earth' remark (made in-house) merely said brazenly what officers commonly said, and kept on saying well into the nineteenth century. Soldiers drawn from the classes of the poor belonged to the culture of the poor.[57]

206

Slow to mobilise, and often troublesome, it is remarkable that the Volunteer system was resorted to in 1803, but what other options did Addington have other than a massive expansion of the unpopular Militia? The failure of the Volunteers led directly to the more formalised Local Militia.

## Merely for Money?

As the previous chapters have shown, five major themes can be identified for reasons why Volunteers joined up in the period 1794–1802: localism, civic pride, politics, religion and nationhood. Indeed, the rapid expansion of the Volunteer movement from 1803, has traditionally been understood to be an expression of nationalist fervour. This as we have seen in the previous chapters is partially true. Yet are we missing the most obvious of the motives? Money! Volunteers were paid in most cases for the giving of their time to the state. In 1794 the East Riding Yeomanry objected to 'the smallness of the pay, from which circumstances one may I think infer two things, first they are aware of the Necessity of the Measure and Secondly in return for their Services they expect a valuable consideration adequate at least to the Profits arising from Labour'.[58] In Pontefract, Earl Fitzwilliam was forcibly told that if the men did not get paid for active service, it would result in 'the immediate dissolution of the corps'.[59]

Money was behind a mutiny in May 1796 when 100 members of the deeply-troubled 'Royal Wakefield Volunteers' took action against Colonel Tottenham for withholding their pay for taking part in the suppression of the Knottingley riot.[60] Tottenham resigned, and the committee of the corps inquired if the accusations were true: his resignation might imply guilt. His resignation was not made public, and many gentlemen left the corps with him, active membership dropping from 170 men under arms in February 1796 to 112 by September. It took two months for a new colonel to be appointed: William Rookes Leeds Serjeantson, a Wakefield man who was appointed on 16 September. He had served in the Flanders campaign, his troop of the King's Dragoon Guards suffering from desertion, sickness and injury, and being noted for its lax discipline.[61] Trouble flared again in January 1804 in the 'Royal Wakefield Volunteers' over the marching guinea. The privates felt that they should be paid this sum as they 'had marched out to buy knapsacks and campaign equipment'. Consequently, at a drill parade, a mutiny occurred with chants of 'stand for your guineas, or down your arms'.[62] When asked to serve beyond the district the rank and file resisted. The reason given was because the pay offered by the government for active service was far less than they would have received for a day's work, and they argued that if they were to be called out, they wanted exactly the same day's wages as if they had been at work. The men proposed that the difference in the money received for active service and the lost days' wages to come from a 'general purse'. The demand was dismissed out of hand.[63]

For a middle-class, plebian organisation like the Royal Wakefields, recruited from artisans, shopkeepers, hairdressers and other professions as we have discussed in a previous chapter, this exposed the weakness of the Volunteering system: many only acted because they were paid and only if the pay was equal to the value of their time. It is undeniable, however, that volunteering had other perks beyond pay: Yeoman were exempt from horse tax, and all Volunteers and Yeoman from paying tax for powdering their hair. In October 1798 Thomas Berry of the Aylesbury Troop withdrew his horse from Yeomanry service and was at once informed that his tax exemption was null and void. To make matters worse, Berry was also told he was in arrears for paying for his uniform and equipment. In August 1803 Henry Chisholm complained to Lord Grenville that he had been accused falsely of wearing hair powder without paying the required tax. He requested a certificate of his Yeomanry service to silence his detractors. Volunteers and Yeoman were furthermore exempted from turnpike tolls when uniformed and on exercise.[64] Substantial cost savings could be made by Volunteering, as well as being exempt from the Militia ballot!

It has often been assumed, that this English national or British patriotism was spontaneous and is directly analogous to the National Guard regiments and other volunteers formed in French communities during 1793–4, in Spain from 1807, and nascent Germany in 1813. It is far too simple to see in the upswell in volunteering from 1803 as the creation of a national identity and consequent fostering of nationalism. Volunteering was not synonymous with loyalism or nationalism. Traditional understanding of this process would have us believe the country was united behind Henry Addington, and was 'champing at the bit' to fight the French to defend 'hearth and home'. Yet, against this cogent argument, we are confronted by the testimony of Francis Ferrand Foljambe, Magistrate and Colonel of the West Riding Yeomanry, dated 21 June 1803:

> I am sorry to say, both from the little observations I have been able to make & from the opinion of some of those I met yesterday, there does appear a degree of apathy and indisposition towards any active measures of defence, that I think more alarming taken all the preparations of the enemy.[65]

A week later he reported to Earl Fitzwilliam that:

> there appears to be an apathy and disinclination towards any exertion . . . it seems to pervade all ranks from the Country Gentlemen to the Labourer. Whether it is that they do not feel the danger or that the protracted Peace of Amiens & the language held by ministers and their speeches want of energy seem to have dampt all military ardour . . . or whether the riches & luxury of the country have got that suspicion of our hearts that we only think of Calculating the expence of defence against the requisitions that might be required by the First Consul of France . . . I do not like the present appearance of things . . . if a different spirit cannot be informed into the people we must undergo the fate of the rest of Europe.[66]

It was not only in Yorkshire that opinion was against, or at least apathetic to, war: M. Luttock of London wrote to his friend in India on 11 July 1803:

> TRADE is entirely stopt, and I fear soon to see revived the disagreeable circumstances which occurred in 1793; for money is very scarce, and confidence decreases daily; so that, except the really good and established houses, none will be able to stand: and even the former will find themselves embarrassed; for unless they can dispose of the goods in their possession, how will they be enabled to make good their payments? In fact, circumstances have never appeared so alarming. The war is certainly not popular; or, perhaps, I should be more accurate in saying, that there is no confidence in the abilities of the present Administration to conduct it with success.[67]

At the same time as the working class and the poor largely opposed the war, so too did swathes of the middle class, fearing a new downturn in trade. A handbill posted in Bradford declared:

> we are to observe that our rulers seem to indicate that the Chief Consul in France is nothing better than a committer of Robberies, Murders & Rapes, and shou'd he succeed in his attempt upon this Island, he'd reduce it to a state of Beggardom. Pray my friends, wou'd he reduce it lower than it is? Where does beggardom originate? . . . To begin with, our supposed invader he has arisen from a very low and obscure rank and birth (yet no lower than Moses who released Legions of people from their Shackles), and according to his time of life, has perform'd wonders . . . Foolish Britons, don't think that your powerful armies you have so wrongfully amassed together from the sweat of the labourers brow can save you from the wickedness of being avenged . . . The great

men seem to say this is a very alarming crisis. The poor who will be found to be the strength of the nation, don't seem to be alarmed, their general cry is Let BONAPARTE COME, how can we be worse.[68]

In such a climate where hundreds of thousands might have flocked to aid Napoleon's forces had he come across the Channel, it is hardly surprising that we see from summer 1803 a change in the media campaign towards the war, driven no doubt by government and elite attitudes. The Tory war faction, as Foljambe eloquently put it, wanted to change public perception: War was good and Napoleon – therefore inter alia democracy, freedom of religion and rights consciousness – was evil. We still grapple with this propaganda construct in current times. We are seeing, as Cookson points out, the creation of something fleeting and transitory, that was fed by the Tory press machine, the creation of the black legend of Napoleon. Volunteering was a 'knee-jerk response' created out of the shadow of a nationalist press which manipulated public imagination against France and above all else, against Bonaparte.[69] This black legend 'tarred with the same brush' English reformist groups, as well as anti-war liberals and the religious left, of being traitors, Jacobins and favouring invasion by France. It was a re-run of the 1790s, but this time, it was a war Pitt sought to win in a crusade to turn the British general public against the Napoleonic regime.[70] So successful was Pitt's propaganda that we still live with this legacy.

Therefore, we must ask, was the mass mobilisation of Volunteers based more on the pragmatism of getting paid in return for time spent in military service rather than an overt display of nationalism? Certainly, for the working men, the chance to earn some extra money, and get a free pair of decent shoes perhaps was a greater draw than any threat from Napoleon. For the officer class, the threat of invasion was real: it was a threat to their way of life. For the average man in the street, war meant starvation, high prices and unemployment. Some 18 months earlier, Magistrate Dawson admitted to Fitzwilliam at the height of the 'Black Lamp' troubles, that 'the rising of the disaffected depends entirely on the Enemy invading'.[71] The same tensions in working-class communities in 1801 to 1802 still existed in 1803, and it would be naïve to believe that the threat of invasion suddenly made anti-government working-class radicals into loyalists. The explosion of working-class discontent in 1811 and 1812 shows that these tensions and hatreds remained and working-class agitation was a central part of the immediate post-war years, centred on the Pentrich rising and Peterloo, which witnessed the implementation of Pitt's sedition legislation and the suspension of habeaus corpus.

The expansion of the Volunteer force owes more to the promise of pay and shoes and to escape the Militia ballot than love of King and Country. For example, in the Barkston Ash and Skyrac Volunteers, raised in 1798, Colonel Gascoigne noted men only volunteered their services because of the promise of pay: he noted in September 1799 that the men were owed five months' pay, and the lack of pay was encouraging men to desert.[72] Clearly, men would volunteer their time, so long as they were rewarded. This was not an outpouring of national sentiment, but a fiscal transaction. Money, a new pair of shoes and an overcoat were at the heart of the new Volunteer forces raised from 1803. Therefore, we ask did the average redcoat know what he was fighting for? Perhaps, but at the same time escaping poverty, getting two meals a day and a new set of clothes was also a draw for many. What was the soldier's motivation? Were some fighting against democracy like the 'Royal Wakefield Volunteers?' We suppose, however, that the Volunteers were far more radicalised in anti-Jacobin and English nationalist sentiment than the regular army. The paymaster of the 5th Foot commented:

> the British soldier, fortunately for himself, is a dunce in politics, it is a subject which he despises . . . to keep his arms in serviceable condition as well as his clothing and appointments, to be patient under privations; cool and steady in dangers; brave and daring in action, to be obedient to orders, and have an honest cheerful heart from the perfection of his character.[73]

We ask, were regular soldiers fighting to save their homeland from 'the other' or did they simply not care? How patriotic was the army? These are all questions for another book. It is impossible to deny that the bounty of £16 14s for short service and £23 for long service in 1813, which had risen from £11 11s and £16 6s respectively in 1808, was a huge draw. Recruits to the army were primarily those made unemployed by the changing nature of the economy. Unemployed and dispossessed Lancashire weavers during the strike of 1807 and 1808 provided over half of the recruits to the 2nd Battalion 6th Foot. We note that it can be reckoned that 46 per cent of the army was recruited from unemployed artisans, the remainder being labourers.[74] They were fighting merely for money just like the Volunteers on the home front.

Chapter 19

# CONCLUSION

Having explored the formation and development of the Volunteer soldier, identified who they were, and assessed the multiplicity of reasons for volunteering, what can we say to conclude our brief resume of the facts? What seems to have initially held the Volunteers together was a collective perception, an attachment, and an idea created by the effective propaganda machine of the Crown: the threat of imminent invasion and a loss of their community and way of life. The Volunteers from 1803 to the battle of Austerlitz shared a willingness to defend the nation – or perhaps their neighbourhood and town – against the invasion of an foreign foe. This patriotism cut across religious and political lines as John E. Cookson and Austin Gee articulated in their own works over two decades ago. The fear of invasion was genuine, but largely 'fake news' to use a modern phrase, local and regional identities were complex to say the least, and were significant in many cases particularly on religious grounds: the hope of unanimity was transitory or unachievable. Civic pride was a major stumbling-block to the forming of more cohesive, larger Volunteer corps through the period. The corps formed in the 1790s, along with the Loyalist Associations of 1792, prior to 1798 were largely a reaction by the 'possessing classes' to the political, ideological and economic stresses of the period which witnessed the burning of effigies of Thomas Paine. The 'possessing classes' or *petit bourgeoise* had a differently mentality to the men who joined up from 1798: their moral economy of class solidarity, enabled them to be effectively utilised as a police and peacekeeping force. After the mutinies of 1800, the Volunteers were hardly ever employed in that role again. Instead, their main focus was to form part of the anti-invasion forces and foster loyalism.

From 1794–1802 corps were anchored in their local communities, and many remained so upon re-formation in 1803, despite the urgings of the Lords Lieutenant. In the West Riding, Earl Fitzwilliam sought to replace localism with broader regionalism, based on wapentake divisions, and when this scheme was fully implemented from 1808 with the Local Militia, localism won out in many placed like Bawtry and Wakefield, where the Volunteer corps refused to become part of the Local Militia: the presence of independent Volunteers made a significant statement to the Riding as a whole. For the local leaders and elites, it gave them an acute sense of self-worth and importance. The urban elite were constantly on their guard against the aristocracy and squirearchy who sought to downgrade them into subservience, and sought to ignore or outmanoeuvre these forces. In Bawtry, Lord Galway sought to have his own army, as suited a man of such pedigree, so too Michael Anglo Taylor with his Barkston Ash Corps as an outward expression of the power and influence they wielded in their own communities, and nationally. The increasingly defined role that the Volunteers occupied from 1803 upon re-formation can be seen as a natural progression of an increasingly militarised society.

It is undeniable, as Linda Colley has shown, that the seeds of nationalism were sown with the localism shown by the earlier Volunteer formations, which promoted civic pride and cemented bourgeois elites in positions of power. However much radicals feared, resented and disagreed with the government's deployment of its security and intelligence services to monitor British society and investigate and repress radical activities and sentiments, they lived in the real world. Mob attacks on homes and businesses, and the Treason Trials, all resulted in the 'realpolitik' decision to assuage the 'Church and King' mob through overtly public displays of patriotism. Volunteering did not always mean approval of the government; it was a display of 'we are all in this together'. The propaganda machine of William Pitt stressed that the 'enemy' wanted to steal the much-vaunted British liberty and carry out bloody repression which was projected in propaganda by Gillray and others. This external threat was seen to be several times greater than that of the native 'old corruption' by the loyalist Tories. To counter this, those excluded from 'British Liberty' on religious and economic grounds never shared this view, and government propaganda probably did not convert the most ardent radicals into diehard loyalists. Indeed 'bloody repression' of the privileged classes was never far from the working-class Jacobin idealism, especially in the crisis years of 1802 and 1812.

For the true loyalist and nationalist, defence of 'British Values' against democracy was never in doubt. Anti-war liberalism was a vocal, influential and prominent minority in the West Riding: but working-class conservatism and nationalism was far more prevalent. We also accept that, then as now, the minutia of the argument against the war and for a free and more tolerant society, was simply ignored by the vast majority of the public, who driven forward by propaganda, and we also suppose nascent nationalism, joined the colours to support 'their way of life'. It is undeniable that, regardless of how and why men came to join the Volunteer movement, the active involvement and participation of thousands of men in the war effort did breed a sense of conservative national feeling which overcame pre-existing political and social divisions.[1]

On the home front, the Napoleonic Wars were by and large a battle between contrasting ideals of 'Britishness' in relatedness to property, law, democracy, the rights of man and religious toleration. Ultimately it was about who had power: the people or a coterie of the elite. This battle of ideology more than anything defined the conflict.[2] 'Britishness' was defined in its opposition to 'the other': by and large 'Britishness' was white, Anglican, pro-slavery, militaristic, nationalist, exclusivist, expansionist – i.e., imperialist – and monarchical. The much-vaunted 'British Liberty' was exclusionist: it said be like us and conform or suffer the consequences.

Moreover, we fully agree that J.E. Cookson's 'National Defence Patriotism' is a broader 'truth' behind reasons for Volunteering at times of national stress from internal and external threats than Colley's thesis that the Volunteer's loyalism marked the birth of a modern nation. If the Volunteers mark the creation of 'Britishness' as Colley argues, therefore the United Englishmen mark the birth of a distinct working-class identity. Furthermore, Colley is right if we rigidly stick to a simplistic nationalist narrative and ignore political and religious divisions. Cookson's thesis, however, underplays the religious-political dimension of the Volunteer movement.

Crucially it must be stressed that in the early nineteenth century, many radicals conceived themselves as being illegitimately excluded from the public space of political debate and appropriated patriotic language and actions to stress their loyalty to the nation and its history in order to legitimise their claims to participate. Rather than advocating revolution and disloyalty to the state *per se*, the radicals stressed their use of constitutional methods and their patriotism – petitioning Parliament and the sovereign; gathering in huge patriotic mass rallies like those held in Halifax or Leeds in 1800 and 1808; joining the Volunteer movement – in which they overwhelmingly wished the state and constitution to remain, but in a fairer and democratic form. Any consensus that had been reached in 1798–1801 and 1803–05, which relied on a just war of self-defence, rapidly evaporated once the nature

214

of the war changed. We need to stress that national identity was a politically-fractured concept, heavily fought over by rival groups who gave it their own distinct interpretations. Patriotism has to be understood as a multi-vocal entity, carrying a plurality of different meanings and, as with all political discourse, intimately connected to the context in which the competing patriotic rhetorical narratives are expressed.

The invasion scares of 1803 brought unlikely allies together for a time to create a sense of national purpose. The state-sponsored patriotism which dominated the era, despite its deep-seated ideological intolerance towards radicals and non-Anglicans, was a flexible concept: the patriotism engendered from 1798 was capable of allowing a wide spectrum of contemporary opinion in its ranks. The success of 'Pittite' patriotism as distinct force manipulated by the state at times of '*la Patrie en Danger*' lay in its ability to focus the multiple identities, and inclinations, of the Whigs and non-Anglicans into acceptance of, and active participation in, the wars against Revolutionary and Napoleonic France, with radicals and loyalists coming together in a Volunteer movement for the defence of the nation, albeit transitorily. This broad-based consensus collapsed with Napoleon's victory at Austerlitz. The concept of civic patriotism had no single monolithic conceptual idealism any more than it did among its participants. Those who wore the mantle of 'Patriotism' were, in a basic sense, continuing the process of self-identification rather than a static collection of prejudices and xenophobia. In Yorkshire, as across Britain at the time, the debate about self-identification involved the relationship of the individual with their locality and wider region, tempered with the demands of identity with the state: for the aspiring bourgeois and urban elites, like the Milnes family who followed an illegal religion, by commanding a troop of Volunteer cavalry cemented their position in the social order, acceptance by their contemporaries and through observance of established hierarchy's with the county nobility. The Crown, magistrates and local elites had no choice but to accept that 'man and woman in the street' might well be patriotic but importantly were not all 'Church-and-King' loyalists in all their views. This inevitably resulted in a compromise between the political aims of the officers on both sides of the debate and also with their men. This compromise was reflected in the nature of radicalism. Wyvill in 1797 argued, supported by Major John Cartwright, that enfranchising the taxpayer was far more achievable and acceptable than the idealism of universal male suffrage.[3]

Outside of this narrow time frame of 1803 to 1806, we are not seeing mass participation of 'the other', i.e., those excluded on religious grounds from full and free participation in the state. Whilst the Loyalist narrative is Trinitarian – largely Anglican and Tory – and therefore exclusive, the argument that Volunteering created a sense of nationhood, is only true when viewed from a narrow Anglican perspective. The resignation, forced or voluntary, of Foxite Whig officers from Volunteer units in 1807 and the withdrawal of anti-war liberals from Volunteer units by 1807, undermines Colley's thesis, and shows that Cookson's 'National Defence Patriotism' was possibly true only for 1803 to 1804, and that the participation of 'the other' in Volunteer corps owed more to the protection of communities by showing that 'they too were loyal' and not fifth columnists: the fear of local repression by 'Church and King' mobs was very real; hatred of Unitarians was very real. Volunteering was one way of showing loyalty. This was pragmatic, and not a true reflection by Unitarians, Whigs and others on their 'love of country'. Yet the values of 'Britishness' that Colley argues were fostered by the Volunteer movement had existed since the 1770s, and its exclusivist rhetoric was in contrast to a differing set of 'British values' encapsulated by 'anti-war liberalism' which emerged in protest to the actions of the British Crown in America. What the Napoleonic Wars witnessed, and the Volunteers helped to foster, was a militant working-class counter-culture. Patriotic sentiment lay at the heart of the relationship between governors and governed, propaganda-makers and readers, church and chapel. Whatever situation the radicals found themselves in, they did not on the whole hold back from volunteering for local defence, once avenues to participation had been created. In contrast to Unitarian publicist William Hazlitt, but agreeing with the Rev. Thomas Belsham and others, the remarkable Hannah Lindsey shifted her sympathy with the French Revolution to a deep suspicion of Bonaparte, coupled with fear of invasion and support for the raising of Volunteer regiments for home defence. In this change of mood, along with many others she embraced a patriotism which decried both overseas and domestic threats to liberty and which placed a higher priority upon the preservation of those liberties than upon a veneration for existing institutions. Yet at the same time she deplored the impact the war was having upon British public life and culture, noting in March 1805 'He [Bonaparte] has done by his threats, what never can be undone, changed the manners and views of this country from Commerce merely, to a Military cast'.[4]

Whilst the country was so divided, the argument that Volunteering created, fostered and built a sense of nationhood is flawed. Indeed, the concept of nationhood as a unifying force owes more to Victorian sentimentality and the politics of the Tory Party, than the thoughts and feelings of the working man in 1805. When we look the figures for the number of Volunteers, 118,000 in 1798, 146,000 in 1801 and 380,000 in 1804, the various corps made up one-third to half of home service forces. When we add in the troops on foreign service, we find the number grows to 800,000 or thereabouts: thus, we see from the available data that one in five adult males participated in military activities.[5] Yet it is undeniable that comparative numbers gave up wages and work to attend the mass radical meetings in 1807, 200,000 signed anti-war petitions in 1808, and similar numbers attended Spa Fields in 1816 or Peterloo in 1819.[6] We often think of France with her *levee en mass* and armies of over 300,000 men as an 'armed nation' with hugely 'militaristic overtones', yet by comparison, so too was Britain. Both nations were militarised, with governments that relied on censorship of the press, spy networks and coercion of the public to achieve the goals and aims of the government/executive. The Crown, in witnessing the civil war in France occasioned by the revolution had sought to control such activities by binding the people to the Crown through loyalist activities, volunteering being the primary *modus operandi* from 1794. Yet the reality, as we have seen, was that the ranks of the Volunteer forces from 1803 were not swelled by patriotism, but by realpolitik. The Levy *En Masse* Act co-opted able-bodied men to serve for compulsory training regardless of their political ideology about the war. The government stated it would suspend the Act, if enough men came forward. Come forward they did in huge numbers! By volunteering the men became exempt from the Militia ballot, the hair-powder tax and, if a member of the Yeomanry, the horse tax. In essence, the government literally forced the hand of hundreds of thousands to enlist: this 'bully-boy tactic' worked. At local community level, men were no doubt persuaded to join to save friends and family from the Levy *En Masse*, at the same time intimidation and confrontation by loyalists no doubt forced others to join. We also note that volunteering was cheaper than paying for a substitute Militiaman. Some men will have joined out of idealism based on nationalism and loyalism to save the country from invasion, but this, as we noted earlier, is a rather too simplistic reading of the evidence. The British Crown from 1799 to 1803 had faced the largest threat to its existence since the 1745 rebellion: the Despard Conspiracy had been a real and present danger. Anti-government feeling simply did not evaporate with the declaration of war against France. That feeling had to be cultivated by propaganda, in which Pitt and his ministers succeeded marvellously; yet he was only 'preaching to the converted' as the strength of anti-war liberalism shows throughout the period. The war was hated, the

Militia was hated, and large swathes of the country took direct political action to end the war. This was not a nation united behind the King, this was a country that was tearing itself apart over political ideology, the most explosive and evident outpouring being the Luddite crisis of 1811–13. Radical religion, Jacobinism and communities under threat from imposed 'top-down change' as well as moral outrage combined in a wave of civil disturbances.

The view of the Volunteers of the Napoleonic War as the 'Dad's Army' of the period, representing the unified will of the people in resisting a common enemy, is wrong: many Volunteers reportedly would have welcomed a French invasion! Yet, we must acknowledge that the club-like structure of Volunteer corps and their largely egalitarian nature stands in hypocritical contrast to many corps' stated aims! This could have given birth to an overtly political force, that posed a threat to established local hierarchies. Commentators at the time noted the political risk came not from the working man, but from the middle class: the very same men who would gain the most from political and economic reform by giving them the vote and thus a legitimate political voice. This was a calculated risk by the government: it is undeniable that the Volunteer forces were a primary factor in the creation of a middle-class identity, just as Jacobinism was increasingly doing for the working man.The expansion of volunteering to encompass the working man was again a risk: the state trained and armed hundreds if not thousands of men, who might use their training ultimately against the state. The Volunteer force needed tighter control, hence the government worked hard to encourage enlistment in the Local Militia when it came. It is also undeniable that the expansion of the Volunteer force harmed both the regular army and also the Militia – men were exempted from the ballot and Volunteering made a show of patriotism without having to go and actually get killed – thus from 1806 we see the working-class man forced out by the ending of his pay and his clothing allowance, and subsuming into the Local Militia on much tighter-controlled terms of service.

The Volunteer movement of 1794–1814 serves to underline the government's success in mobilising large bodies of men without creating a strong body of opinion against such a move, through carefully crafted propaganda. The Crown sought to encourage those who the state considered men 'fit to join the ranks' of the propertied classes, to strengthen local ties of allegiance. The reasons for Volunteering went far beyond the concept of nationalism. That the Volunteer forces were successful and creating a largely Anglican, pro-war, pro-Tory organisation is without doubt; a force that foreshadowed the development of a police force. Certainly from 1795 to 1802, the Volunteers' primary goal, and real achievements, lay in local policing, and 'stamping out' local unrest and threats to the Volunteer's own stake in society. Yet this simplifies the tensions within Volunteer corps between the 'haves' and the 'have nots'. By controlling civilian disorder, a hugely unpopular task, the Volunteer solider branded himself an enemy of the community which he came from. The deliberate expansion of the Volunteer force from 1803 to encompass a broader cross section of society led to the movement's downfall. The political unreliability of the working class, and the burden of state subsidy for their clothing and equipment, as well as the terms of service which allowed men to resign at will, resulted in the Local Militia Act, and a professionalisation of the Volunteer solider.

The Volunteer force was at its most useful before 1802, and the recreation of the force in 1803 was surely a stop-gap measure till a new way of bolstering national defence could be formulated. Driven more by localism than nationalism, the Volunteer force was fickle and fragile, a costly and inefficient force. Yet, the Volunteers, despite their failings, led directly to the Territorial Army, and ultimately 'Dad's Army'. We conclude by remarking that the rationale for Volunteering intersects with the entirety of an individual's plural lives; cultural and political: state loyalist propaganda and romantic illusions of being a soldier; religious: to maintain Protestantism from the atheism and religious plurality; and finally personal and communal pressures – not wishing to have one's masculinity shamed in the eyes of a sweetheart or friends through accusations of cowardice.[7] These and many other reasons led men to join Volunteer units.

219

# NOTES

## Preface

  1  Glenn A. Steppler (1992), *Britons, to Arms*. Stroud: Alan Sutton.

## Chapter 1: Defending the Nation

  1  Richard Price (1789), *Discourse delivered on the love of our country*. London: J Johnson. pp. 49–50.
  2  John Seed (1985), 'Gentlemen Dissenters: The Social and Political Meanings of Rational Dissent in the 1770s and 1780s', *The Historical Journal*, 28(2), pp. 299–325.
  3  Nick Mansfield (2022), *Soldiers as Citizens*. Liverpool: Liverpool University Press, p. 59.
  4  Emma Vincent Macleod (1998), *A War of Ideas: British Attitudes to the War Against Revolutionary France 1792-1802*. London: Routledge, pp. 13–27.
  5  David Eastwood (1991), 'Patriotism and the English State in the 1790s', in Mark Philp (ed.), *The French Revolution and British Popular Politics*. Cambridge: Cambridge University Press, p. 154.
  6  British Library Add. MS 16,921, f. 117, Anon. – Reeves, 10 December 1792; See also Add. MS 16,920, ff. 129-30, 'Pacificus' – J. Reeves, 5 December 1792.
  7  Sheffield City Archives [hereafter SCA] WWM/Y17/5, Beckett – Fitzwilliam, 22 April 1794.
  8  *Leeds Intelligencer* – Monday 17 December 1792.
  9  *Leeds Intelligencer* – Monday 24 December 1792.
10  Nicolas Rogers (1999), 'Burning Tom Paine: Loyalism and Counter-Revolution in Britain, 1791-1793', *Histoire Sociale*, Novembre 1999, pp. 139–71.
11  Macleod, p. 17.
12  The National Archives [hereafter TNA] Home Office Papers [hereafter HO] 42/32/269 Information of Pauncefort Cooke sworn before William Wickham, 30 June 1794.
13  North Yorkshire Record Office [hereafter NYRO], Wyvill Papers, Samuel Shore to Wyvill, 20 June 1794.
14  Edward Palmer Thompson (2013), *Making of the English Working Class*. London: Penguin Classics, pp. 137–8.
15  J.R. Western (1965), *English Militia in the Eighteenth Century - the Story of a Political Issue, 1660-1802*. London: Routledge & Kegan, p. 129. See also ibid., pp. 290–1.
16  Linda Colley (2005), *Britons: Forging the Nation 1707-1837*. London: Yale University Press, p. 287.
17  Geoffrey Cousins (1968), *The Defenders. A History of the British Volunteer* London: Frederick Muller, p. 75.

## Chapter 2: The Volunteer Infantry

1   Paul L. Dawson (2019), *Lexington to Waterloo: Westgate Chapel and National Politics*. Wakefield: Westgate Chapel, pp. 161–2.
2   Ibid., pp. 174–5.
3   Macleod (1998), p. 39.
4   Ibid., pp. 75–6.
5   Ibid., p. 76.
6   *Sheffield Register, Yorkshire, Derbyshire, & Nottinghamshire Universal Advertiser* – Friday 21 March 1794
7   Austin Gee (2003), *The British Volunteer Movement 1794-1814*. Oxford: Oxford University Press, p. 66
8   Ibid., p. 68
9   Peter Hicks, 'The Militarisation of Society in Georgian Britain and Napoleonic France', *Napoleonica. La Revue*, 2008/1 (N° 1), pp. 136–47.
10  North Yorkshire Record Office (hereafter NYRO) ZDW 7/2/87/9.
11  Ibid., ZDW 7/2/88/1, Hildyard to Wyvill, 24 May 1794.
12  Ibid., ZDW 7/2/87/14, Wyvill to Hildyard, 28 May 1794.
13  Ibid., ZDW 7/2/88/9, Dealtry to Wyvill, 10 June 1794.
14  Ibid., ZDW 7/2/88/11, John Yorke to Wyvill, 14 June 1794.
15  Hicks, pp. 136–47.
16  *Leeds Intelligencer* – Monday 21 April 1794.
17  *Leeds Intelligencer* – Monday 28 April 1794.
18  Ibid.
19  *Leeds Intelligencer* – Monday 14 April 1794.
20  Ibid.
21  Anthony Leslie Dawson (1999), *Wakefield's Dads Army During the Napoleonic Wars*. Unpublished research project, p. 5.
22  *Leeds Intelligencer* – Monday 2 June 1794.
23  *Leeds Intelligencer* – Monday 26 May 1794.
24  Richard Warren pers comm.
25  East Riding Archives zDDX17/1/2/9. See also Ibid. zDDX17/1/2/16.
26  Ibid., zDDX17/1/2/16.
27  Ibid., zDDX17/1/2/22.
28  *Hull Advertiser and Exchange Gazette*, 16, 30 August, 6 December 1794.
29  *Leeds Intelligencer* – Monday 28 April 1794.
30  *Leeds Intelligencer* – Monday 14 July 1794.
31  TNA HO 50/346, Wilberforce to Portland 1 November 1794.
32  *Leeds Intelligencer* – Monday 1 September 1794.
33  *Leeds Intelligencer* – Monday 9 June 1794.
34  *Leeds Intelligencer* – Monday 7 July 1794.
35  *Leeds Intelligencer* – Monday 9 August 1802.
36  *Leeds Intelligencer* – Monday 16 January 1797.
37  Westgate Chapel Wakefield Archives, Pew Rent Register 1761-1803.
38  Sheffield City Library, notes and cuttings.
39  Anthony Dawson, pers comm. 2 May 2022.
40  TNA HO 50/536, Letter Rev. James Wilkinson 7 May 1794
41  TNA HO 50/346, Busfield, Bradford – Dundas, 10 June 1794.
42  TNA HO 42/30, ff. 52-3, J. Russel – Dundas, 12 May 1794.
43  TNA HO 50/49, Fitzwilliam to Dundas, 10 February 1801.
44  Kevin Linch (2001), 'A Geography of Loyalism? The Local Military Forces of the West Riding of Yorkshire, 1794–1814', *War & Society*, 19:1, p. 18.

45  John Goodchild Collection: Wakefield Royal Wakefield Volunteers, list of members 30 August 1795 compared to pew rent register for Westgate Chapel, Wakefield 1797-1799 held in Westgate Chapel Archives and West Parade Wesleyan Chapel records in the John Goodchild Collection. See also John Goodchild Collection: Poll for the Knights of Shire, Yorkshire 1807.
46  John Goodchild pers comm 1 October 2012.
47  WYAS Wakefield, YAS QE13/1/38 1751.
48  Anthony L. Dawson (1998), *Wakefield's Volunteers in the Napoleonic Wars, 1794-1814. The Royal Wakefield Volunteers.* Consulting appendix 1 and 3, compared to Westgate Chapel pew rent registers and baptismal register.
49  SCA WWM Y20/29a Resolutions of the Committee, Whitaker to Fitzwilliam 27 April 1798.
50  Gee, pp. 151–2.

## Chapter 3: The County Yeomanry

1   Richard Warren pers comm.
2   *Leeds Intelligencer* – Monday 12 May 1794.
3   *Leeds Intelligencer* – Monday 26 May 1794.
4   Ibid.
5   *Leeds Intelligencer* – Monday 9 June 1794.
6   Ibid.
7   SCA WWM Y17-17/14, Bacon Frank to Earl Fitzwilliam, 1 June 1794.
8   Suffolk Record Office [hereafter SRO] Mileson Edgar Papers. HD80/3/1 pp. 165–6.
9   Doncaster Archives [here after DA]. DD/DC/M1/24, Copy address of Bryan Cooke to the Volunteers of the Doncaster Troop on disbanding 27 April 1802.
10  *Leeds Intelligencer* – Monday 26 April 1802.
11  TNA HO 42/65/343, Fitzwilliam to Home Office, 20 July 1802.
12  https://www.historyofparliamentonline.org/volume/1790-1820/member/spencer-stanhope-%28formerly-stanhope-%29-walter-1750-1821.
13  SRO Mileson Edgar Papers. HD80/3/1 pp. 165–6.
14  TNA HO 42/66/74 Folios 224-225, Hobart to Fitzwilliam, 6 September 1802.
15  DA DD/DC/M1/31, Copy of Circular letter to officers of the Doncaster Pontefract and Barnsley Troops to meet Lord Fitzwilliam, 24 October 1802.
16  *Leeds Intelligencer* – Monday 20 June 1803.
17  SCA WWM Y17/34, Bacon Frank to Earl Fitzwilliam, 10 July 1794.
18  Ibid. WWM Y17 34 Allowances.
19  Ibid. WWM Y17 35 Allowances.
20  Ibid. WWM Y17/36, Bacon Frank to Earl Fitzwilliam, 7 March 1795.
21  Ibid.
22  SCA WWM/F Y/27.
23  Anthony L. Dawson (1999), p. 2.
24  Ibid, pp. 2–4.
25  TNA HO 42/28, Folio 197, Buckingham – Grenville 2 February 1794.
26  TNA HO 50/88, Richmond – Hobart, 8 August 1802.
27  TNA HO 42/51, ff. 286-287B, Monckton – Portland, 19 September 1800.
28  WYAS Bradford West Riding Yeomanry Cavalry, records. MMC/22 List of men enrolled in Lord Ribblesdale's troop 1798.
29  Ibid.
30  BL, Add Mss 59291.
31  SCA WWM Y41/1/1.
32  TNA WO 13. Pay Allowances, Volunteers, Yeomanry, armed associations.

## Chapter 4: The Provisional Cavalry

1 Roger A. Wells (2011), *Wretched Faces: Famine in Wartime England, 1793-1801*. London: Breviary Stuff, Tables 1–12, pp. 357–69.
2 SCA WWM Y17/42, Spencer Stanhope to Earl Fitzwilliam, 6 August 1795.
3 SCA WWM Y16/96/c, Reasons and Orders.
4 Ibid., WWM Y17/42, Spencer Stanhope to Earl Fitzwilliam, 6 August 1795.
5 Ibid., WWM Y17/42, Thomas Lister to Earl Fitzwilliam, 13 February 1796.
6 Ibid., WWM Y17/55, William Markham to Earl Fitzwilliam, 7 May 1796.
7 TNA HO 42/35/377, Wilson to Portland, 9 August 1795.
8 SCA WWM F 44/45, M.A. Taylor to Fitzwilliam. See also *The Iris* – 26 June 1795.
9 *Leeds Intelligencer* – Monday 24 August 1795; *Leeds Intelligencer* – Monday 10 August 1795.
10 SCA WWM F45-a/102, Fitzwilliam to Burke, 9 August 1795.
11 John Bohstedt (1983), *Riots and Community Politics in England and Wales, 1790–1810*. Cambridge: Cambridge University Press, pp. 1–3.
12 *York Herald* – 8 August 1795.
13 TNA HO 42/35 Folios 32-33, Magistrates of Birmingham to Portland, 23 June 1795.
14 TNA War Office Papers [hereafter WO] 1/1082, Folio 157, Francis Annesley to Windham, 6 June 1795; See also TNA WO 1/1083, Folio 205, Baker to Windham, 29 July 1795; WO 1/1094, Warwick to Windham, 27 December 1795.
15 TNA HO 50/26, Marquis of Buckingham to Portland, 17 and 18 December 1796. See also TNA HO 50/26, Northampton – Portland, 9 December 1796.
16 TNA WO 1/1090, Folios 441-2, Mundey to Windham, 4 August 1795.
17 HO 42/50, Folios 365-6, Ruggles to Portland, 6 July 1800.
18 TNAWO 17/1015-23, Yeomanry Cavalry Returns, 1795.
19 *The Oracle* – 18 July 1795.
20 *Hampshire Chronicle* – Saturday 12 November 1796.
21 *Hampshire Chronicle* – Saturday 16 December 1797.
22 *Leeds Intelligencer* – Monday 21 November 1796.
23 *Gloucester Journal* – 13 March 1797.
24 *Hull Advertiser and Exchange Gazette* – 18 March 1797.
25 M.Y. Ashcroft, *To Escape the Monster's Clutches*, North Yorkshire County Record Office, 1977.
26 *Shrewsbury Chronicle* – 23 March 1798.
27 *Leeds Intelligencer* – Monday 16 January 1797.
28 *Leeds Intelligencer* – Monday 19 June 1797.
29 *Leeds Intelligencer* – Monday 15 May 1797.
30 *Leeds Intelligencer* – Monday 13 February 1797.
31 *Leeds Intelligencer* – Monday 13 March 1797.
32 *Leeds Intelligencer* – Monday 20 February 1797.
33 *Leeds Intelligencer* – Monday 17 April 1797.
34 *Leeds Intelligencer* – Monday 13 February 1797.
35 *Leeds Intelligencer* – Monday 12 June 1797.
36 Ibid.
37 *Leeds Intelligencer* – Monday 16 April 1798
38 John E. Cookson (1997), *The British Armed Nation*. Oxford: Clarendon Press, p. 33.
39 *Leeds Intelligencer* – Monday 2 April 1798.
40 *Leeds Intelligencer* – Monday 30 April 1798.
41 Author's collection.
42 *Leeds Intelligencer* – Monday 9 April 1798.

43  Ian Beckett (2011), *Britain's Part-Time Soldiers: The Amateur Military Tradition: 1558–1945*. Barnsley: Pen & Sword Military. p. 77.
44  https://bmmt.co.uk/wp-content/uploads/Chapter-Four-1792-1815.pdf
45  *Leeds Intelligencer* – Monday 26 December 1796.
46  *Leeds Intelligencer* – Monday 2 January 1797.
47  *Leeds Intelligencer* – Monday 16 January 1797.
48  Ibid.
49  *Leeds Intelligencer* – Monday 23 January 1797.
50  *Leeds Intelligencer* – Monday 13 February 1797.
51  *Leeds Intelligencer* – Monday 22 May 1797.
52  SCA WWM Y20/14/a, Godfrey Wentworth Wentworth to Earl Fitzwilliam, 15 April 1798.

## Chapter 5: Invasion Scare

1  TNA HO 50/346 Cockell to Portland, 30 May 1797. See also ibid., Cockell to Portland, 7 June 1797.
2  *Leeds Intelligencer* – Monday 28 August 1797.
3  *Leeds Intelligencer* – Monday 4 September 1797.
4  TNA HO 50/346 Cockell to Portland, 30 May 1797. See also ibid., Cockell to Portland, 7 June 1797.
5  SCA WWM Y20/4 Cockell to Fitzwilliam, 26 March 1798. See also ibid., Y16/105, Cockell to Fitzwilliam, 21 April 1801; TNA HO 50/50, Cockell to Dundas, 9 April 1801; ibid., 50/52, Cockell to Hobart, 7 October 1801; ibid., 50/53 Cockell to Hobart, 12 January 1802.
6  TNA HO 50/50, Cockell to Fitzwilliam, 9 April 1801.
7  West Yorkshire Archive Service [WYAS here after] Quarter Sessions QS1/137/4 Pontefract Quarter Sessions, April 1798.
8  *Leeds Intelligencer* – Monday 10 September 1798.
9  *Leeds Intelligencer* – Monday 5 August 1799.
10 *Leeds Intelligencer* – Monday 27 October 1794.
11 https://www.historyofparliamentonline.org/volume/1790-1820/member/sotheron-william-1755-1806
12 https://www.62ndregiment.org/William_Sotheron.htm
13 SCA WWM Y16/105, Teesdale Cockell to Earl Fitzwilliam, 21 April 1801.
14 TNA WO 79/2, Minute Book Royal Preston Volunteers.
15 Ibid.
16 *Chester Chronicle* – 9 June 1797.
17 *Chester Courant* – 12 December 1797.
18 *Chester Courant* – 1 July 1794.
19 *Chester Chronicle* – 4 July 1794.
20 *Gloucester Journal* – 20 February 1797.
21 SCA WMM Y16/35 Gascoigne to Fitzwilliam, 23 September 1798.

## Chapter 6: 1798 Armed Associations

1  Jenny Graham (2000), *The nation, the law and the king: reform politics in England, 1789–1799*, 2 vols. University Press of America, p. 754.
2  John Goodchild collection: Richard Munkhouse DD, Sermon Delivered at the Parish Church of St John the Baptist Wakefield, 19 December 1797.
3  Graham, pp. 843–6.
4  TNA HO 42/46/173 Folio 369, Extract of Information Respecting the United Irishmen.

5   Ibid., HO 42/43/12 Folios 33A-33B, Letter from George Cartwright, 6 May 1797.
6   NYRO ZDW 7/2/88/9, Wyvill to Buchan, 13 February 1798.
7   TNA WO 1/922/297 Folios 297-300, Bouillon to Huskisson, 28 December 1797.
8   TNA HO 42/46/173 Folio 375, Rev. Thomas Bancroft to Home Office.
9   Gee, pp. 121–2.
10  Ibid., pp. 38–9.
11  H.F.B. Wheeler (1907), *Napoleon and the Invasion of England: The Story of the Great Terror*. London: John Lane, pp. 275–9.
12  John Goodchild Collection: MSS Notes Wakefield Armed Association pers comm 11 March 1996.
13  John Goodchild Collection: Officers' commission Wakefield Armed Association.
14  *Leeds Intelligencer* – Monday 16 April 1798.
15  SCA WWM Y/20 Armed associations.
16  SCA WWM Y20/20 William Rawson to Earl Fitzwilliam, 21 April 1798.
17  Ibid., WWM Y20/39/a Castleford Potteries Declaration, 10 May 1798.
18  Ibid., WWM Y20/39/b Castleford Potteries Declaration, 10 May 1798.
19  Ibid., WWM Y/20/54 J A Busfield to Fitzwilliam 19 May 1798.
20  *Leeds Intelligencer* – Monday 30 April 1798.
21  SCA WWM Y20/26, Pontefract Armed Association to Earl Fitzwilliam, 25 April 1798.
22  Ibid. WWM Y20, Armed associations.
23  Ibid. WWM Y20/43b, Offer of Service 4 May 1798.
24  Harry Dickinson (1990), 'Popular Loyalism in the 1790s' in Eckhart Hellmuth (ed.), *The Transformation of political culture: England and Germany in the late eighteenth century*. Oxford: Oxford University Press, p. 511.
25  SCA WWM Y20/43c, Offer of Service, 4 May 1798.
26  Ibid., WWM Y20/32, John Rayner to Earl Fitzwilliam, 30 April 1798.
27  Ibid., WWM Y20/53/a, Thomas Fenton to Earl Fitzwilliam, 19 May 1798.
28  Ibid., WWM Y20/53/b, Thomas Fenton to Earl Fitzwilliam, 19 May 1798.
29  Ibid., WWM Y20, uncatalogued Resolutions at Doncaster, 7 May 1798.
30  Anthony L Dawson pers comm 25 July 2021.
31  *Leeds Intelligencer* – Monday 30 April 1798.
32  SCA WWM Y20/, Armed Association Commissions.
33  Ibid., WWM Y20/17/1, Henry Peterson to Earl Fitzwilliam, 24 May 1798.
34  Ibid., WWM Y20/41/a, Walter Ramsden Fawkes to Earl Fitzwilliam, 12 May 1798.
35  Ibid., WWM Y20/41/b, Walter Ramsden Fawkes to Earl Fitzwilliam, 12 May 1798.
36  Ibid., WWM Y20.
37  Ibid., WWM Y20/66, Samuel Tooker to Earl Fitzwilliam, 7 June 1798.
38  Ibid., WWM Y20/67, Samuel Tooker to Earl Fitzwilliam, 10 June 1798.
39  *Leeds Intelligencer* – Monday 31 December 1798.
40  SCA WWM Y20/71, Resolution of Meeting in Leeds, 27 June 1798.
41  Ibid.
42  Ibid.
43  Emily Hargrave (1926), *The Early Leeds Volunteers*. Publications of the Thoresby Society, Vol XXVIII, Miscellanea, pp. 290–2.
44  John Goodchild pers comm 22 June 1996.
45  TNA HO 40/1/1, Huddersfield Petition, 29 April 1812.
46  SCA WWM Y20/67, Robinson to Fitzwilliam, 7 June 1798.
47  TNA HO 50/458/4, Grenville to Portland, November 1797.
48  TNA WO 6/197, 14 May 1798.

49  Ibid., WO 6/197, 9 June 1798.
50  Ibid., WO 6/197, 18 May 1798.
51  NYRO ZDW 7/2/120/11, Wyvill to Fauconberg, 31 May 1798.
52  Beckett, p. 80.
53  *Shrewsbury Chronicle* – 18 June 1798.
54  *Shrewsbury Chronicle* – 21 September 1798.
55  Howard Clayton (1971), *Coaching City: A Glimpse of Georgian Lichfield*. Bala: Dragon Books, p. 88.
56  John Goodchild Collection: Wakefield Armed Association MSS Notes list of members 30 April 1798 compared to pew rent register for Westgate Chapel, Wakefield 1797-1799 held in Westgate Chapel Archives and West Parade Wesleyan Chapel records in the John Goodchild Collection. See also John Goodchild Collection: Poll for the Knights of Shire, Yorkshire 1807.
57  SCA WWM Y20/29a, Whittaker to Fitzwilliam, 27 April 1798.
58  Anthony Dawson pers comm citing membership list of Wakefield Armed Association 30 April 1798 allied to Westgate Chapel pew rent register 1797 and 1798.
59  John Goodchild Collection: Wakefield Royal Wakefield Volunteers, list of members 30 August 1795 compared to pew rent register for Westgate Chapel, Wakefield 1797-1799 held in Westgate Chapel Archives and West Parade Wesleyan Chapel records in the John Goodchild Collection. See also John Goodchild Collection: Poll for the Knights of Shire, Yorkshire 1807.
60  SCA WWM Y20/53, [illegible] to Earl Fitzwilliam, 19 May 1798.

## Chapter 7: Association Cavalry

1  Cookson, p. 67.
2  Hicks, p. 140.
3  Gee, p. 111.
4  Ibid., p. 89.
5  Anthony Skelsey (2018), 'The Loyal Birmingham Light Horse Volunteers', *The Military Historical Society Bulletin*, Vol. 68, Issue 271, February 2018, pp. 118–21.
6  https://thisreilluminatedschoolofmars.wordpress.com/notes-on-the-dress-of-Volunteers-Yeomanry-and-armed-associations/shropshire-independent-Yeomanry-and-association-cavalry/ accessed 13 August 2022
7  *Birmingham Gazette* – 16 April 1798.
8  https://www.olddeptfordhistory.com/2011/06/deptford-volunteeer-1798by-jhon-ashton.html?fbclid=IwAR1ELJ472opJbFeraizccmuohHqZ4oSWgHxAhyjPO6L5mJMGUKEW9kW-nsE accessed 13 August 2022
9  *Salopian Journal* – 9 May 1798.
10  *Manchester Mercury* – 23 June 1799.
11  Richard Warren pers comm 30 May 2022.
12  *Hull Advertiser and Exchange Gazette* – Saturday 4 August 1798. See also *Leeds Intelligencer* – Monday 6 August 1798.
13  TNA WO17/1037.
14  SCA WWM Y20/18/b, Broadsheet, dated 16 April 1798.
15  Ibid. WWM Y20/18/c, Declaration, 21 April 1798.
16  *Leeds Intelligencer* – 4 November 1799.
17  *Leeds Intelligencer* – Monday 16 July 1798.
18  SCA WWM Y20/5, Regulating Code of Laws for the Halifax Volunteer Cavalry, 1798.
19  *Leeds Intelligencer* – Monday 10 June 1799.

20  SCA WWM Y20/13, James Wilkinson to Earl Fitzwilliam, 4 April 1798.
21  Ibid., WWM Y20/64, Charles Hawksley Webb to Earl Fitzwilliam, 4 June 1798
22  *Sheffield Iris* – 2 November 1798. See also *Leeds Intelligencer* – Monday 5 November 1798.
23  *Sheffield Iris* – 9 December 1798.
24  SCA WWM Y20/64, Charles Hawksley Webb to Earl Fitzwilliam, 4 June 1798.

## Chapter 8: 1803: New Formations

1  Leslie Mitchell (2004), *'Fox, Charles James (1749–1806)'*. Oxford Dictionary of National Biography.
2  John Goodchild Collection: Richard Munkhouse DD. Sermon Delivered on the necessity of War, 3 September 1803.
3  https://bmmt.co.uk/wp-content/uploads/Chapter-Four-1792-1815.pdf
4  NYRO Wyvill Papers, Samuel Shore to Wyvill, 23 December 1803.
5  NYRO Wyvill Papers, Rev Theophilus Lindsey to Wyvill, 22 July 1803.
6  Olivier Blanc (1995), *Les espions de la Révolution et de l'Empire*. Paris: Perrin, pp. 219–24.
7  https://www.Napoléon-series.org/research/government/diplomatic/letters/c_letters52.html. Accessed 11 November 2021.
8  Mike Jay (2004), *The Unfortunate Colonel Despard*. London: Bantam Press.
9  *Leeds Intelligencer* – Monday 20 June 1803.
10  *Leeds Intelligencer* – Monday 4 July 1803.
11  *Leeds Intelligencer* – Monday 25 July 1803.
12  *Leeds Intelligencer* – Monday 1 August 1803.
13  TNA HO 42/72/227, Anonymous to I H Browne, 24 August 1803.
14  *Leeds Intelligencer* – Monday 25 July 1803.
15  TNA HO 42/72/227, Anonymous to I H Browne, 24 August 1803.
16  *York Herald* – Saturday 10 September 1803.
17  *York Herald* – Saturday 22 October 1803.
18  Gee, p. 152.
19  TNA HO 50/123, Bacon Frank to Home Office, 3 February 1804.
20  Gee, p. 241.
21  Ibid., p. 43.
22  *York Herald* – Saturday 20 August 1803.
23  *Leeds Intelligencer* – Monday 15 August 1803.
24  Ibid.
25  Anthony L. Dawson (1999), p. 8
26  *Leeds Intelligencer* – Monday 5 September 1803.
27  *Leeds Intelligencer* – Monday 10 October 1803.
28  *Wakefield Star* – 13 January 1804.
29  *Wakefield Star* – 3 February 1804.
30  *Wakefield Star* – 24 February 1804.
31  Anthony L. Dawson (1998), pp. 40–1.
32  Ibid.
33  *Leeds Intelligencer* – Monday 25 July 1803.
34  *York Herald* – Saturday 20 August 1803.
35  *Leeds Intelligencer* – Monday 5 September 1803.
36  *York Herald* – Saturday 20 August 1803.
37  *York Herald* – Saturday 14 January 1804.
38  *Leeds Intelligencer* – Monday 5 September 1803.
39  *York Herald* – Saturday 2 July 1803.

40  *Leeds Intelligencer* – Monday 18 July 1803.
41  *Leeds Intelligencer* – Monday 29 August 1803.
42  *Leeds Intelligencer* – Monday 3 October 1803.
43  *Lancaster Gazette* – 3 March 1804.
44  Ibid.
45  *Leeds Intelligencer* – 23 January 1804.
46  *Leeds Intelligencer* – Monday 8 August 1803.
47  *Leeds Intelligencer* – Monday 15 August 1803.
48  *Leeds Intelligencer* – Monday 29 August 1803.
49  Gregory Claeys (2007), *The French Revolution Debate in Britain*. London: Palgrave MacMillan, pp. 69–70.
50  *Leeds Intelligencer* – Monday 22 August 1803.
51  *Leeds Intelligencer* – Monday 15 August 1803.
52  Gee, p. 45.
53  SCA WMM/Y10/73, Foljambe to Earl Fitzwilliam, 24 April 1798.
54  Ibid. WWM F45/e/120, Earl Fitzwilliam to Pelham, 29 August 1803.
55  Ibid. WWM Y16/155/a, Busfield to Earl Fitzwilliam, 12 August 1803.
56  TNA HO 50/91, Earl Fitzwilliam to Hobart, 13 August 1803.
57  Ibid.
58  SCA WWM Y37/20, List of Volunteers.
59  TNA HO 50/91, Fitzwilliam to Yorke, 31 October 1803.
60  WYAS JG 0001459, Bacon Frank MSS, Earl Fitzwilliam to John Shillito, 21 September 1803.
61  SCA WWM Y30/18, John Halliley to Earl Fitzwilliam, 18 August 1803.
62  Ibid. WWM Y30/66/a, John Halliley to Earl Fitzwilliam, 2 October 1803.
63  Ibid. WWM Y30/66/b, John Halliley to Earl Fitzwilliam, 24 October 1803.
64  Ibid. WWM Y30/26, Rev. Edward Kilvington to Earl Fitzwilliam, 20 August 1803
65  Ibid. WWM Y30/48, Articles of Enrolment of the Ossett Corps of Volunteer Infantry.
66  Ibid. WWM Y16/153, John Halliley to Earl Fitzwilliam, 29 August 1803
67  Ibid. WWM Y16/162, John Hague to Earl Fitzwilliam, 17 September 1803; Y16/166 Abraham Greenwood to Earl Fitzwilliam, 17 September 1803; Y16/194 John Halliley to Earl Fitzwilliam, 5 November 1803.
68  SCA WWM Y16/149, Richard Carr to Earl Fitzwilliam, 4 August 1803.
69  Ibid. WWM Y30/49, Richard Carr to Earl Fitzwilliam, 1 September 1803.
70  WYAS Wakefield, JG 001459, Bacon Frank MSS.
71  SCA WWM Y20.
72  WYAS JG001459 Bacon Frank MSS. West Riding Volunteer Regiments.
73  *Sheffield Iris* – 26 April 1804.
74  WYAS JG001459 Bacon Frank MSS. West Riding Volunteer Regiments.
75  *York Herald* – Saturday 15 October 1803.
76  *York Herald* – Saturday 17 December 1803.
77  WYAS JG001459 Bacon Frank MSS. West Riding Volunteer Regiments.
78  *Leeds Intelligencer* – 21 May 1804.
79  *Leeds Intelligencer* – 30 April 1804.
80  *York Herald* – Saturday 26 November 1803.
81  *Leeds Intelligencer* – Monday 28 November 1803.

## Chapter 9: Men, Uniforms and Equipment

1  *Leeds Intelligencer* – 5 September 1803.
2  National Army Museum [NAM hereafter] 1959-07-53.
3  NAM 1987-08-12.

4   NAM 1992-05-36.
5   Leeds City Museum LEEAG.2008.0006.0004.
6   Portrait of Captain Thomas A. Ward, Sheffield Museum Trust.
7   Coat on display in the Piece Hall, Halifax.
8   NAM 1958-05-17.
9   George Walker (1814), *Costumes of Yorkshire*. Leeds: Robinson and Son.
10  John Goodchild Collection, Portrait William Rooks Leeds Serjeantson.
11  *York Herald* – Saturday 10 September 1803.
12  *York Herald* – Saturday 17 September 1803.
13  *York Herald* – Saturday 3 December 1803.
14  *York Herald* – Saturday 17 September 1803.
15  Ibid.
16  *York Herald* – Saturday 1 October 1803.
17  Ibid.
18  *York Herald* – Saturday 3 December 1803.
19  *York Herald* – Saturday 24 December 1803
20  *Leeds Intelligencer* – Monday 21 November 1803.
21  *Leeds Intelligencer* – Monday 7 November 1803.
22  *Leeds Intelligencer* – Monday 31 October 1803.
23  SCA WWM Y20/223/a, Thomas Fenton to Earl Fitzwilliam [illegible], January 1808.
24  Ibid., WWM Y16/287, Thomas Fenton to Earl Fitzwilliam, 3 November 1807.
25  *Leeds Intelligencer* – Monday 12 October 1807.
26  WYAS Bradford Volunteer Papers, DB17 C3/2.
27  SCA WWM Y30/60, List of men enrolled 18 September 1803.
28  John Goodchild MSS Notes Walkers of Rotherham.
29  Gee, pp. 151–2.
30  Cookson (1997), pp. 209–20.
31  Colley (2005).
32  Gee, p. 152.
33  https://bmmt.co.uk/wp-content/uploads/Chapter-Four-1792-1815.pdf
34  SRO Mileson Edgar Papers. HD80/3/2 pp. 165–6.

## Chapter 10: Officers and Gentlemen

1   Anthony L. Dawson (1999), p. 42.
2   SCA WWM Y17/45, Teesdale Cockell to Fitzwilliam, 6 October 1795.
3   TNA HO 50/91, Fitzwilliam to Hobart, 13 August 1803.
4   Gee, p. 122.
5   John Goodchild Collection, MSS Notes Brandling family and Middleton colliery.
6   Anthony Dawson pers comm.
7   https://www.historyofparliamentonline.org/volume/1790-1820/member/taylor-michael-angelo-1757-1834
8   https://www.historyofparliamentonline.org/volume/1790-1820/member/monckton-arundell-robert-1752-1810
9   https://www.historyofparliamentonline.org/volume/1820-1832/member/wrightson-william-1789-1879
10  York City Library. WYV/1/39/25, Letter from Gamaliel Lloyd of Leeds, 3 April 1780. See also ibid. WYV/1/39/48, Letter from Gamaliel Lloyd of Leeds, 17 April 1780; WYV/1/39/66, Letter from Gamaliel Lloyd of Leeds, 17 May 1780; WYV/1/39/120, Letter from Gamaliel Lloyd of Leeds, 14 January 1781; WYV/1/39/150, Letter from Gamaliel Lloyd of Leeds, 28 March 1782; WYV/1/39/162, Letter from Gamaliel Lloyd of Leeds, 29 October 1782.

11  Derbyshire Record Office. D5369/19/20-22. Three letters to William Smithson of Leeds Esq.
12  Paul Lindsay Dawson (2021), *A Potted History of Wakefield*. Stroud, Amberley Publishing.
13  https://www.historyofparliamentonline.org/volume/1790-1820/member/milner-sir-william-mordaunt-1754-1811
14  John Newman (2006), '"An Insurrection of Loyalty": The London Volunteer Regiments' Response to the Invasion Threat', in Mark Philp (ed.), *Resisting Napoleon: The British Response to the Threat of Invasion, 1797-1815*. Aldershot: Ashgate, pp. 78–9.
15  Ibid., p. 75.
16  Sometimes also written as 'Awdry', see *London Gazette*, 8 July 1794. https://www.thegazette.co.uk/London/issue/13681/page/685 [accessed 4 August 2022], p. 685.
17  https://www.historyofparliamentonline.org/volume/1790-1820/member/cooke-bryan-1756-1821
18  SCA WWM Y27/11, Lord Ribblesdale to Earl Fitzwilliam, 1 August 1798.
19  https://www.historyofparliamentonline.org/volume/1790-1820/member/chaloner-robert-1776-1842
20  https://www.historyofparliamentonline.org/volume/1790-1820/member/foljambe-francis-ferrand-1750-1814
21  https://www.historyofparliamentonline.org/volume/1790-1820/member/spencer-stanhope-%28formerly-stanhope-%29-walter-1750-1821
22  https://www.historyofparliamentonline.org/volume/1790-1820/member/stuart-wortley-james-archibald-1776-1845
23  *Leeds Intelligencer* – Monday 3 October 1803.

## Chapter 11: The Local Militia

1   Beckett, pp. 100–04.
2   *York Herald* – Saturday 25 February 1804.
3   *York Herald* – Saturday 5 May 1804.
4   *Leeds Intelligencer* – Monday 2 January 1804.
5   Cookson, pp. 81–4.
6   *Leeds Intelligencer* – Monday 1 December 1806.
7   Gee, p. 46.
8   *Leeds Intelligencer* – Monday 26 October 1807.
9   *Leeds Intelligencer* – Monday 16 November 1807.
10  SCA WWM Y16/224/a, Proceedings of Court Martial, 8 August 1806.
11  Ibid., WWM Y16/227, Earl Fitzwilliam to Home Office, 26 August 1806.
12  Gee, p. 156.
13  *Leeds Intelligencer* – Monday 2 March 1807.
14  SCA WWM Y16/223, Fitzwilliam to the Home Secretary, 31 May 1807.
15  Gee, p. 47.
16  *Leeds Intelligencer* – Monday 25 April 1808.
17  WYAS Bradford, SpSt 10/7/79, Francis Lindley Wood to Spencer Stanhope, 14 May 1808.
18  SCA WWM Y16/200, Fitzwilliam to Beckett, 21 December 1808.
19  *Leeds Intelligencer* – Monday 13 June 1808.
20  *Leeds Intelligencer* – Monday 18 July 1808.
21  *Leeds Intelligencer* – Monday 13 June 1808.
22  *Leeds Mercury* – Monday 27 August 1808.
23  *Leeds Mercury* – Saturday 23 July 1808.

24  *Leeds Intelligencer* – Monday 3 October 1808.
25  *Leeds Intelligencer* – Monday 16 May 1808
26  *Leeds Intelligencer* – Monday 8 August 1808.
27  https://www.woodbrooke.org.uk/wp-content/uploads/2017/02/Volume_5.pdf
28  *Leeds Intelligencer* – Monday 9 October 1809.
29  Ibid.
30  *Leeds Mercury* – Saturday 21 October 1809.
31  TNA HO 50/301, Wroughton to Sidmouth, 21 December 1813.
32  W.B. Crump (1931), *The Leeds Woollen Industry 1780-1820*. Leeds: Thoresby Society, p. 96.
33  This would be one of the grandsons of John James Bischoff (1729–1806), whose son George married twice into the Whitaker family of Call Lane Unitarian Chapel. His son James married Peggy Stansfeld, sister to Thomas Wolrich Stansfeld.
34  Crump pp. 120–1.
35  Ibid., pp. 138–9.
36  *Leeds Mercury* – Saturday 14 July 1810.
37  TNA HO 50/301, John Hill to Serjeantson, 25 November 1811.
38  SCA WWM Y10/206, Sidmouth to Fitzwilliam, 15 December 1812.
39  *Wakefield Herald and West Riding Advertiser* – 20 March 1813.
40  Anthony L. Dawson (1999), p. 14.
41  *Wakefield Free Press* – 5 June 1880.
42  SRO Mileson Edgar Papers. HD80/2, p. 288.
43  *Leeds Mercury* – Saturday 20 April 1816.
44  Gee, p. 49.
45  Ibid., p. 337.

## Chapter 12: Defending Hearth and Home?

1  John Goodchild Collection: Richard Munkhouse DD. Sermon Delivered at the Parish Church of St John the Baptist, Wakefield, 9 February 1798.
2  *Leeds Intelligencer* – Monday 28 April 1794.
3  *Sheffield Register, Yorkshire, Derbyshire, & Nottinghamshire Universal Advertiser* – Friday 6 June 1794.
4  SCA WWM Y17//5, Beckett to Fitzwilliam, 22 April 1794.
5  *Leeds Intelligencer* – Monday 28 August 1797.
6  SCA WWM Y17/43, Broadsheet Pontefract, 5 September 1795.
7  *Leeds Intelligencer* – Monday 14 July 1794.
8  TNA H0 50/346, Wilkinson to Portland, 7 May 1794.
9  Cookson (1997), pp. 209–20.
10  Colley (2005).
11  *Leeds Intelligencer* – Monday 28 April 1794.
12  John Goodchild Collection: Richard Munkhouse DD Sermon for thanksgiving of plenty 1801.
13  WYAS Wakefield QS1/137/4 April 1798.
14  *York Herald* – Saturday 14 January 1804.
15  SCA WWM Y16/34, Gascoigne to Fitzwilliam, 20 September 1798.
16  Ibid., WMM Y16/35, Gascoigne to Fitzwilliam, 23 September 1798.
17  Ibid., WWM Y16/44, Gascoigne to Fitzwilliam, 1 April 1799.
18  *Leeds Intelligencer* – Monday 5 March 1804.
19  SCA WWM Y41 Volunteer strength returns.
20  TNA HO 50/159, M.A. Taylor to Bacon Frank, 23 July 1806.

21  Steppler, p. 79.
22  Ibid., p. 66.
23  David Clammer (2011), 'Dorset's Volunteer Infantry 1794–1805', *Journal of the Society for Army Historical Research*, vol. 89, no. 357, pp. 6–25. JSTOR, http://www.jstor.org/stable/44231815. Accessed 8 August 2022.
24  Oldham Local Studies. Standing Orders Oldham Local Militia.
25  SCA WWM Y10/101, Yorke to Fitzwilliam, 15 November 1803.
26  Steppler, p. 65.
27  TNA HO 50/30/61, unsigned to Duke of Leeds, 27 October 1803.
28  SCA WWM Y17/17, Thomas William Tew to Earl Fitzwilliam, 5 June 1794.
29  Ibid., WWM Y17/18, Bacon Frank to Earl Fitzwilliam, 1 June 1794.
30  Ibid., WWM Y17/20, Bacon Frank to Earl Fitzwilliam, 10 June 1794.
31  Ibid., WWM Y17/21, Joseph Hunter to Earl Fitzwilliam, 10 June 1794.
32  Ibid., WWM Y39/3, Richard Medley to Committee, 29 June 1801.
33  TNA HO 42/65/343, Fitzwilliam to Home Office, 20 July 1802.
34  Ibid., WWM Y17/34, Bacon Frank to Earl Fitzwilliam, 10 July 1794.

## Chapter 13: Civic Pride

1   *Leeds Intelligencer* – Monday 9 June 1794.
2   *Leeds Intelligencer* – Monday 3 November 1794.
3   *Leeds Intelligencer* – Monday 19 January 1795.
4   *Leeds Intelligencer* – Monday 26 January 1795.
5   *Leeds Intelligencer* – Monday 6 June 1796.
6   *Leeds Intelligencer* – Monday 17 June 1799.
7   *Leeds Intelligencer* – Monday 6 March 1797.
8   *Leeds Intelligencer* – Monday 4 April 1796.
9   *Leeds Intelligencer* – Monday 12 March 1798.
10  *Hull Advertiser and Exchange Gazette* – Saturday 6 September 1794.
11  *Leeds Intelligencer* – Monday 31 December 1798.
12  *Leeds Intelligencer* – Monday 9 January 1804.
13  SCA, 'Newspaper cuttings relating to Sheffield', series S Vol 10. See also ibid., Bland Collection, Cuttings.
14  Ibid.
15  *Leeds Intelligencer* – Monday 7 May 1804.
16  *Leeds Intelligencer* – Monday 3 June 1805.
17  *Leeds Intelligencer* – Monday 16 December 1805.
18  *Leeds Intelligencer* – Monday 27 May 1805.
19  *Leeds Mercury* – Saturday 16 May 1812.
20  *Leeds Intelligencer* – Monday 28 April 1794.
21  *Leeds Intelligencer* – Monday 16 June 1794.
22  *Leeds Intelligencer* – Monday 12 May 1794.
23  *Leeds Intelligencer* – Monday 7 July 1794.
24  *Leeds Intelligencer* – Monday 7 July 1794.
25  *York Herald* – Saturday 10 September 1803.
26  *York Herald* – Saturday 17 September 1803.
27  *York Herald* – Saturday 14 January 1804.
28  *Leeds Intelligencer* – Monday 12 December 1803.

## Chapter 14: Volunteers and the 'Moral Economy'

1   *Leeds Intelligencer* – Monday 10 September 1798.
2   *Leeds Intelligencer* – Monday 19 December 1803.

3   *Leeds Intelligencer* – Monday 8 June 1801.
4   *Leeds Intelligencer* – Monday 6 February 1804.
5   *Leeds Intelligencer* – Monday 8 July 1805.
6   Anthony Dawson pers comm citing *Leeds Mercury*.
7   NYRO ZFW 7/2/87/23, Hutchinson to Chaytor, 15 June 1794.
8   *Leeds Intelligencer* – 30 June 1794; See also 'Wakefield Volunteers', *Leeds Intelligencer* – 30 June 1794.
9   TNA HO 42/30/20 Folios 52-53. Letter from Rev. J Russell of Dronfield 12 May 1794.
10  Ibid. HO 50/536 Letter Rev. James Wilkinson 7 May 1794.
11  Gee, p. 33.
12  Cookson (1997), p. 27.
13  TNA HO 42/30, Folios 21-22, Brooke to Dundas, 6 May 1794.
14  Ibid., WWM F44/39, J.A. Athorpe to Earl Fitzwilliam, 12 December 1792.
15  Ibid., H0 50/346, Wilkinson to Portland, 7 May 1794.
16  SCA WWM F44/38, Rev. James Wilkinson to Earl Fitzwilliam, no date, the next letter in sequence is 12 December 1792, so presumably this letter is from the last quarter of 1792.
17  TNA HO 50/346, James Wilkinson, Sheffield to Dundas, 7 May 1794.
18  *Leeds Intelligencer* – Monday 30 April 1798.
19  SCA WWM F/38/18, Letter from Col. Teesdale Cockell, Pontefract, to Fitzwilliam, 23 February 1802.
20  Ibid WWM/F38/1,1 Letter from Col. Teesdale Cockell, Pontefract, to Fitzwilliam, 22 February 1802.
21  TNA HO 50/50, Lt Col. Teesdale Cockell to Hobart, dated Pontefract 9 April 1801.
22  Ibid.
23  Ibid., HO 50/50, Letter Lt Col Teesdale Cockell, dated Pontefract 25 May 1801.
24  https://www.historyofparliamentonline.org/volume/1790-1820/constituencies/pontefract
25  TNA HO 50/123, Fitzwilliam to Hawkesbury, 11 August 1804.
26  *Leeds Intelligencer* – Monday 12 August 1805.
27  *Hull Advertiser* – 15 November 1806.
28  SCA WWM F45/e/123-2, Earl Fitzwilliam to Lord Pelham, 25 May 1807.
29  Ibid.

## Chapter 15: Church and State

1   Linda Colley (1986), 'Whose Nation? Class and National Consciousness in Britain 1750-1830', *Past & Present*, 113, p. 107.
2   Gee, p. 313
3   Ibid., p. 310.
4   Ibid., p. 106.
5   Robert Poole (2019), *Peterloo: The English Uprising*. Oxford University Press, p. 22.
6   TNA HO 42/62, Hay to Portland, 24 May 1801. See also ibid., Radcliffe to Portland, 23 May 1801.
7   Henry Redhead Yorke (1794), *Thoughts on Civil Government: Addressed to the Disfranchised Citizens of Sheffield*. London: D. I. Eaton, p. 38.
8   Gee, p. 105.
9   https://bmmt.co.uk/wp-content/uploads/Chapter-Four-1792-1815.pdf
10  SCA WWM Y20/32, John Rayner to Earl Fitzwilliam, 30 April 1798.
11  *Leeds Intelligencer* – Monday 21 July 1794.

12  *Leeds Intelligencer* – Monday 8 September 1794.
13  Ibid.
14  *Leeds Intelligencer* – Monday 11 May 1795.
15  *Leeds Intelligencer* – Monday 20 November 1797.
16  Ibid.
17  *Leeds Intelligencer* – Monday 5 November 1798.
18  Ibid.
19  *Leeds Intelligencer* – Monday 17 June 1799.
20  Macleod, pp. 204–05

## Chapter 16: Loyalism and Dissent

 1  Cookson (1997), pp. 23–7.
 2  Edmund Burke (1812), *Speech on the Petition of the Unitarians, in The Works of the Rt. Hon. Edmund Burke*. London: Rivington.
 3  Clammer, p. 6.
 4  John Goodchild pers comm.
 5  Alan Brooke and Lesley Kipling (1993), *Liberty or Death: Radicals, Republicans and Luddites 1793-1823*. Huddersfield: Garian Press, pp. 5–6.
 6  John Goodchild Collection: MSS notes Wakefield Armed Association
 7  SCA WWM Y16/24, Teesdale Cockell to Fitzwilliam, 21 April 1798.
 8  Ibid., WWM Y17/45, Teesdale Cockell to Fitzwilliam, 6 October 1795.
 9  Ibid., WWM Y17/47, Teesdale Cockell to Fitzwilliam, 16 October 1795.
10  TNA HO 42/46/173 Folio 375, Rev. Thomas Bancroft to Home Office, 24 April 1799.
11  SCA WWM Y17/47, Teesdale Cockell to Fitzwilliam, 16 October 1795.
12  TNA HO 50/89, Earl of Warwick to Charles Yorke, 28 September 1803.
13  Katrina Navickas (2006), 'The defence of Manchester and Liverpool in 1803: conflicts of loyalism, patriotism and the middle classes', in Mark Philp (ed.), *Resisting Napoleon. The British Response to the Threat of Invasion, 1797–1815*. Aldershot: Ashgate, pp. 61–73.
14  SCA WWM F44/17, Rev. Henry Zouch to Earl Fitzwilliam, 13 June 1792.
15  *York Herald* – Saturday 14 February 1801.
16  John Goodchild pers comm.
17  *Leeds Intelligencer* – Monday 3 October 1803.
18  NYRO Wyvill Papers, James Milnes to Wyvill, 22 November 1795.
19  Navickas, pp. 61–73.
20  Anthony Dawson pers comm.
21  Oates (1752–1811) was the grandson of Joseph Oates (1675–1729), and his uncle was George Oates who married Mary Hibbert the daughter of a slave trader. His father Samuel Oates (died 1789) had married Mary Hamer, the granddaughter of James Ibbetson, builder of Call Lane Unitarian Chapel in 1691. Samuel Hamer Oates married Mary Sarah Coape: her sister married General Sir John Sherbroke.
22  John Goodchild pers comm 17 June 2017.
23  Richard George Wilson (1971), *Gentlemen Merchants: The Merchant Community in Leeds 1700 – 1830*. Manchester: Manchester University Press, pp. 188–90.
24  *York Herald* – Saturday 31 January 1801.
25  North Riding Record Office, Wyvill Papers.
26  *Leeds Intelligencer* – Monday 11 June 1807.
27  Albert Goodwin (1979), *The Friends of Liberty: The English Democratic Movement in the Age of the French Revolution*. London: Routledge, p. 231.
28  *Leeds Intelligencer* – Monday 31 December 1792.

29  SCA WWM Y30/ Hand Bill, Halifax, 3 August 1803.
30  John Goodchild Collection: Trustees Minute Books Northgate End Chapel, Halifax. List of trustees, 1782,1797, 1822.
31  TNA HO 42/72/1 Folios 548-550. A letter from R. Fletcher, Bolton, 4 August 1803.
32  Navickas, pp. 53–61.
33  Charles Wellbeloved (1800), *The Principles of Roman Catholics and Unitarians Contrasted: A sermon*. York: Thomas Wilson, p. 34.
34  Ibid., pp. 35–7.
35  TNA HO 42/61/380, Letter from [the Reverend William Atkinson], chaplain to the Bradford Volunteers [Yorkshire West Riding], to Home Office, 30 March 1801.
36  Macleod, pp. 130–2.
37  Ibid., p. 96
38  Colley (2005), p. 337.
39  *Leeds Intelligencer* – Monday 30 July 1798.
40  *The Anti-Jacobin Review* 1798, pp. 210–11. See also, *The Anti-Jacobin Review* 1799, pp. 83–90 and 213–15.
41  *Leeds Intelligencer* – Monday 15 June 1807.
42  *Leeds Mercury* – Saturday 19 May 1810.
43  John E. Cookson (1982), *The Friends of Peace. Anti-war liberalism in England 1793-1815*. Cambridge: Cambridge University Press, p. 200.
44  Ibid., p. 204.
45  Brooke and Kipling, p. 14.
46  *The New Annual Register, Or General Repository of History* Volume 29, 1801, p. 281.
47  https://api.parliament.uk/historic-hansard/commons/1808/mar/18/petition-from-manchester-respecting-peace
48  *Cowdray's Manchester Gazette* – 12 March 1808.
49  *Leeds Intelligencer* – Monday 7 December 1807. See also *Leeds Intelligencer* – Monday 14 December 1807.
50  *Leeds Intelligencer* – Monday 29 February 1808.
51  Cookson (1982), pp. 239–44.
52  Benjamin Naylor (1803), *The Right and Duty of a Defensive War*. London: J. Johnson.
53  Cookson (1997), p. 244.

## Chapter 17: A Public Nuisance?

1  Nick Mansfield (2021), *Soldiers as Workers*. Liverpool: Liverpool University Press, pp. 165–6.
2  Gee, pp. 258–9.
3  Roger A.E. Wells (1977), *Dearth and Distress in Yorkshire 1793-1802*. York: Borthwick Institute, pp. 29–34.
4  SCA WWM Y34/d/1-4, Disputes between Wath Troop & Sergeant Crossley, 21 January 1808.
5  Ibid., HO 42/45/133 Folio(s) 520-521, Examination on oath, before magistrates Thomas Butterworth Bayley and John Floud, 17 April 1798.
6  SCA WWM Y22/1, Colonel J A Athorpe to Fitzwilliam, 1 March 1798.
7  TNA HO 42/42/145 Folios 332-335, Secret information, 12 March 1798.
8  TNA PC 1/44/A161, Foxley to Belgrave, August 1799.
9  TNA HO 42 44 Folio 100, Thomas Bancroft to W. Wickham, 2 July 1798.
10  Ibid., HO 42/47, Folio 18, Thornton to Wickham, 2 April 1799.

11  Ibid., HO 42/61/79 Folio(s) 222-22, Letter from the Reverend Thomas Bancroft, 14 March 1798.
12  SCA WMM F45/d/65, Anonymous to Earl Fitzwilliam, 24 July 1802.
13  TNA HO 42/65/347, Fitzwilliam to Home Office, 20 July 1802.
14  SCA WWM F45/d/57, John Dixon to Earl Fitzwilliam, 17 July 1802.
15  TNAHO 42/72/339, Home Office to Fitzwilliam, 31 August 1803.
16  SCA WWM Y16/155/a, Busfield to Fitzwilliam, 12 August 1803.
17  TNA HO 42/51, Folio 127, Anonymous Address, 'Brother Brittons', n.d. [September 1800]; HO 42/52, Folio 36, Anonymous Handbill, 'People Arouse', c. 7 October 1800.
18  *Leeds Intelligencer* – Monday 27 January 1800.
19  Wells (1977), pp. 33–4.
20  *Leeds Intelligencer* – Monday 2 December 1799.
21  WYAS Radcliffe Papers MSS 578-579.
22  TNA HO 50/91, Taylor to Dundas, 30 September 1800.
23  Ibid., HO 42/51/180 Folio(s) 80-83, Letter from Earl Fitzwilliam, 8 September 1800.
24  Ibid., HO 42/51/215, Fitzwilliam to Portland, 3 September 1800.
25  Ibid., HO 42/51 Folio 80, Fitzwilliam to Portland, 8 September 1800.
26  Ibid. HO 42/51/84, Fitzwilliam to Portland, 8 September 1800.
27  Ibid.
28  TNA HO 42/51/88, Rev. James Wilkinson to Portland, 8 September 1800.
29  Ibid.
30  TNA HO 42/51/97, Fitzwilliam to Portland, 10 September 1800.
31  Ibid. HO 50/47, Rev. James Wilkinson to Portland, 19 June 1800.
32  Gee, p. 31.
33  TNA HO 42/51/321, Benjamin Gott to Portland, 21 September 1800.
34  TNA HO 42/53/20 Folio(s) 54-55, Thomas Bancroft to Home Office, 3 November 1800.
35  Gee, p. 235.
36  Bohstedt, pp. 124–8.
37  TNA HO 42/55/60 Folios 163-176.
38  Bohstedt, pp. 224–5.
39  TNA HO 42/36/25, Henry Cholmeley to Portland, 15 November 1795.
40  TNA HO 42/124, Stevenson to Sidmouth, 23 June 1812.
41  TNA HO 50/291, Fenton to Ryder, 22 April 1812.
42  Ibid., HO 42/125, John Lloyd to Home Office, 7 July 1812.
43  SCA WWM/F/45/126, Letter from William Dawson, Wakefield, to Fitzwilliam, 7 April 1812.

## Chapter 18: Democratic Soldiers?

1  Roger Wells (1982), 'The Militia Mutinies of 1795', in J. Rule (ed.), *Outside the Law: Studies in Crime and Order 1650-1850*. Exeter: University of Exeter, pp. 48–52.
2  *William Cobbett's Political Register*, January to June 1804, Vol. V col. 40.
3  Ibid., col. 41.
4  Gee, p. 221.
5  TNA HO 51/75, Charles Yorke to William Sharpe, 1 November 1803.
6  Gee, p. 211.
7  SCA WWM Y22/2, Colonel J.A. Athorpe to Fitzwilliam, 1 March 1798.
8  Ibid. WWM Y22/3, Colonel J.A. Athorpe to Fitzwilliam, 8 March 1798.
9  Ibid. WWM Y22/5, Captain Fenton to Earl Fitzwilliam, 9 June 1799.
10  TNA HO 50/46, Samuel Peat to Henry Dundas, 27 August 1799.

11  SCA WWM Y10/112, Tottenham to Fitzwilliam, 19 January 1804.
12  Ibid., WWM Y10/107, Orderly Room, 11 January 1804; See also ibid., 108b Yorke to Fitzwilliam, 11 January 1804; 11b 'A friend to Yorke', 30 January 1804; 112 Tottenham to Fitzwilliam, 19 January 1804; 109 Tottenham to Dr Bacon, 17 January 1804.
13  Ibid., WWM Y16/195, Resolutions of meeting, 5 February 1804.
14  Ibid.
15  Ibid.
16  *Wakefield Star* – 13 January 1804.
17  *William Cobbett's Political Register*, January to June 1804, Vol. IV, col 835.
18  Ibid., cols. 927-928.
19  *Leeds Intelligencer* – Monday 20 February 1804.
20  Ibid.
21  *Wakefield Star* – 24 February 1804.
22  *Hull Advertiser and Exchange Gazette* – Saturday 8 May 1813.
23  *Leeds Intelligencer* – 21 May 1804.
24  SCA WWM Y16/248a, Francis Lindley Wood to Fitzwilliam, 23 July 1807.
25  Ibid., WWM Y16/248b, Francis Lindley Wood to Fitzwilliam, 24 July 1807.
26  *Leeds Intelligencer* – Monday 23 January 1804.
27  *Leeds Intelligencer* – Monday 29 July 1805.
28  *Leeds Intelligencer* – Monday 5 August 1805.
29  *Leeds Intelligencer* – Monday 26 November 1804.
30  TNA HO 50/148, misunderstanding in the Ripon Volunteer Corps. See also SCA WWM Y34/c, Disputes, Colonel Wood Ripon Volunteers.
31  Ibid., HO 42/82/443, John Charnock to Fitzwilliam, 23 April 1805.
32  Ibid., HO 42/82/444, Wood to Fitzwilliam, 23 April 1805.
33  Ibid., HO 42/82/446, John Charnock to Fitzwilliam, 24 April 1805.
34  SCA WWM Y34/c/4, Letter to Earl Fitzwilliam, 15 August 1808.
35  Ibid., WWM Y34/c/8, Sworn Statement Captain John Charnock.
36  Ibid., WWM Y34/c/10, John Charnock to Fitzwilliam, 18 September 1805.
37  Ibid., WWM Y10/112, Tottenham to Fitzwilliam, 19 January 1804.
38  Steppler, p. 75.
39  *William Cobbett's Political Register*, January to June 1804, Vol. IV, cols 287. Ibid., cols 348-349.
40  TNA HO 50/47, Dundas to Sutherland, 17 June 1800.
41  Ibid., H0 50/92, Hobart to Aukland, 30 January 1804.
42  Ibid., HO 50/123, Horton to Fitzwilliam, 2 October 1804; ibid., HO 50/81 Folio 425, Hawkesbury to Fitzwilliam, 8 October 1804; ibid., Folios 482-483, Hawkesbury to Fitzwilliam, 19 October 1804.
43  *York Herald* – Saturday 15 October 1803.
44  *Leeds Intelligencer* – Monday 17 March 1806.
45  TNA HO 50/234, Fenton to Fitzwilliam, 24 July 1809.
46  *Leeds Intelligencer* – Monday 14 October 1805.
47  *Leeds Intelligencer* – Monday 28 October 1805.
48  *Leeds Intelligencer* – Monday 25 November 1805.
49  *Leeds Intelligencer* – Monday 3 November 1806.
50  *Leeds Intelligencer* – 28 November 1803.
51  SCA WWM Y16/337, Hewitt to Fitzwilliam, 21 June 1808. See also ibid., Y16/340 Hewitt to Fitzwilliam, 24 July 1808; ibid., Y16/341 Hewitt to Fitzwilliam, 26 July 1808.
52  Gee, p. 227.
53  *Leeds Intelligencer* – Monday 29 April 1811.

54  *Leeds Mercury* – Saturday 7 December 1811.
55  Steppler, p. 65.
56  Beckett, p. 118.
57  John E. Cookson, (2008), 'Regimental Worlds: Interpreting the Experience of British Soldiers of the Napoleonic Wars', in Alan Forrest, Karen Hageman and Jan Rendell, *Soldiers, Citizens and Civilians: Experience and Perceptions of the Revolutionary and Napoleonic Wars 1790-1820*. Basingstoke: Palgrave, p. 26.
58  R.S. Norfolk (1965), *Militia, Yeomanry and Volunteer Forces of the East Riding 1689-1908*. East Yorkshire History Society, p. 15.
59  SCA WWM Y16/9, Teesdale Cockell to Earl Fitzwilliam, 5 March 1798.
60  *Leeds Intelligencer* – Monday 9 May 1796.
61  Anthony L. Dawson (1998), pp. 7–8.
62  SCA WWM Y10/112, Tottenham to Fitzwilliam, 19 January 1804.
63  Ibid.
64  https://bmmt.co.uk/wp-content/uploads/Chapter-Four-1792-1815.pdf
65  SCA WWM Y16/137, Francis Foljambe to Earl Fitzwilliam, 21 June 1803.
66  Ibid., WWM Y16/141, Francis Foljambe to Earl Fitzwilliam, 28 June 1803.
67  https://www.napoleon-series.org/research/government/diplomatic/letters/c_letters69.html
68  SCA WWM Y16/154/b, Busfield to Earl Fitzwilliam, 13 August 1803.
69  Simon Burrows (2006), 'The Black Legend of Napoleon', in Mark Philp (ed.), *Resisting Napoleon: The British Response to the Threat of Invasion, 1798-1815*. Aldershot: Ashgate, pp. 141–57.
70  Simon Burrows (1997), 'The struggle for European opinion in the Napoleonic Wars', *French History*, Vol. 11, Issue 1, March 1997, pp. 29–53.
71  SCA WWM/F/45/28, William Dawson to Fitzwilliam, 7 September 1801.
72  Ibid., WWM Y16/44, Gascoigne to Fitzwilliam, 1 April 1799.
73  Mansfield (2022), p. 13.
74  Kevin Linch (2011), *Britain and Wellington's Army*. London: Palgrave Macmillan, pp. 90–1.

## Chapter 19: Conclusion

1  Colley (2005), p. 307.
2  MacLeod, pp. 204–05.
3  NRYO ZFW uncatalogued, Wyvill to Cartwright (illegible), 1797.
4  Anthony L. Dawson pers comm 7 March 2021.
5  Mark Philp (2017), *Reforming Ideas in Britain: Politics and Language in the Shadow of the French Revolution, 1789-1815*. Cambridge: Cambridge University Press, p. 83.
6  It is estimated that 60,000 went to hear Henry Hunt at Manchester's St Peter's Field in 1819 and 100,000 at London's Spa Fields three years earlier.
7  Colley (2005), pp. 300–08.

# BIBLIOGRAPHY

## Archive Sources

Barnsley Local Studies and Archives.
    Spencer Stanhope Papers, 60556
British Library Newspaper Collection.
    *Cowdray's Manchester Gazette, Hampshire Chronicle, HullAdvertiser and Exchange Gazette, Sheffield Register, The Times, The Anti-Jacobin Review, The New Annual Register, William Cobbett's Political Register, York Herald.*
Derbyshire Record Office.
    D5369/19/20-22. Smithson papers
Doncaster Archives.
    DD/DC/M1/Yeomanry Papers
John Goodchild Collection: formerly at Registry of Deeds Wakefield.
    MSS Notes Andrew Peterson
    MSS Notes Bradford Volunteers
    MSS Notes Brandling family and Middleton colliery
    MSS Notes Royal Wakefield Volunteers
    MSS Notes Wakefield Armed Association
    MSS Notes Walkers of Rotherham
    MSS Notes Pontefract Volunteers
    Northgate End Chapel Archive
    Westgate Chapel (Unitarian) Archive
North Yorkshire Record Office.
    Wyvill papers ZFW
Oldham Local Studies.
    Regimental Standing Orders, Oldham Local Militia
Sheffield City Archives.
    Bland Collection, Cuttings
    Misc. Papers 1063M. Rules and Regulations for the corps of Loyal Independent SheffieldVolunteers
    Newspaper cuttings relating to Sheffield
    *Sheffield Iris*
    *Sheffield Register*
    Wentworth Woodhouse Muniments F38, F44, F45, F46, G83, Y10, Y16, Y17, Y20, Y30,Y34, Y37, Y39

Suffolk Record Office.
Mileson Edgar Papers. HD80/3/1, HD80/3/2, HD30/3/3
The National Archives.
    Home Office papers HO 30/29, HO 33/1, HO 40/1, HO 40/2, HO 40/3, 40/9,
        HO 42/30,HO 42/32, HO 42/33, HO 42/34, HO 42/35, HO 42/47, HO
        42/51, HO 42/61, HO 42/62,HO42/65, HO 42/66, HO 42/72, HO 42/74,
        HO 42/83, HO 42/117, HO 42/118, HO42/119, HO42/120, HO 42/121,
        HO 42/122, HO 42/123, HO 42/124, HO 42/125, HO 42/126, HO42/127,
        HO 42/128, HO 42/129, HO 42/130, HO 42/131, HO 42/132, HO 50/91
    War Office Papers WO/1, WO/17
Wakefield Museum and Local Study Centre.
    *Leeds Mercury*
    *Leeds Intelligencer*
    *Wakefield Star*
    *Wakefield Herald and West Riding Advertiser*
West Yorkshire Archive Service.
    Bradford Volunteer Papers, DB17 C3/2.
    JG 1402 Town Constables Book
    JG 1459 Bacon Frank MSS
    SpSt 10/7/79
    Quarter Session Records, 1637-1914
    West Riding Yeomanry Cavalry, records. MMC/22 List of men enrolled in
        LordRibblesdale's troop 1798
York City Library.
    Yorkshire Association papers.

## Digital Sources

https://bmmt.co.uk/wp-content/uploads/Chapter-Four-1792-1815.pdf

## Printed Works

Beckett, Ian (2011), *Britain's Part-Time Soldiers: The Amateur Military Tradition: 1558–1945.* Barnsley: Pen & Sword Military.

Bohstedt, John (1983), *Riots and Community Politics in England and Wales, 1790-1810.* Cambridge: Cambridge University Press.

Brooke, Alan, and Kipling, Lesley (1993), *Liberty or Death: Radicals, Republicans and Luddites 1793-1823.* Huddersfield, Garian Press.

Burke, Edmund (1796), *Thoughts on the Prospect of a Regicide Peace, in a Series of Letters.* London: J. Owen.

_____ (1812), *Speech on the Petition of the Unitarians, in The Works of the Rt. Hon. Edmund Burke.* London: Rivington.

Burrows, Simon (1997), 'The struggle for European opinion in the Napoleonic Wars', *French History*, Volume 11, Issue 1, March 1997, pp. 29–53.

_____ (2006), 'The Black Legend of Napoleon', in M. Philp (ed.), *Resisting Napoleon: The British Response to the Threat of Invasion, 1798-1815.* Aldershot: Ashgate.

Claeys, Gregory (2007), *The French Revolution Debate in Britain.* London: Palgrave MacMillan.

Clammer, David (2011), 'Dorset's Volunteer Infantry 1794–1805', *Journal of the Society for Army Historical Research*, vol. 89, no. 357, pp. 6–25.

Clayton, Howard (1971), *Coaching City: A Glimpse of Georgian Lichfield*. Bala: Dragon Books.

Cockell, Teesdale (1799), *Instructions for the Pontefract Battalion of Volunteers, etc.* Pontefract: J. Fox.

Colley, Linda (1986), 'Whose Nation? Class and National Consciousness in Britain 1750-1830', *Past & Present*, 113, pp. 97–117.

_____ (2005), *Britons: Forging the Nation 1707-1837*. London: Yale University Press.

Cookson, John E. (1982), *The Friends of Peace. Anti-war liberalism in England 1793-1815*. Cambridge: Cambridge University Press.

_____ (1997), *The British Armed Nation*. Oxford: Clarendon Press.

_____ (2008), 'Regimental Worlds: Interpreting the Experience of British Soldiers of the Napoleonic Wars', in Alan Forrest, Karen Hageman and Jan Rendell, *Soldiers, Citizens and Civilians: Experience and Perceptions of the Revolutionary and Napoleonic Wars 1790-1820*. Basingstoke: Palgrave, pp. 23–42.

Cousins, Geoffrey (1968), *The Defenders. A History of the British Volunteer*. London: Frederick Muller.

Crump, W.B. (1931), *The Leeds Woollen Industry 1780-1820*. Leeds: Thoresby Society.

Dawson, Anthony L. (1998), *Wakefield's Volunteers in the Napoleonic Wars, 1794-1814. The Royal Wakefield Volunteers*. Unpublished research project.

_____ (1999), *Wakefield's Dads Army During the Napoleonic Wars*. Unpublished research project.

Dawson, Paul L. (2019), *Lexington to Waterloo: Westgate Chapel and National Politics*. Wakefield: Westgate Chapel.

_____ (2020), *Wakefield at Work*. Stroud: Amberley Publishing.

Dickinson, Harry (1990), 'Popular Loyalism in the 1790s', in Eckhart Hellmuth (ed.), *The Transformation of Political Culture: England and Germany in the Late Eighteenth Century*. Oxford: Oxford University Press.

Eastwood, David (1991), 'Patriotism and the English State in the 1790s', in Mark Philp (ed.), *The French Revolution and British Popular Politics*. Cambridge, Cambridge University Press.

Gee, Austin (2003), *The British Volunteer Movement 1794-1814*. Oxford: Oxford University Press.

Goodwin, Albert (1979), *The Friends of Liberty: The English Democratic Movement in the Age of the French Revolution*. London: Routledge.

Graham, J. (2000), *The nation, the law and the king: reform politics in England, 1789-1799*, 2 vols. University Press of America.

Hargrave, Emily (1926), *The Early Leeds Volunteers*. Publications of the Thoresby Society, Vol XXVIII, Miscellanea.

Hicks, Peter (2008), 'The Militarisation of Society in Georgian Britain and Napoleonic France', *Napoleonica. La Revue*, 2008/1 (N° 1), pp. 136–47.

Lees, J.H. (1811), *Recollections and Attentions for the Officers and Non-commissioned Officers of the Staincross and Osgoldcross regiment of Local Militia*. Barnsley: C. Greaves.

Linch, Kevin (2001), 'A Geography of Loyalism? The Local Military Forces of the West Riding of Yorkshire, 1794–1814', *War & Society* 19.

_____ (2011), *Britain and Wellington's Army*. London: Palgrave Macmillan.

Macleod, Emma Vincent (1998), *A War of Ideas: British Attitudes to the War Against Revolutionary France 1792-1802*. London: Routledge.

Mansfield, Nick (2021), *Soldiers as Workers*. Liverpool: Liverpool University Press.

_____ (2022), *Soldiers as Citizens*. Liverpool: Liverpool University Press.

Mitchell, Leslie (2004), 'Fox, Charles James (1749–1806)'. Oxford Dictionary of National Biography Online.

Navickas, Katrina (2006), 'The defence of Manchester and Liverpool in 1803: conflicts of loyalism, patriotism and the middle classes', in Mark Philp (ed.), *Resisting Napoleon. The British Response to the Threat of Invasion, 1797–1815* Aldershot: Ashgate, pp. 61–73.

Naylor, Benjamin (1803), *The Right and Duty of a Defensive War*. London: J. Johnson.

Norfolk, R.S. (1965), *Militia, Yeomanry and Volunteer Forces of the East Riding 1689-1908*. East Yorkshire History Society.

Philp, Mark (2017), *Reforming Ideas in Britain: Politics and Language in the Shadow of the French Revolution, 1789-1815*. Cambridge: Cambridge University Press.

Poole, Robert (2019), *Peterloo: The English Uprising*. Oxford: Oxford University Press.

Price, Richard (1789), *Discourse delivered on the love of our country*. London: J. Johnson.

Rogers, Nicolas (1999), 'Burning Tom Paine: Loyalism and Counter-Revolution in Britain, 1791-1793', *Histoire Sociale* Novembre 1999.

Skelsey, Anthony (2018), 'The Loyal Birmingham Light Horse Volunteers', *The Military Historical Society Bulletin* Vol. 68 Issue 271, February 2018, pp. 118–21.

Steppler, Glenn A. (1992), *Britons, to Arms*. Stroud: Alan Sutton.

Thomas, Captain George (1812), *The Local Militia Paymaster; or, Military Friend*. London: Thomas Egerton.

Wells, Roger A.E. (1977), *Dearth and Distress in Yorkshire 1793-1802*. York: Borthwick Institute.

_____ (1982), 'The Militia Mutinies of 1795', in J. Rule (ed.), *Outside the Law: Studies in Crime and Order 1650-1850*. Exeter: University of Exeter.

_____ (1986), *Insurrection: The British Experience 1795-1803* Stroud: Sutton Books.

_____ (2011) *Wretched Faces: Famine in Wartime England, 1793-1801*. London: Breviary Stuff.

Western, J.R (1965), *English Militia in the Eighteenth Century - the Story of a Political Issue, 1660-1802*. London: Routledge & Kegan.

Wheeler, H.F.B. (1907), *Napoleon and the Invasion of England: The Story of the Great Terror*. London: John Lane.

Wilson, Richard George (1971), *Gentlemen Merchants: The Merchant Community in Leeds 1700 – 1830*. Manchester: Manchester University Press.

Wood, William (1801), *A Sermon preached at Mill-Hill Chapel, in Leeds, on the commencement of the Nineteenth Century*. Leeds: Edward Baines.

Yorke, Henry Redhead (1794), *Thoughts on Civil Government: Addressed to the Disfranchised Citizens of Sheffield*. London: D. I. Eaton.

# INDEX